To Dad
Happy birthday 2004
lots of love
Lisa + Mark
x x

HEADINGLEY HEROES

Leeds RLFC in the 60s and 70s

Phil Hodgson

Best wishes

Best wishes

Best wishes

Vertical

VERTICAL EDITIONS

First published in the United Kingdom in 2004 by Vertical Editions, 7 Bell Busk, Skipton North Yorkshire BD23 4DT

Copy Editor, Valerie Rice

ISBN 1-904091-10-5

Jacket design and typeset by HBA, York

Printed and bound by the Cromwell Press, Trowbridge

CONTENTS

Introduction	7
1. The Holy Grail to Headingley	10
2. The Wilderness Years?	21
3. On the Cusp of Great Deeds	31
4. The Dawning of an Era	39
5. At the Peak of Greatness	49
6. Trophies Galore!	63
7. Points and Pragmatism	80
8. Triumph and Tragedy	89
9. The H Bombs Arrive	104
10. Maestro or Mug?	117
11. A Season in the Dark	133
12. Francis returns	142
13. More Silver amassed	151
14. Rising to the Occasion	159
15. Wonder Wembley Win	169
16. Leaving it late	177
League Tables	185
Index	190

ACKNOWLEDGEMENTS

It would not have been possible to contemplate writing this book without the help, both direct and indirect, of many others.

I owe a great debt to the many wonderful chroniclers of the period, whose reports of the matches and events of the era have been both evocative and invaluable.

Journalists such as Brian Batty, Alfred Drewry, Raymond Fletcher, Arthur Haddock, John Robinson, Leslie Temlett, Eddie Waring and Trevor Watson provided a highly informed backdrop to Leeds' many achievements and I have leaned heavily, and gratefully, on their informed analysis.

Ken Dalby's many works on the Loiners have also been essential, as have recent tomes by Phil Caplan, Paul Hardisty and the Yorkshire Evening Post's Peter Smith. And no writer could manage without the essential, but now abandoned, Rothmans Year books, compiled for many years by Raymond Fletcher and David Howes, the old John Player Yearbooks which were edited by Jack Winstanley, and the many books with which Rugby Football League Media Manager John Huxley and the historian supreme Robert Gate have been involved.

It would be remiss not to thank the staff, particularly Jane, at the Yorkshire Post Photographic Library, Rugby Football League historian Tony Collins and Martin Hawksworth and Ian Nutbrown of the Pontefract & Castleford Express. And the book would perhaps not have got off the ground without access to scrap books loaned by long-time Leeds fans Denise Thompson (nee Reardon) and Trevor Lamb, or of assistance by such as Graham Morris and Billy Thompson.

The 'life' of this book, however, is in the interviews with the players, and others, who were involved in taking the Loiners to new heights in the 1960s and the 1970s. I have been moved by the willingness of almost all of them to contribute their time, led by Derek Hallas, the secretary of the Leeds Past Players Association, and my particular thanks also go to Peter Astbury, John Atkinson, Ray Batten, Mick Clark, Phil Cookson, Kevin Dick, Les Dyl, Graham Eccles, Neil Hague, Gary Hetherington, John Holmes, Syd Hynes, Harry Jepson, Lewis Jones, John Langley, Alex Murphy, Steve Pitchford, Bill Ramsey, Bev Risman, Alan Smith, John Sykes, David Ward and Billy Watts.

Others who have also been instrumental in helping to pull this book together include: Ray French, Graham Morris, Alan Parker, Charlie Seeling, Dave Smart, Ken Sykes, Alan Thomas, Keith Thompson and Dennis Whittle.

My ever-indulgent and always supportive publisher, Karl Waddicor, was unfailingly unflappable, and last, but not least, my long-suffering wife Julia who in addition to transcribing many of the interviews has forborne, stoically and (almost) uncomplainingly, the disruption to our family life throughout the past year.

Phil Hodgson

July 2004

FOREWORD BY ALAN SMITH

Little was I to know that signing for Leeds RL in June 1962 was to see a significant change in my life. For a farm labourer's son still basking in Rock and Roll and motorcycling, to be asked to play under 19 amateur Rugby League at the age of 17 didn't seem like a bad idea. To be thrust into the professional arena at Headingley eighteen months later was daunting.

Walking into the dressing rooms passing amongst the likes of Lewis Jones, Brian Shaw, Ken Thornett, Jack Fairbank and many other accomplished stars only served to remind me how little I knew about the arts and skills of rugby. It was learn quick or get out! Leeds' long time baggage man Arthur Crowther, God rest his soul, spotted my plight and quickly became my father figure.

Signing for Leeds might as well have been in Lapland as far as my own father was concerned. His comments 'are you sure you're mixing with the right company lad?' still ring in my ears. But mixing with the right company was my privilege for the next 21 years. This book by Phil Hodgson will evoke memories and emotions to the privileged supporters and players of that era. It cannot and does not try to draw comparisons. If you are a lover of yesteryear, of statistics and skills long gone then you will enjoy walking hand in hand (particularly with some of the forwards I knew) down memory lane. I would like to thank Phil for asking me to write a foreword for this very special book made possible by some very special people.

Alan Smith

August 2004

INTRODUCTION

It's an eternal aspect of the human condition that disappointment is almost a certainty; the cliché 'It will all end in tears' may reflect a pessimistic outlook on life but clichés are clichés because they are usually true.

Usually, but not always. My experience in writing and, resoundingly, in researching this book is a strong case in point.

It had often seemed to me that the achievements of the various Leeds sides of the 1960s and 1970s were founded not only on high skills levels and peak fitness but also on very strong, indeed indomitable, team spirit.

Photographs of the successful sides of the era invariably reveal a bunch of lads who you suspect would be just as happy playing for each other on a park pitch in a local cup final as in hoisting aloft Lewis Jones or Mick Clark or Barry Seabourne or Syd Hynes or David Ward at Wembley or at any of the major grounds in the north of England.

Appearances can often be misleading. Not, though, in this case.

A strength of the Leeds players throughout an era in which a major trophy was won in every season from 1966-67 until 1980-81 is that what you saw was what you got.

Team spirit, an elusive chemistry which in truth can never really be created artificially, was as high as it's probably possible to get at Headingley and that attribute, when added to players of world class abilities, produced a heady mix.

The term 'team spirit' can, in this case, be extended way beyond its usual meaning. Coaches such as Roy Francis and Syd Hynes were, in their different ways, important figures in sustaining the quality, as was Dai Prosser, the coach who helped steer Leeds to their first Championship success in 1960-61.

The senior management was also highly important. It's a truth which is often overlooked that no set of players or coach, no matter how talented, can achieve very much without effective management and leadership behind the scenes.

Leeds had that; never more so than in what appear, superficially, to have been several mediocre seasons, from 1961-62 to 1965-66.

During that period the Loiners slipped from top of the table to seventh (twice), then thirteenth, followed by a rise to tenth and, in 1965-66, sixth.

Hindsight – a wonderful thing – tells us that Leeds, during that period, had talents such as Mick Shoebottom, Alan Smith, Seabourne and Hynes coming through who would provide the backbone of the team which enjoyed the glory years of the late 1960s.

A more valuable commodity than hindsight is foresight, which the Leeds board of the early 1960s possessed in abundance, together with a strong streak of courage.

It would have been easy, in the spring of 1963, for men such as AB Sharman, Jack Myerscough, Alf Rutherford, Noel Stockdale, Joe Warham and Noel Shuttleworth to have taken the popular option, as they headed for a slump to thirteenth the following season.

The Leeds directors could have been tempted to splash out on a big name player, either from within the Northern Rugby League or from the Valleys of South Wales.

An expensive capture by what was known as the 'Bank of England' club would have placated the demanding supporters and would, quite possibly, have set Leeds on a path towards short term, and short-lived, success.

Instead the Leeds board invested over £6,000 on the famous 'electric blanket' and made it known that they were actively pursuing a policy of developing young, local talent.

Both initiatives were to reap rich dividends over the next 17 years or more. Deservedly so for a group of men, 'Champagne Charlies' all and with the marvellous Jack Myerscough to the fore, who embodied the qualities of the old-style 'gentleman director,' now an almost an extinct breed in any walk of life.

It has to be said that, for Leeds, 'local talent' meant, as often as not, lads from Hunslet. And it also has to be said that my choice, as a long-standing Hunslet supporter, to write a book in praise of the Loiners has surprised, to say the least, many of my family and friends.

I may even have placed myself in some physical danger by writing positively about a club which is not so much 'north of the river' to some people I know but measured, rather, as being several thousand miles away by the

Hunslet Juniors 1968/69. Harry Jepson first left, back row. Phil Hodgson second from right, middle row. The poplar trees in the background are all that remains of the famous Parkside ground.

preferred southerly route.

Indeed any funds that may come my way from this book could well end up in the coffers of kneecap replacement specialists, with the originals having possibly been shattered by members of my own family.

No matter. It was hardly the fault of the enterprising Leeds board that their counterparts at Parkside lacked the qualities needed to run another great club properly.

That fact was, perhaps, recognised by Hunslet's long-serving Secretary Harry Jepson, who I first met when I played for Hunslet Juniors. Harry left Hunslet for Leeds two or three years before the sale of Parkside in 1973 for development and continued the habit of sound stewardship at Leeds that defined Messrs Myerscough and co.

Having paid homage to management, however, sport is fundamentally about players. The word 'great' is one that I use sparingly, if at all. But during the 1960s and 1970s Leeds certainly had many players of whom the adjective could at least be seriously considered.

In addition to that, they are invariably top blokes. And they have certainly not disappointed, for which I will be lastingly grateful.

This book, ultimately, is in praise of them. With their unfailing help, in many enjoyable interviews, I hope to have given a 'feel' of a special body of men who, over two decades, thrilled not only their own supporters but all true lovers of Rugby League. Their epitaph is not only in the record books but also in the memories of supporters privileged to have seen them in glorious action. And my own epitaph? If I'm found somewhere in a ditch: 'It's a Hunslet supporter what did it!'

Phil Hodgson
July 2004

1. THE HOLY GRAIL TO HEADINGLEY

Leeds entered the 1960s as unarguably one of the strongest clubs in the game but carrying the unwanted mantle of underachievers.

The Loiners had featured regularly in the code's glamour occasion, the Challenge Cup Final, and had lifted the trophy as recently as 1957 when skipper Keith McLellan carried the cup down the famous steps after the 9-7 victory over Barrow.

But, despite having been recognised as one of the leading lights of the game since the days of the Northern Union, Leeds had consistently been denied the major prize of the Championship.

The Loiners, indeed, had been unable to reach the Championship Final – and with it the opportunity to be recognised as unarguably the finest side in the country – since 1938, when neighbours Hunslet won the huge Elland Road derby 8-2 before a then-record crowd of 54,000.

As the austere 50s drew to a close there was little sense that the long wait was about to come to an end.

The month of December 1959 finished with four successive defeats. Halifax toppled Leeds 20-13 at Thrum Hall, Batley edged the Loiners 8-6 in a depressing Christmas Day defeat at Mount Pleasant, and Wakefield Trinity swept to a shattering 39-5 victory at Headingley on Boxing Day.

A miserable Christmas was compounded by the 27-7 setback at Huddersfield two days later and, with only seven wins from their first 21 games, Leeds were in real danger of finishing in

Headingley Hero

Wilf Rosenberg

South African winger Wilf Rosenberg spent less than three years at Headingley. His achievements, however, will be remembered for as long as Leeds play Rugby League.

Rosenberg set a post-war record of 44 tries in the Loiners' inaugural Championship-winning season of 1960-61 and two of those were vital in accounting for St Helens in the Top Four semi-final.

Moreover, Rosenberg added an exotic panache to the Headingley scene, in common with other South African flyers who plied their trade elsewhere in the Northern Rugby League.

The decisions of Tom Van Vollenhoven and Jan Prinsloo to join St Helens in the late 1950s awoke Rosenberg to the potential of a career in the professional code. At 25 years of age he turned his back on the Springboks, with whom he had played three Tests against the 1955 British Lions, followed by a tour to Australia and New Zealand and a Test against France in 1958.

Rosenberg was no stranger to foreign climes. His parents had emigrated to Australia when he was a babe in arms, returning home when he was 14.

Tempted by the chance to study dentistry at Leeds University, the three-quarter joined the Loiners early in 1959, making his debut at home to Barrow on 28 February. After failing to impress at centre, Rosenberg switched to the wing and, in March 1960, forging a highly productive partnership with Derek Hallas and a friendship with the Great Britain centre which was to prove lifelong.

Hallas sent Rosenberg over for 11 tries in their first nine games together, many of them scored with his trademark swallow dive, and the fans found the

Continued...

combination, and the flair of the rest of the side, irresistible as it became obvious that something special was on the horizon.

Ten of the last 11 games of the 1959-60 season were won; a complete transformation, 17 of the previous 27 league games having been lost. The Loiners, despite their status as a big city club and a host of cup successes, had found the Championship elusive but with Rosenberg rattling up the tries Leeds eased to the head of the table as the 1960-61 campaign got under way and rarely looked like falling from grace. The South Stand was packed as the fans revelled in Rosenberg's feats, aware that Drew Turnbull's post-war record of 42, set in 1954-55, was under threat. Many of those fans, as Lewis Jones explains, were new to the game. 'The shrewdest thing that Leeds did was signing Wilf Rosenberg. If they were weak in any area then they went out and bought. With Wilf, they didn't just get a very good player. They also attracted a hell of a big Jewish following. A lot of my friends are Jewish and I'm glad to say that I'm accepted as one of them. Our following in the Jewish community while Wilf was here was huge.

'For some reason or other it stopped and it turned out that they had all gone to Elland Road.'

The exodus may have coincided with Rosenberg's departure to Hull. The slightly built speedster, who stood 5 feet 10 inches and weighed in at 11 stone 6 pounds, had sustained a broken jaw in a torrid game at Hunslet in the early stages of the 1961-62 season and, less than keen on recovering form and confidence in the A team, requested a transfer which was reluctantly granted.

Wilf Rosenberg's last game for Leeds was at Headingley, against Dewsbury, on Mischievous Night 1961. He had scored a total of 73 tries for Leeds in only 81 appearances, a remarkable strike record. Perhaps fittingly his epitaph – other than his two touchdowns in the Lazenby Cup 'friendly' win over Hunslet – was the last try he scored for the Loiners in official competition; the second touchdown against St Helens in the wonderful Championship semi-final victory, recorded forever in a classic photograph which captures the South African flyer high in the air with a despairing Mick Sullivan unable to prevent the clinching score.

the bottom half of the table for the first time since the aberration of 1945-46, when the side closed at twenty-third of the 27 clubs in the post-war rebuilding period.

But a massive improvement in form in the second half of the campaign led to Leeds securing fourteenth spot, for the third successive season, in the 30-team league.

The fixture format of the period involved a Yorkshire League and a Lancashire League made up of 15 teams each. Five cross-county opponents helped provide 38 league games, with a top four play-off settling the Championship.

What were to become the greatest two decades in the club's history opened on 2 January 1960 at York in the champagne style that is synonymous with the name 'Leeds.' The Minstermen, a decent enough outfit that would finish twenty-first in the table with 17 wins, was put to the sword in a 44-9 romp in which Derek Hallas and Delmos Hodgkinson raced over for two tries each. The legendary Lewis Jones landed 10 goals in the Loiners' biggest win of the campaign, and Leeds' other tries went to Jackie Pycroft, Eric Horsman, Eddie Ratcliffe and Gordon Brown.

One absentee from the score-sheet that day was Wilf Rosenberg. The South African winger topped the Loiners' try scoring list in the 1959-60 season with 27 tries, 11 of which had been scored prior to the turn of the year. After Leeds had seen out January with a 9-7 Headingley win

Eddie Ratcliffe tackles Billy Boston while Brian Shaw looks on.

over Hull Kingston Rovers and defeats against Hull and Hunslet, Rosenberg returned to try-scoring action with a hat trick in the 31-4 defeat of Doncaster.

Rosenberg also scored a crucial try, seven days later, in the 8-5 Challenge Cup win over Hull Kingston Rovers, when Hodgkinson grabbed the other try and Jones added a conversion. The Loiners, though, went out of the competition in the second round at Wigan, 14-11 (just a week after the 9-0 defeat at Central Park by the Pie Eaters), leaving the way open for the pursuit of respectability in the league.

Leeds went on to lose just one more league game in a run of form which augured well for the following season.

Rosenberg and Hallas scored a try apiece and Jones kicked a couple of goals in the 10-0 defeat of a powerful Oldham side, and revenge was more than sweet when Batley were beaten 16-8, courtesy of tries by Hallas, Rosenberg, Colin Evans and the fine Australian Test full-back Ken Thornett.

More big wins followed against Keighley (23-9), Bradford Northern (29-4), York (22-2), Hunslet (17-5) and Bramley, who were beaten 22-8, before Castleford halted the seven-match winning run with a 19-17 victory at Wheldon Road.

Leeds, however, closed the campaign with a 'double' over a Featherstone side which had plenty at stake and which needed to take three points from the two matches to nose ahead of Wigan into the top-four play-offs. Those wins ensured that the Loiners had triumphed in more games than they had lost, with 20 victories from their 38 games. Only two days after having raced to a 35-8 win at Dewsbury – with Rosenberg scoring a hat trick and Jones scoring a try and seven goals – Leeds won 10-7 at Post Office Road, thanks to tries for Ratcliffe and Bernard Prior and two Jones goals. The Loiners went on to edge Rovers less than a week later 15-11 at Headingley, Rosenberg grabbing his side's only try and Jones kicking six important goals.

The Welshman finished with 109 goals that season, his five tries producing a tally of 233

A Loiner Looks Back

Derek Hallas

'Leeds treated us well. I was drafted into the Great Britain side when Neil Fox was unfit in January 1961. We beat France 27-8 at St Helens. Leeds were playing that day at Keighley, and won. I got £18 for playing for Great Britain, and I got paid winning money of £14 by Leeds for the victory at Keighley in line with the policy at the time. No other club would do that.'

points, and his prowess with the boot was to prove a vital factor as Leeds secured the Championship for the first time the following season.

1960-61 opened with 12 wins in the first 13 games, the only setback being the 6-4 home defeat at the hands of Oldham on 20 August when Lewis Jones scored Leeds' only points with two goals.

The Loiners, firmly focused under coach Dai Prosser and with Joe Warham as Football Manager, had already opened with comfortable victories over sides with strong ambitions of their own in Workington Town and Huddersfield. Few teams would opt for a campaign opener at Derwent Park but there was no Cumbrian flu in the Leeds camp as the Loiners eased to a 21 3 success with five tries, Rosenberg crossing twice and supporting scores going to Hodgkinson, Bernard Prior and Barry Simms.

That was to be Prior's last try for the club as Leeds splashed out £13,500 to Hunslet for loose forward Brian Shaw. The total was a world record, although not as a cash sum. £9,500 was paid to the Parksiders, with Bernard Prior, valued at £3,500, and Norman Burton (£250) also heading to south Leeds in exchange.

Leeds fans scented that something special could be on the agenda when Huddersfield travelled to Headingley four days later and returned to Fartown having suffered in similar fashion to Workington. Leeds again netted five tries, Rosenberg grabbing another brace and

A Loiner Looks Back

Lewis Jones

Ken Thornett in action in the 1961 Championship Final.

'For many years, Leeds had had good players but that didn't necessarily bring success. In 1957, when we won the Challenge Cup, and in 1961 when we won our first Championship we had very good sides and on both occasions we had very good odds against at the bookies.

'The two players who came into the team in 1960/61 were the unsung heroes. Trevor Whitehead had an excellent game in the Championship Final. I don't think he'd ever played in the front row prior to that season, he was a big lumbering centre really. Somebody wasn't available and they decided to put him at prop and he was a revelation. And Vince Hattee was drafted into the centre when Fred Pickup was injured. They are names which do not readily jump to mind for most, but they do to me. With hooker Barry Simms, they were the men of the match. Australian Ken Thornett was the best full-back I ever saw and a pleasure to have played with. Jack Fairbank and Dennis Goodwin were a fine second row and worked well with loose-forward Brian Shaw. Don Robinson was a good experienced prop and there has to be a word for coach Dai Prosser who made sure that the spirit in the camp was second to none. The players were amazed that he was not retained after that season.

'Joe Warham was the Team Manager and Dai was one of the lads, he created a great spirit amongst us. If you've got a team of good players, you don't have to coach them. And you can't coach a team if they're not good players.'

Billy Boston scores for GB against New Zealand at Headingley

Derek Hallas, Don Robinson and Fred Pickup adding supporting scores.

And after the setback against Oldham the Loiners were not to taste defeat in the league until late November.

The trip to Post Office Road, never easy, ended in a 12-4 victory over the ever-pragmatic Featherstone Rovers, earned with tries for Pickup and Rosenberg and three Jones goals.

That success was followed by two 'derby' clashes in a week. Hunslet travelled across the river to Headingley in the first round of the Yorkshire Cup and were accounted for 16-0 through a try and two goals for Jones and touchdowns by Hodgkinson, Rosenberg and second row Jack Fairbank. And Bramley were put to the sword at the Barley Mow, the Loiners netting seven tries and six goals in the 33-4 'derby' victory with Hallas registering 18 of his side's points with two tries and, in the absence of Jones, six goals.

Jones, back in action, landed five important goals, Rosenberg stealing the only try, as Dewsbury almost pulled off a shock with a 13-13 draw at Crown Flatt in the second round of the Yorkshire Cup. It was tough, too, in the replay where Rosenberg was again a shining light with a hat trick in the 22-16 win. Skelton, Tomlinson and Thornett also raced over, with Jones adding a couple of goals.

Loiners Big Match

6 May 1961, Championship Semi-Final, Leeds 11 St Helens 4, Headingley

It takes rather more to win a Championship than a good, or even a great, performance in a final.

The title reflects a team's achievements over an entire season with, from 1906-07 to 1961-62, the top four playing off on a straight knockout basis to determine the crown. First hosted fourth and second entertained third, with the final played on neutral territory before crowds which often equalled and occasionally surpassed those for the Challenge Cup Final.

Leeds made history after winning 30 of their 36 league fixtures – their best record by some distance – to finish top of the pile and reach the top four play-offs for the fist time since 1957 when, with a Wembley date with Barrow on their minds, they had lost 22-12 at eventual champions Oldham.

Four years on, pole position secured a home game with fourth-placed St Helens, who arrived at Headingley for the first meeting of the sides that season with a well-deserved reputation as one of the most attractive sides in the league and with the little matter of a Challenge Cup Final against old rivals Wigan a matter of only seven days away.

If they'd forgotten that fact, they were soon reminded. Centre Derek Hallas, now Secretary of the Leeds Past Players Association, recalls: 'Our second row forward, Jack Fairbank, was a hard, hard man, frightened of no one. St Helens had a very good pack and had their own characters, including Don Vines, Vince Karalius – the Wild Bull of the Pampas – and Dick Huddart. Anyway, Fairbank gave them his warning at the first scrum: 'Any of you so-and-sos want to play at Wembley next week keep out of my so-and-so way!' I've got to admit, if I'd been playing at Wembley I'd have been thinking about it. They weren't too happy, and they'd a crack side out. Alex Murphy was at stand-off that day, to stop Lewis Jones, and Lewis ran

Continued...

rings around him. When Lewis Jones decided he was going to play, he could play. If he decided he didn't feel like it, he didn't bother. It had nothing to do with the nature of the game, he was just that sort of person. He wasn't the kind of skipper that inspired you with 'into the breaches speeches.' He'd just walk in, blowing smoke out of his mouth; he'd been having a fag in the shower. He was the only person I've ever known do that at Leeds. He'd pick the ball up off the table and be half way out of the dressing room door, with "let's go lads," and that was it.

'We tackled well against Saints. People were covering each other all the game, Vines looked like he was through and then he was smothered, and Fairbank was in typically ferocious mood; he and hooker Barry Simms were the tough guys up front.'

Both – Simms in particular – were capable of footballing finesse in a pack which included former three-quarters Dennis Goodwin in the second row and Trevor Whitehead at prop. Goodwin's old centre skills came in useful when he broke down the right, sending South African winger Wilf Rosenberg over with an exquisitely timed pass. That try, Rosenberg's 43rd of the season, broke the Loiners' post-war record and, following stand off Lewis Jones' earlier long range penalty, gave Leeds a 5-point lead.

Jones, whose defensive skills were all too often overlooked during his illustrious career, denied St Helens a gilt-edged chance when he brought down centre Brian McGinn. And winger Eddie Ratcliffe, drafted in to keep tabs on the legendary Tom Van Vollenhoven, proved his worth with a series of telling stops.

The Lancastrians, though, kept the 19,000 crowd on its toes in the biting late-spring wind with a penalty by Austin Rhodes, the full-back landing his second goal after young Leeds centre Vince Hattee, a late replacement for the injured Fred Pickup in the centre, repaid the faith shown by coach Dai Prosser by forcing his way over for a try that gave the Loiners a four-point cushion.

Leeds knew that another score was necessary to secure a first appearance in the Championship Final

Continued...

The Loiners had, between those two County Cup clashes, hosted Hull at Headingley where the Airlie Birds went down to a 19-15 defeat in which Rosenberg once again proved his immense value to the side with a brace of tries; Hallas netted the remaining Leeds touchdown and Jones added what was becoming a customary five goals.

The Welsh maestro had the same number of successes with the boot in his next two games, at Bradford Northern and at home to Hunslet, in 16-7 league victories which kept the Loiners riding high in the table. Rosenberg, an absentee from the try scoring lists in those fixtures and the subsequent 15-2 win at York, posted his intent in the next match, the Yorkshire Cup semi-final at Headingley against Huddersfield.

Fartown had the better of Leeds on that occasion, winning 12-9 despite scoring only two tries to the Loiners' three, which included two for the South African flyer and an effort by Hodgkinson. Leeds, however, recovered from the setback by continuing their fine league form with four wins on the hoof, while Huddersfield were to experience disappointment on their return to Headingley for the final with a 16-10 defeat by Wakefield Trinity.

The Lions of Swinton were scuttled 12-2 at home in a vital game, and that epic victory was followed by an equally momentous 20-5 triumph at a Leigh side which was to finish sixth in the table. It was harder, though, at mid-table Hull KR, where a try each for Rosenberg and Hallas and two Jones goals helped snatch a 10-9 win,

Wilf Rosenberg scores the winning try despite a despairing tackle by Mick Sullivan.

since 1938 (when neighbours Hunslet had won 8-2 before a 54,000 Elland Road crowd). And that score was a real classic, a truly sensational effort as well as being one of the most important touchdowns ever scored on the famous turf.

It fell to Rosenberg, the darling of the South Stand, three minutes from time. Scrum-half Colin Evans and hooker Simms were the catalysts, creating space for centre Derek Hallas whose finely honed partnership with his flying winger worked, once more, to perfection.

Rosenberg, freed 40 yards out, still had plenty to do with craggy Cockney prop Cliff Watson, winger Mick Sullivan and Rhodes, internationals all, ready to set a testing examination paper.

Hallas, the man with the best view in the stadium of possibly the best-ever try scored at Headingley, tells the story: 'Sullivan had come inside and I gave Wilf the ball. Watson tried to knock him into touch and missed. Rhodes had him on the touchline side and instead of tackling him, he was that close he tried to shoulder him in. How the hell Wilf got through I don't know. Then, from what seemed to be about 35 yards, he just sort of took off and scored in the corner with Mick Sullivan hold of his ankles, both off the ground. The stand just went barmy, stamping on their seats. Wilf always calls it 'That Try', he views it as his most important try for the club.'

Leeds: Thornett; Rosenberg, Hallas, Hattee, Ratcliffe; Jones, Evans; Robinson, Simms, Whitehead, Fairbank, Goodwin, Shaw.
St Helens. Rhodes; Vollenhoven, Donovan, McGinn, Sullivan; Murphy, Smith; Terry, Dagnall, Watson, Vines, Huddart, Karalius.
Referee: Mr T Watkinson (Manchester)
Leeds. T: Rosenberg 2, Hattee. G: Jones.
St Helens. G: Rhodes 2.
Attendance: 19,000

but York were no match for the Loiners when Pickup grabbed a hat trick and Rosenberg and Thornett had two tries apiece in a 37-4 stroll.

No side can go through an entire campaign without an indifferent spell and Leeds' came with two successive trips across the Pennines in the murk of autumn. Swinton, who were to finish third in the table, limited the Loiners to a Rosenberg try and Jones goal in a 19-5 defeat at Station Road and, as the season drifted into December, Leeds went down to Oldham 7-0 at the Watersheddings.

The Challenge Cup apart, the Loiners were only to taste defeat on two more occasions that season.

Lewis Jones had a try and five goals in the 22-8 win at Castleford, when supporting touchdowns came from Hallas, Thornett and Evans. And obdurate Dewsbury, always ready to test Leeds, were edged 10-7 at Crown Flatt, where Rosenberg sniffed out two tries and Jones kicked the goals.

The big Boxing Day clash with Wakefield turned a little sour when Trinity prevailed 14-9, but it was plain sailing for Leeds throughout the remainder of Christmas and January.

Two Hallas tries, a Rosenberg touchdown and two Jones goals helped earn a 13-0 winning pay packet at Mount Pleasant, Batley, and Bradford Northern could do little to deny Leeds on New Year's Eve at Headingley, when Rosenberg netted another brace in the 19-3 win.

Leeds stayed unbeaten in the league until the excursion to Huddersfield on 18 March, which ended in a 15-5 defeat despite a Rosenberg try and Hattee goal. Hallas scored two tries and a goal in the 22-6 victory at Doncaster, Pickup and Rosenberg had a brace apiece as the Loiners had it a little easier than usual at Dewsbury in the 23-12 verdict, and the prolific Pickup strode over for a hat trick to lead Leeds to a 26-3 triumph at Keighley.

Jones helped Leeds grind out a 6-0 win over Leigh at Headingley with three penalties before Leigh's neighbours, Wigan, dumped the Loiners out of the Challenge Cup, forcing a 5-5 draw in Yorkshire and winning the Central Park replay 32-7 when the Loiners could only muster a try and two goals by Jones.

That setback, however, was possibly a key factor in Leeds' subsequent Championship success. Freed of any Wembley diversions the Loiners won 10 of their last 12 league games to seal pole position, a healthy five points ahead of nearest challengers Warrington.

The 'double' was completed over Batley who, as at Mount Pleasant, went down by 13 points. Brian Shaw scored his first try for the club in the 22-9 win, when Thornett kicked a goal, Vince Hattee landed four and there were touchdowns for Simms, Ratcliffe and Rosenberg.

Shaw was again on the score-sheet seven days later against Keighley who offered little resistance in the 33-10 defeat; coincidentally, the 23-point margin which matched the win at Lawkholme Lane a month earlier.

Rosenberg had two tries against Keighley and maintained that rate in the subsequent home victories over Featherstone Rovers (16-9) and Workington Town, who were left trailing 26-17.

Loiners Big Match

20 May 1961, Championship Final, Leeds 25 Warrington 10, Odsal Stadium, Bradford

The Loiners, incredibly, had failed to win the Rugby League Championship prior to the 1960s. Despite having been recognised as one of the code's glamour sides, particularly from the 1930s onwards, the accolade of being unarguably the best team in the game had proved frustratingly elusive.

Leeds had reached the Championship Final, contested by the survivors of a top-four play-off, five times, each occasion ending in disappointment.

The Loiners' conquerors, on three of those occasions, were Huddersfield. Harold Wagstaff's 'All Four Cups' side of 1914-15 won 35-2 – a margin likely to remain a record in the final – and followed up that success with a 2-0 win in 1928-29 and a 10-0 success (after a 2-2 draw) 12 months later.

It was Swinton's turn to deny Leeds the following year, winning 14-7 at Wigan, and neighbours Hunslet toppled Leeds 8-2 in the famous all-Leeds final, at Elland Road, in 1937-38.

Semi-finals in 1946-47, 1954-55 and 1956-57 were as close as the Headingley men came to breaking their duck until the 1960-61 season began with high hopes after the capture of Great Britain loose forward Brian Shaw from Hunslet for a reputed world-record fee of £13,250, which included hooker Bernard Prior and Norman Burton in part-exchange.

Lewis Jones, the 'Golden Boy' signed from the valleys for £6,000 nine years earlier, was still in his prime and captained a side that also included star Australian full-back Ken Thornett, flying South African wingman Wilf Rosenberg and classically-gifted centre Derek Hallas.

The portents were good when Leeds reached their first Championship Final in 23 years courtesy of a home semi-final win over St Helens. The Loiners' opponents were Warrington who, coincidentally, had

Continued...

been the last remaining hurdle in the Challenge Cup Final when Leeds tasted Wembley success for the first time. A crowd of 52,177 turned up at Odsal on Saturday 20th May 1961, half of them praying passionately for a historic Leeds win.

The other half were baying for a Warrington outfit that boasted Australian winger Brian Bevan in what was to be the living legend's last major final.

Bevan and his team mates were, however, upstaged on a day dominated by Jones and Hallas, working from a fine platform laid by a pack in which hooker Barry Simms won the scrums 3-1.

Leeds went into a lead they were never to lose when second row Dennis Goodwin, who had set up the Loiners' first try in the semi-final win over St Helens, sent his partner Jack Fairbank over for a try, Jones adding the goal.

Making the most of two missed penalty attempts by Wire full-back Eric Fraser, the Loiners stretched their lead to 10 points by half time with a try for scrum-half Colin Evans who burrowed over from acting half-back after Thornett, Hattee and Hallas had combined in a length-of-the-field attack to send Jones close.

Two quick tries in the second half for Hallas, from exquisite passes by Thornett and prop Trevor Whitehead, one of which Jones improved, put Leeds in sight of the trophy. And although Warrington enjoyed a rally in which Jim Challinor crossed twice, Laurie Gilfedder adding each goal, one of the Leeds club's great victories was wrapped up in style with a sparkling solo try by Jones, who had responded to Challinor's scores with a penalty and also converted his own touchdown.

The Welsh maestro's score denied the supporting Hallas a hat trick but the former Roundhay Rugby Union man had no complaints. The important job had been done; Leeds, unquestionably, were the finest team in the land.

Try awarded!

Says Hallas: 'I got two tries, these things happen. Wilf wanted to score but didn't; he dropped one on the line. I happened to be there to finish off the rounds of passing that brought me two tries. The memory I've got is that I missed a hat trick because Lewis didn't pass me the ball. He got through, had the full-back to beat with me in support, but just rounded Eric Fraser and scored under the posts.

'We got £35 for winning the Championship; maybe two week's wages. On the other hand there were over 50,000 people there. But, apart from the medal, it was the fact that we'd won the title, something that had never been done before by Leeds, which made it so memorable. We beat St Helens and Warrington, two good sides, in the play-offs and we fully deserved to win it. And, in the final, we could have had 40 points, we were in such fine form.'

Leeds: Thornett; Rosenberg, Hallas, Hattee, Ratcliffe; Jones, Evans; Robinson, Simms, Whitehead, Fairbank, Goodwin, Shaw.

Warrington: Fraser; Bevan, Challinor, Pickavance, O'Grady; Greenough, Edwards; Brindle, Harper, Arkwright, Gilfedder, Major, Naughton.

Referee: Mr R Gelder (Wilmslow)

Leeds: T: Hallas 2, Fairbank, Evans, Jones. G: Jones 5.

Warrington: T: Challinor 2. G: Fraser 2.

Attendance: 52,177

Huddersfield broke the spell at Fartown, before Leeds had the better of Hull KR at Headingley, Rosenberg and Hallas crossing in the 14-2 win, and at Parkside, where Hunslet were undone by two Lewis Jones goals; the only scores of a typically defence-dominated 'derby.'

Bramley offered stiffer resistance at Headingley than they had done on their own ground, holding Leeds to a 16-6 win on April Fools' Day in which Trevor Oldroyd scored a try and two goals, Fairbank, Hodgkinson and Hattee also crossing. Castleford also conceded

A Loiner Looks Back
Derek Hallas

Derek Hallas scores in the 1961 Championship Final.

'When we went to Hull we'd meet at the Griffin, have a meal and go on the train and by taxi to the ground. One afternoon their hooker Tommy Harris sprained his ankle in the first couple of minutes. We were all rubbing our hands, we were playing against 12 men and we'd got the match. Bernard Prior was our hooker. At the next scrum there was a crack, the scrum broke up and the referee's blowing his whistle and pushing everybody back. Prior's spark out and Hull's Mick Scott said, "Ah, well, looks like 12-a-side from now then." Poor old Bernard didn't remember going to Hull; you could get away with that in those days.

'Many a time you'd hear a thump and the whole scrum would go up. And when it broke up there'd be some poor bloke, nearly always the hooker, laid out. What a position to play.'

the 'double' pushing Leeds all the way before slipping to a 16-12 defeat at Wheldon Road in which Hodgkinson, Ratcliffe, Fairbank and Jones forced their way over, Hallas adding a couple of goals.

It was, however, one-way traffic in the next game as hapless Doncaster, the league's bottom side, were brushed aside in a 53-6 win. Goodwin netted a hat trick in the stroll, Rosenberg, Shaw and Hallas had a brace apiece and Hattee scored a try and six goals.

That routine run-out was, perhaps, a long way from ideal preparation for a trip to the Boulevard where Hull FC ground out a 13-7 victory in the penultimate league match of the campaign, Fairbank crashing over for Leeds and Jones contributing two goals.

But Leeds, already certain of top spot and of the Yorkshire League title, gave themselves a timely boost for the play-offs with a 15-8 success at Wakefield Trinity in their final league game. Not only was this victory satisfying revenge for the Boxing Day defeat at Headingley. It also denied Trinity the chance of breaking into the top four, the men from Belle Vue finishing two points behind St Helens who would also have

Headingley Hero
Jack Fairbank

All Rugby League sides need an enforcer. The man whose sheer physical presence will help concentrate the opposition's minds is an essential part of any team's armoury, not least from the perspective of the creative players who are aware that the hatchet men on the other side will be loathe to ply their trade should retribution be swift and effective.
Leeds' first Championship success in 1960-61 was due in no small measure to just such a character. Jack Fairbank, the tough tackling, aggressive second row forward played a huge part in the Loiners' success. And his activities remain legendary.
Such was Fairbank's reputation as an uncompromising player that he didn't necessarily even have to do anything. His impact on the top four semi-final win over St Helens began with his simple

Continued...

question to the Saints players, who were due to play Wigan in the Challenge Cup Final the following week – 'do you want to play at Wembley? If so, keep out of my way' – which had the desired effect.

The farmer from Halifax, however, contributed far more to the Leeds cause than sheer aggression. A talented footballer who could fire out a telling pass when need be, he was also a rangy, powerful runner and a better reader of the game than he was perhaps given credit for.

His tackling, however, was his real forte, and it was a rarity for any opposing player not to feel for some time the effects of one of his bone-crunchers.

Fairbank extended the philosophy into training and into the Loiners' other off-field activities.

Known affectionately in the dressing room as the 'maniac in the second row', he was a naturally strong man and disdained the introduction of weights and circuit training in the early 1960s. He didn't need to build up his upper body strength, not according to centre Derek Hallas, who recalls: 'Nobody liked playing touch and pass against Jack, because he'd break your back with a tick. He was a real character. We used to go to the Turkish Baths in Harrogate and they had to ban him. We had the place to ourselves and Jack has to be Jack. We're in the steam room one night, it was fairly crowded and Jack came in with the fire hose and rinsed us all out. You couldn't stand up, you'd be lying there having a nap and he'd come in and drop a freezing towel on you. You always have to have somebody in a team who is prepared to do things like that.

'When we were playing away the team sheet would go up on Tuesday night with the travel arrangements. At the bottom, underlined in red, was the message: blazers will be worn. Otherwise you wouldn't be allowed on the bus. We used to pick Jack up on the way to games in Lancashire and one day he turned up with a flat cap on, donkey jacket and his khaki coat, which was full of milk money. His Wellington boots were covered in cow dirt. George Airey, (Mr George, son of Edwin Airey) was sitting at the front and saw him. He said to our manager Joe Warham, 'tell Fairbank he will not be required this afternoon.' Jack got back off the bus, he was just standing there. We're all laughing through the windows taking the mick – you know what players are like – but we were all sorry he wasn't playing because we knew that the opposition was never happy about playing against Jack.

'He was great to have around though. If you said, "do me a favour Jack, stop so-and-so, he's having a go," he'd say, "which is that?" "Number 4." "Leave it with me," and the next thing the bloke would be flat out. He'd do that to you if you weren't careful. That's what he was like, he had a presence, a big, strong lad. One of the funniest things was when he and Eric Ashton got sent off at Wigan. Ashton fighting with Jack Fairbank, can you imagine it? But he got sucked in.'

Dai Prosser and a bunch of young fans welcome Trevor Whitehead, Tony Skelton, Barry Simms and Jack Fairbank.

had to lose their last match to be denied by Trinity.

Indeed, Leeds' victory over Wakefield ensured that the Saints would be the visitors to Headingley for the play-offs, with second-placed Warrington hosting Swinton (third) in the other semi-final.

The Wire overcame the Lions 13-5 to book their spot at Odsal and Leeds, whose last appearance in the Championship Final had been in 1938 at Elland Road against Hunslet, secured their own role on centre stage with an 11-4 win over St Helens, Rosenberg's sensational try in that epic success helping him set a new post-war record for the club of 44 in a season.

2. THE WILDERNESS YEARS?

After the heady heights of the club's first-ever Championship, hopes were high that the Loiners would consolidate and remain at the top of the Rugby League tree for the foreseeable future.

It wasn't to be.

The Leeds side broke up fairly quickly and slipped immediately from their exalted position at the head of the Northern Rugby League to seventh in 1961-62. The departure of Wilf Rosenberg, who scored two tries in the pre-season Lazenby Cup win over Hunslet but transferred to Hull shortly afterwards, was a blow, as was the loss of his centre Derek Hallas to Keighley.

Two Divisions were introduced in 1962-63 in a planned three-year experiment which only lasted for two seasons as attendances generally failed to hold up. The Loiners completed the 1962-63 campaign in seventh spot and finished fifth in the Eastern Division, which had been introduced to provide the 'derby' fixtures lost following the abolition of the County Leagues.

New Zealand score a try against Great Britain at Headingley in 1961

Headingley Hero

Lewis Jones

To Lewis Jones fell the honour of being the first man to captain Leeds to the Championship. When the Welsh stand-off lifted the Championship cup at Odsal in 1961 he and his team-mates had ended what, for such a major club, had been an unlikely 65-year drought.

That fact alone ensures Jones' status among Headingley greats. So, too, do the statistics of 2,920 points for the club, from 144 tries and 1,244 goals, in a glittering career spanning 12 years from 1952, when he made his debut against Keighley at Headingley on 8 November, to 30 March 1964 with the home game against Halifax.

Jones, in addition, holds Leeds' record for points in a season, totalling 431 from 33 tries and 166 goals in 1956-57, the campaign in which he made his sole Wembley appearance.

Those figures, however, convey little of the majesty of the 'Golden Boy' who came north as a 21-year-old prodigal from Wales Rugby Union and left for the Australian club Wenworthville 12 years later with the praises of an entire city ringing in his ears.

Lewis Jones remains adored in Leeds as one of the most gifted men to have played Rugby League or, for that matter, in any other sport.

The possessor of an astonishing change of pace, a bewildering sidestep and swerve and a spectral 'double-kick' acceleration, the man from Gorseinon, near Swansea, was a real crowd-pleaser whether at centre, full-back or stand-off and more than repaid his £6,000 signing on fee.

Continued...

The 1963-64 season proved to be worse. Leeds plummeted to 13th in the top flight, although the Headingley outfit held firm at fifth in the Eastern Division.

With the return to a 30-team league in 1964-65, Leeds' fortunes improved, but only slightly, the Loiners rising to tenth in the table.

The relative lack of success in league football was matched in the Challenge Cup. The Loiners, after overcoming Bramley in the first round in 1961-62 in a game in which centre

Leeds XIII (combined Bramley, Hunslet and Leeds) take on New Zealand in 1961

His approach, endearingly and occasionally infuriatingly, could be seen as close to casual and there were critics who suggested that his commitment to the cause was less than it should have been, particularly in defence.

Others, however, spring quickly to his cause. Says John Atkinson: 'Lewis Jones once wrote, 'If you're on the floor, you can't contribute to the game.' It stuck in my mind. Lewis shadowed people until he was ready. If they made a mistake, not only was he there to take advantage, he was also in a position that if they didn't make a mistake he'd still tackle them.'

Derek Hallas, the right centre in the 1961 side, recalls: 'Lewis Jones was an enigma, there's no question about that. But people like that can just come up with something and slip you through half a gap with a little pass.

'Alex Murphy was at stand-off when we played St Helens in the 1961 Championship Final, with the aim of stopping Lewis Jones, and Lewis ran rings around him. When Lewis Jones decided he was going to play, he could play. If he decided he didn't feel like it, he didn't bother. It had nothing to do with the nature of the game, he was just that sort of person.

'Lewis used to hang the ball out, scrum-half Colin Evans would run round him, back pass to Ken Thornett on the burst and I would follow Ken through. I've scored more than one try like that and so did my winger Wilf Rosenberg.'

Graham Eccles didn't have the opportunity to play with Lewis Jones but, as a youngster, he had the thrill of watching the maestro from the Headingley terraces. He says: 'The thing that stood out was his change of pace. It was devastating. He changed from cruising to full stride in an instant. Pace makes the difference between a mediocre player and a top player. There's no substitute for it.'

Many other fans, too young to have seen Lewis Jones in his prime, had an opportunity to catch a glimpse of his talents when he played in Alan Smith's Testimonial Match in 1973. One cameo moment will live forever in the memory. Having come on as a second half substitute, Jones sent a short pass to a forward coming up 'on the bump.' The distance of the pass would have been two feet, three feet at the most. The remarkable thing was that the ball seemed to hang in the air for several seconds until his team-mate's arrival. An astonishing moment which would have perplexed Sir Isaac Newton and one that perhaps sums up the genius of Lewis Jones.

Geoff Wriglesworth netted four tries, were drawn at Leigh in the second round and after forcing a 7-7 draw at Hilton Park were dumped out in the Headingley return 17-16. Wriglesworth, a try-scorer in each of the ties against the Lancashire side, may have had mixed feelings about the competition that year! Not Leigh, however, who had gushed in their programme notes: 'Whatever the result, whatever the day and whatever the occasion it cannot be denied that the Leeds team is always a big attraction. The reason: the Headingley men play attractive football for which the RL followers are always yearning.'

Despite – or perhaps because of – that reputation, the Loiners also slipped in the second round the following year. Castleford, about to emerge as a long-lasting power in the game, were beaten 10-8 at Wheldon Road at the first stage but Wigan, so often the Loiners' bêtes noires in the competition, prevailed 20-11 at Central Park in the next round.

It got worse the following year when Leeds were drawn at Salford in the first round. The Red Devils, at the time, were at a very low ebb indeed and had languished in the lower reaches of the league for several years. The previous season, Salford had finished 12th of the 14 clubs in Division Two and they were destined to retain that sorry status in 1962-63.

Leeds, who finished fourth from bottom in Division One – only two clubs were relegated in the experimental period – should in theory have had few problems at The Willows but Salford, who would lose 10-4 at home to Barrow in the next round, produced a major upset with a 10-6 victory, limiting the Loiners to three Lewis Jones goals.

There were, though, signs of a revival the following season when Leeds battled their way to the quarter-finals. Helped – and on this occasion, making full use of – relatively kind

A Loiner Looks Back

Lewis Jones

Jones gives John Holmes goalkicking tuition.

Lewis Jones' main attribute, in the opinion of most judges, was his devastating change of pace, a facility which, self-effacingly, he still finds difficult to explain. 'It was just something that happened. Everybody's got a method of beating a man, whether it's a sidestep or whatever or purely barging through the opposition. It was all I could rely on really, I didn't have very much but what I did have was pace off the mark, that was very important for me anyway.

'I was always going to run into trouble with a sidestep, unlike Brian Bevan, he had a sidestep which was unbelievable. It didn't matter if you let him go, you'd think, "I've got the speed to catch him." You hadn't! Then again you might think, "right, I'll go straight in," but he'd come off his right foot and leave you for dead. Oh, he was impossible. He never slackened speed; even though he sidestepped a couple of yards inside you, he never lost pace. Most people do, but he just kept going. It was unbelievable. You looked at him and saw little knobbly knees, and he used to take his teeth out. He was transparent at times! You can see how Leeds made a mistake when they sent him away just after the war, saying he wasn't big enough, but he was a great player.'

Sign of the times?

The Leeds programme notes for the home fixture with Hull on 23 August contained the following: 'One of the most disturbing features of recent years has been the poor sportsmanship of many boys attending RL matches, particularly shown by booing opponents when taking attempts at goal, but are we adults blameless? Children usually follow the lead they are given so let our aim at Leeds for 1961-62 be to gain a reputation second to none for sportsmanship and to teach the younger generation to appreciate the other team's play and to accept that referees are only human and on average over the year any errors made have a way of cancelling each other out.'

draws, and both at home, the Loiners overcame Liverpool City 19-6, followed by Bramley, who were accounted for by 13-9, to set up a big third round tie at Hunslet.

Trevor Foster (facing sideways) had a spell as a Leeds coach in the early 1960s with Roy Francis (centre) on Wales trip to France.

The Parksiders, however, were a power at the time and the south Leeds club's ranking as favourites was justified by the 7-5 win which enabled Hunslet to meet Wakefield Trinity at Headingley, securing the 8-0 win which led to the classic final at Wembley against Wigan.

For Leeds, the defeat was part of a learning curve which would stand many promising youngsters in fine stead over the next few years.

One facet of the Leeds club – a point made on occasion by winger Alan Smith – is that while other clubs may rise and fall, the Loiners are always there or thereabouts. That truth was confirmed by Leeds' appearance in two Yorkshire Cup Finals during their 'lull'. Both,

A Loiner Looks Back

Alan Smith

Atkinson, Smith, Dyl and Holmes.

'Leeds wanted to sign me in 1962, and Joe Warham asked me to go to Headingley to look around. We were from a little farming community, Overton, near Wakefield. I don't think my mum and dad had been to Leeds in all their lives. Going to Horbury was big time but to go to Leeds! It worried them. They said, "make sure you don't get into the wrong company," and to be certain they sent my brother-in-law, Geoffrey, with me.

'We had a lovely day. Joe Warham entertained us so well and I was so impressed by the stadium, the cricket field, the rugby field, the tradition. Lewis Jones was there and all I could think was, "what am I doing here?" Joe persuaded me to sign with a £300 cheque. Wakefield were also after me and their contract was worth £1,000 in £250 increments; £250 to sign on, £250 after so many games, £250 for Yorkshire and £250 if you played for Great Britain. It was a lot of money but whether I was going to get the next £750 I didn't know. So I signed for Leeds and took the cheque home. "Dad I've got a cheque." He said, "a cheque, what's that? What good is it lad?" I loved him and my mum. They never saw a rugby game in their lives, never even saw me play, but I was brought up on love. I'd no pressure and I was always questioned, "are you doing the right thing?"'

A Loiner Looks Back

Derek Hallas

'Joe Warham, a school teacher, was our team manager. During the Championship season they took the coaching off Joe and gave the job to Dai Prosser. I was on the pitch after we beat Warrington at Odsal there were loads of people on the pitch with Dai Prosser. Joe came up to him, shook his hand, and said, "congratulations, Dai, but I don't know how you've done it."

'Dai was a lovely fella. If ever I went to York I'd go to his fish and chip shop and he always gave me twice even if I didn't want twice.

*'In training he'd say, "OK, lads, four laps." We'd groan, "oh, f*** off, Dai," but we'd do it for him, because he was that sort of bloke.'*

Joe Warham pictured third from left.

admittedly, ended in defeat, and both convincingly at the hands of Wakefield Trinity, who won 19-9 at Odsal in 1961-62 and 18-2 at Fartown in 1964-65.

Leeds, however, had at least been involved and the experiences, which added to the development of some highly talented youngsters, were to help reap rich dividends for the rest of the decade. What appears to be a sorry record masks a period of rebuilding which led to the club's finest era, one almost unmatched in the history of the sport.

Leeds signed and blooded a number of fine youngsters in the early 1960s, with two of the Loiners' brightest stars emerging in half-backs Mick Shoebottom and Barry Seabourne. The pair bucked the long-established tradition among Hunslet lads of automatically heading, almost without question, to Parkside and are among the first examples of a Headingley policy which was to provide the backbone of the side for years to come. And the decision to appoint Hull FC boss Roy Francis as coach in 1963 proved to be the catalyst for a run of success secured with style.

Shoebottom made his debut on 24 February 1962, bagging his first try for the club in the 34-8 league victory at Tatters Field, Doncaster. Shoey had a few more outings the following year, snaffling four tries including two against

Fairest and Most Loyal Player

The Yorkshire Federation of Rugby League Supporters Clubs, which was founded in 1923, introduced the James Harrison Trophy, in recognition of the 'Fairest and Most Loyal Player' throughout the county, in 1958. Named in honour of the former Bramley player, who was a member of the Federation, the prestigious trophy was twice won by Leeds players between 1960 and 1980.

Lewis Jones was honoured in 1963 and Ray Batten became the second Loiners recipient in 1971.

Headingley Hero

Barry Simms

Barry Simms is arguably the great lost talent of Rugby League. The young hooker, who had been a major figure in the Championship-winning side of 1960-61, appeared to be set for a glittering career at domestic and international levels until a bizarre injury put paid to his dreams.

Simms' rugby future was effectively ended when, as the half time whistle blew during Leeds' game against Castleford he kicked a loose ball away as he was leaving the pitch. His knee gave way on the follow-through, the hooker was carried off and, at the age of just 23, his days as a leading light were effectively over.

Simms made a brave bid to return to action but he was never the same again. But what a player he had been in his relatively short sojourn on centre stage! Introduced to the first team in 1958, he made an immediate impact and as a 19-year-old played a central role as Leeds beat Wakefield Trinity in that year's Yorkshire Cup Final – his first game in the competition.

Such were his talents that Bernard Prior, a quality hooker who would go on to represent Great Britain with Hunslet and earn a Championship medal with Wakefield Trinity in 1967, became surplus to requirements and moved to Parkside as part of the deal that brought Brian Shaw to Headingley.

A creative player with a fine turn of pace and a sidestep to match, Simms also possessed an abrasive edge which endeared him to the Headingley crowd and to his fellow players.

Derek Hallas, the Loiners' centre in the Championship-winning side, recalls: 'He wasn't big but, with Jack Fairbank, he was one of the tough guys

Continued...

Workington Town at Headingley on 8 May. The youngster had already shown his mettle by scoring against very tough opposition, including a try in the notable 30-3 victory over eventual champions Swinton and a try at Wilderspool in a 22-14 defeat. The battling spirit for which Shoebottom was to become famous was already very much in evidence!

A little over a fortnight after Shoebottom's exploits against Workington a productive midfield partnership went into germination with Seabourne's first venture into the first team in the match at Hull KR on 24 May 1963. Seabourne, gradually blooded, scored three tries the following season including two in the 30-7 home victory over Hull.

Another scorer on that early November afternoon was a man who, like Seabourne, would make his name as a creator rather than as a finisher and, with Shoebottom, would complete a powerful midfield triangle from which the Loiners would prosper.

That player, one of the most skilful and intelligent footballers ever to grace the sport of Rugby League, was Ray Batten, a capture from the Heworth club who was to delight Leeds fans in particular and Rugby League fans in general for many a year with his sublime and subtle approach.

A young winger by the name of Alan Smith, meanwhile, was struggling to make his mark. The former Brookhouse, Wakefield, amateur scored five tries in 1962-63 – including four on his debut in the 55-2 Eastern Division romp *in the pack. We played Hull at Headingley and Bill Drake kicked me off my feet at a play-the-ball in front of the stand. Barry hit him. The referee blew the whistle and my lasting memory is Drake, who was six foot two, and Simms at five foot nine, and the referee's looking up and down at each as he's telling them off. It looked so ridiculous.'*

The immortal Lewis Jones, Simms' captain, rated Simms very highly. 'He was the great lost player. The Man of the Match award didn't exist when we won the Championship Final in 1961 but if it had it would undoubtedly have gone to Barry Simms. These were the days when the ball had to be put into the scrum straight, a good scrum-half was quite essential and so was a good hooker. Barry would win the ball against the head and that was a big factor in us winning the Championship. I found myself embarrassed with the amount of ball I received from the scrums, and he gave me my try in that game on a plate. He stood up in the tackle, got the ball to me and I only had to run about 10 yards. Barry was never recognised as a great player but if you played with him you knew he was.'

over Dewsbury in August – and two in each of the following two seasons.

However, the greatest loss to the Loiners during the period perhaps overshadowed the emergence of precocious young talents. Lewis Jones, a true legend of the sport after having come north in 1952, was the original Golden Boy and a consummate rugby artist. The Welshman, the first Leeds captain to lift the Championship, had been offered a highly attractive deal by Wentworthville and the maestro made his last appearance for the club in the 14-4 league win at Knowsley Road, St Helens on 22 February 1964.

That victory confirms that, despite their fall from the higher echelons, Leeds were still capable of matching the best. But the overall scoring record for that season tells its own story. Wriglesworth topped the try-scoring list with 12, ahead of Scotchman Drew Broatch (10) and Ron Cowan (7). Jones, meanwhile, landed 66 goals in his curtailed season, the first time he had been unable to pass the century mark for eight years.

All that was to change as Francis transformed the fortunes of the club and reaffirmed Leeds' reputation as a glamour side of the game; one which had never quite been lost as testified by Workington Town who, when the Loiners travelled to Cumbria on 30 March 1963, stated in the Derwent Park programme: 'Today we are proud to entertain Leeds, Bank of England side,

A Loiner Looks Back

Derek Hallas

'When I was at Keighley, playing Leeds was our big match. We played them at Headingley once, beat them, and I scored a hat trick. It was absolutely fantastic, in front of a big crowd; I thought Christmas had come early. It wasn't long after that I signed for Leeds, to replace Keith McLellan. I realised then what it was like playing for Leeds against the so-called smaller clubs, going to Batley and Bramley and especially Keighley. They'd been cheering for me three weeks before and they booed me off the pitch! Going to places like Dewsbury and Featherstone, my God they were tough matches; I'd rather have played in Lancashire. Every team had good players and you were fortunate to have been picked out to play for Leeds. There may have been players at other clubs who may have been just as good if not better than you, so you had to feel that you were lucky to be the one to be asked to sign. When I got the Leeds blazer, from Rawcliffes, I felt I was somebody. When I went shopping in town I always wore my Leeds blazer because it guaranteed me a discount.'

A Loiner Looks Back

Lewis Jones

Leeds sides containing men of the calibre of Lewis Jones attracted massive crowds. 38,000 packed Headingley on one occasion for a game with Wigan, just 22,000 turning up for a match at Elland Road between Leeds United and Manchester United on the same day. The Loiners, however, watched the purse strings. Jones, who had joined Leeds for £6,000 in 1952, vividly remembers quibbling over his expenses with Club Secretary George Hirst.

'I used to get half a crown expenses and I once said "hey George, half a crown expenses?" He answered, "how many times have you been down this week?" I said, "three times, Tuesday, Wednesday and Saturday." He asked "what's the tram fare from West Park to Headingley?". I replied "five pence each way, George, that's ten pence return." George said, "you've been down three times, that's 30 pence, yes, half a crown expenses. Oh, but hold on, hold on, Tuesdays and Thursdays you come training, fair enough, but I don't have to pay you for Saturday because you're coming to your place of employment! That's two 10 pences, that's one shilling and eight pence." So next week I had 1s 8d in my bloody pay packet!

'I've been down at Headingley watching from behind the posts when there has been 11,000 or 12,000 in and I swear my legs were off the ground on occasions. I thought to myself, how the hell did they get 38,000 in here?'

Jones back in Blighty, assisting Eric Ashton.

containing Scottish, Welsh and Great Britain internationals, to say nothing of their South African and Australian importations. Glamour has always been a part of their make-up, so much so that they have been one of the game's finest attractions for well over 40 years. Probably the best known member of the side is Lewis Jones, but let us not lose sight of the fact that they thought fit to pay a world record price to Hunslet for Brian Shaw.'

That outstanding potential was echoed by Hull KR for Leeds' visit in February 1965. Said Rovers: 'Today we greet Roy Francis and his men from Headingley, always considered one of Rugby League's glamour clubs. Yet in spite of their wealth of talent, the hallmark of Leeds often seems to be inconsistency. This season, however, the Leeds record has given cause for greater satisfaction. They are in sixth position, and were also defeated Yorkshire Cup finalists, last November. Since Roy Francis left Humberside for Headingley no less than seven new forwards have been transferred to Leeds from other senior clubs, several of them having distinct Humberside connections. Alan Lockwood and Les Chamberlain went from Rovers, Bill Drake from Hull, and Peter McVeigh from Batley after trials at the Boulevard. Others were Mick Clark, Albert Firth and Ron Morgan, the latter at £4,500 the costliest of the lot. Yet despite this accumulation of newcomers Leeds were scouting around for forwards before the cup register closed.'

Leeds' hunger for success, illustrated by that never-ending search for improvement, was echoed by the supporters. In his address at the close of the 1964-65 campaign Tom Steel, President of the Supporters' Club, wrote: 'Until

Alf Meakin

There was a rare failure in November 1964. Leeds signed Alf Meakin after witnessing the success of another Olympic sprinter, Berwyn Jones, at Wakefield Trinity. Welshman Jones, who gained three Great Britain caps, had a rugby pedigree and had represented Wales Schoolboys at Rugby Union. Meakin, a novice to the oval ball, looked like a fish out of water on his televised debut at Headingley and moved to Blackpool Borough after three trial games. He did, however, settle reasonably well on the Lancashire coast and headed Blackpool's try scoring list in 1965-66 with 12 touchdowns.

Alan Smith trained alongside Meakin during his short spell at Leeds. He recalls: 'They thought if anybody would tire him out it would be me. I didn't. He was an out and out sprinter; when he had the ball in his hands he lost his balance. It wasn't a good signing, it was made in response to Wakefield signing Berwyn Jones. You can't get it right all the time.'

late in the season they only held fifth place, reached the final of the Yorkshire Cup and only went under to Hunslet in the RL Cup by two points. This reads like a successful side but I don't think anybody would claim that we have reached the point where the supporter can be very confident of victory against strong opposition, so whilst accepting that the players give of their best one is entitled to query is the best of some good enough?'

Football Chairman Jack Myerscough was mindful of the need for improvement and wrote: 'Although it is the best of the outdoor games, Rugby League has now to compete with so many other attractive and even domestic diversions that there is not the same density of supporters who really are always able to come and watch a match. Those who do come are mainly the keen and interested types who are very selective and study their football and are not easy to please if the performance is of a poor standard.

'Our endeavour at Headingley therefore is to get together a well-knit and useful side which can be developed to stand up to a three-year period at the least, and during the course of the future, to pep up the team with any superior acquisitions as we may develop, or who might become available from time to time.'

Joe Warham echoed those sentiments and his quotes in the same Leeds Supporters Yearbook can be seen as prophetic: 'Never was the junior field more assiduously combed than it is today. With the ban on overseas signings, and because the welfare state has removed much of the compulsion to leave South Wales, clubs largely confine themselves to recruitment from Lancashire, Yorkshire and Cumberland. Recognising this a few years ago, the Leeds club took directly under its wing the teams successfully established by Ken Dalby at the Headingley boys club.

'A group of intermediates just then emerging included such as Eddie Ratcliffe, Fred Pickup, Jack Rogers, John Sykes, Norman Burton and Gilbert Ashton who, together with Barry Simms and others, gave us an A team which in 1959-60 established itself as the best in the game. Their success in senior football is mixed, but Simms and Pickup gained international and county selection respectively. This is indicative of the ratio anticipated. If one or two emerge annually who are capable of top performances (I suggest Robin Dewhurst as one) then over a period the nucleus of a successful side can be established.

'More recently the juniors, under Jack Nelson, have virtually "swept the board." They have won five out of six available trophies in the past two years and only lost the "one that got away" because of an unfortunate leg injury to promising half-back Trevor Briggs. Recruitment to this team was from a wide area of the West Riding and perhaps especially from South of the river.

'Barry Seabourne, Robert Smith, Peter Astbury, Stuart Coulthard, Alan Gardner and Roger Smith all became professionals. All of them except the last two have tasted league football, and Roger has not had the chance because of a leg injury. Of last year's team Burke and Brown are already professionals and among others Briggs, Canister, Clay, Eardley, Paddington, Horsman, Lamond, Nicholson, Higginbottom, the Morton brothers, Rider and Ward must surely make their mark.

'Just how successful all this is may at the moment be debatable in some minds – though not in mine. Judgement now is premature. I've heard youngsters of barely seventeen criticised for not fulfilling expectations! If in another five years these boys have not established themselves then we can accept that they have failed.

'The Castleford stars of today are ex-juniors who have had a few years experience of senior football before emerging as fully fledged performers. Leeds have taken over the role of others who have ruled the roost in Junior football.

'What we now aim to do is to perpetuate this ascendancy and then assuredly the seniors will benefit and will themselves attain that leading position we are all striving to regain!'

Chairman Alf Sharman was similarly forthright: 'No disappointed supporter feels his disappointment more keenly than does the administration. Our shortcomings in recent seasons have most certainly not been the outcome of complacency and that is emphatically not the reigning mood at the moment.

'We confidently hope that next season, given at least average luck with health and injury, and with our younger players a year nearer maturity, a real step towards rehabilitation will be seen. We aim to build on this a team worthy of that staunch and loyal body of supporters we have in this city. Time was when almost overnight one or two dramatic "captures" could change the whole picture. Those days are not now with us. But we do pledge to you the will and the vigilance to seek always progressive steps towards improvement, fully conscious of the difficulties but with sober optimism and sure faith that ultimate success will be ours.'

With the board clearly looking to the future, the Leeds Supporters Club was also looking ahead and opened its new headquarters on the site of the old bowling club at the rear of the South Stand.

3. ON THE CUSP OF GREAT DEEDS

Leeds, after two mediocre seasons in the First Division, began to prosper on the return to a single 30-team league.

Mick Shoebottom continued to learn his trade at stand off, working with Ken Rollin – signed from Wakefield Trinity – at half-back, and loose forward Ray Batten made eight appearances, serving under the apprenticeship of veteran

Harry Poole, who had been captured from Hull Kingston Rovers.

New signing John Atkinson, a free-scoring winger enticed from Roundhay RUFC, also emerged, with four tries, but the pace man would have to wait awhile before breaking Scottish winger Ron Cowan's productive partnership with centre Geoff Wriglesworth. Cowan topped the Headingley try-scoring list with 23 touchdowns as the side rose to sixth in the table.

The trophy cabinet again remained bare but the signs in 1965-66 were there for all to see that the Loiners were on the verge of great things under Roy Francis whose training methods, particularly his focus on fitness, were beginning to have an effect.

One team, in particular, provided an obstacle to Leeds' prospects: Wigan.

The Pie Eaters ended Leeds' bid for Wembley with a 7-2 verdict in the Challenge Cup semi-final at Fartown, Huddersfield, and the men from Central Park put paid to Leeds' Championship prospects two weeks later with a 22-5 victory in the second round of the top-16 play-offs.

The controversial format, introduced the previous season, was to remain in place until the reintroduction of two divisions in 1973-74 and

A Loiner Looks Back

Alan Smith

Alan Smith typically in action.

'I scored four tries from the left wing on my debut. It was against Dewsbury at Headingley on 29 August in an Eastern Division Championship game and the team was: Dewhurst; David, Hallas, Thornett, Smith; Jones, Evans; Robinson, Charlesworth, Terry, Tomlinson, Fairbank, Pickup.

'Dewsbury kicked off and Jack Fairbank caught it. He looked like a giant to me and it seemed as if all the Dewsbury team parted to let him through. He went steaming down the middle and scored. I thought, "hell, we're alright here."

'I was opposite a lad called Ken Teasdale, who was a local star making his debut for Dewsbury. Fred

Continued...

Pickup got him. They carried poor Ken off and I thought, "oh dear, what's he done that for?" There were no substitutes in those days and I finished up getting four tries. The first one, Lewis Jones drifted out to the left and he just looked at me, almost motioning me keep going. He grubber-kicked the ball, it settled over the line, and I was on my little rails in a straight line for my first try for Leeds. It was a night to remember, a great start. But I couldn't sustain the first team. I wasn't good enough, I was inexperienced, my handling was suspect, and my tackling was suspect. Then I broke my leg in the October, which put me out for a season.'

was never wholly popular as it gave a side finishing below halfway in the table the chance to lift the Championship.

Indeed, Leeds' play-off defeat the previous year, as the tenth side in the table, was at Halifax, who had finished seventh and went on to win the title from that relatively lowly position.

Remarkably the men from Thrum Hall retained the Championship in 1965-66, despite having slipped to tenth in the league. Any doubts Leeds fans may have had over the new system were, perhaps, eased by the fact that Fax included among their victims Wigan, who were toppled 25-12 in the semi-final at Central Park.

Leeds, though, had only themselves to blame for the Challenge Cup reverse. Wigan had been considered in some quarters to have been fortunate to prevail after Loiners' hooker Tony Crosby had secured possession for his side by a 12-1 ratio in the second half. Wigan, as to be expected, didn't hold with that view and sniffily reported in the programme for the Championship clash with Leeds: 'This is, of course, the second meeting between the clubs in the past fortnight. After our victory in the Semi-Final of the Rugby League Challenge Cup at Huddersfield many people expressed the opinion that we were very fortunate to win this game. We, of course, think differently, and at the same time would say that any side who wins possession 12-1 as Leeds did in the second half and plays the type of football they played that

Headingley Hero

Roy Francis

Francis with Shoebottom after the 1968 Cup Final.

It's often said that Roy Francis, the coach who moulded Leeds into a side that could seriously challenge for the accolade as the most attractive club team in history, was ten years ahead of his time.

The truth may be that Francis was after his time, with an important passing nod to the demands of Rugby League in the 1960s.

The Welshman, who had come north from Brynmawr in 1936 to join mighty Wigan as a free-scoring winger, had learned his Rugby League trade in an era when coaches were a relatively new phenomenon.

Teams were brought to a peak of fitness by a trainer and it was the players, and particularly the captains, who dictated tactics.

It was an approach which Francis utilised to great advantage at Headingley – bringing to bear skills

Continued...

Leeds v Australia matchday programme

day certainly cannot expect to go to Wembley.'

Ironically Wigan stumbled to a heavy defeat at the hands of St Helens in the final, again finding themselves starved of possession as, without suspended hooker Colin Clarke, they struggled in the scrums against a St Helens side which appeared to stray offside deliberately whenever Wigan had possession. Saints, it was alleged, could do that secure in the knowledge that the Pie Eaters, obliged under the then rules to kick to touch, would be unlikely to win the resultant scrum.

That, though, was scant consolation for the Loiners who had battled their way through to the last four with comfortable wins over York and Hull before losing to Warrington, after a replay, in the third round.

Former England Rugby Union stand off Bev Risman, signed from Leigh at the turn of the year, soon settled into the side and confirmed his pedigree as one of the sons of the legendary Gus with several seasons of excellent service.

Taking over goal-kicking duties which had previously been shared principally by Robin Dewhurst and Mick Shoebottom, Risman was an instant success with the boot and also provided extra attacking options from full-back where he emulated a trend instigated by other former stand off halves such as Brian Jefferson

developed in adversity.

After having moved to Barrow within two years of his arrival at Wigan Francis, in common with so many others, found his playing career disrupted by the Second World War. Unlike the majority of his contemporaries, however, Roy Francis may have benefited from the conflict. Along with many other leading players, he turned out regularly for Eddie Waring's Dewsbury side and it's reasonable to speculate that the young Francis learned much about presentational skills from the redoubtable Waring, who went on to become the voice of Rugby League, as far as the national TV audience was concerned, throughout the 1960s and 1970s.

Perhaps more importantly, Francis honed his skills as a fitness instructor with the commandos, who he trained to a peak of fitness on the north-west coast of Scotland, then as a remedial instructor.

Francis missed out on Dewsbury's 1942-43 Challenge Cup Final because of those commitments, but the lessons learned in the services would stand him in good stead when his playing days came to an end.

After glittering spells with Warrington and Hull, he turned to coaching at the Boulevard and subsequently with Leeds.

Francis' impact as a player, notable as it was, was eclipsed by his impact as a coach. He had learned much from his role as remedial instructor during the war, when he was handed the task of rebuilding shattered minds. Interested in psychology, he realised that players must be as happy off the field as on it and pioneered the practice of organising coach travel and match tickets for the players' wives.

His attention to detail paid off. Hull won the Championship in 1956 and 1958, finishing as runners up in the intervening season, and were Challenge Cup runners-up in 1959 and 1960 when injury crises wrecked both bids.

His exploits attracted the admiration of the ambitious Leeds board who saw Francis as the man best suited to guiding the many talented youngsters then emerging at Headingley.

Continued...

He was appointed as coach in the same year – 1963 – as the Loiners installed the underground heating system. Both moves were inspired.
Francis had a simple philosophy. He bought the right players – and many of his acquisitions were judicious to a degree with men such as Mick Clark and Bev Risman enjoying new leases of life at Headingley – and got them super fit.
Having taken care over his purchases, and instructed them to adopt an expansive style, he let them get on with the job in hand once they were out on the field.
Within three years the Loiners were embarking on a glorious epoch in which they would finish top of the table for four successive seasons, Francis' legacy long outliving his exit late in 1968.
Six months prior to his departure to North Sydney, Francis had witnessed his charges at their peak with the wonderful 25-4 victory over Wigan in the Challenge Cup semi-final.
The final itself, against Wakefield Trinity, was won – or, more accurately, not lost – 11-10 in a game ruined by a saturated pitch, but at least Roy Francis had the satisfaction of having secured the sport's major prize after the disappointments of 1959 and 1960. And with two Yorkshire Cup successes and a couple of Yorkshire League Championships, the results were exactly what the Leeds fans desired.
Equally importantly, those trophies were won in style. Leeds always had men in support and were always prepared to keep the ball moving as the hard work on the training ground paid off.
Francis' spell in Australia was ill-fated in terms of results, although his legacy Down Under may still be seen through the adoption of his methods by many Aussie coaches. He returned to England where he rejoined Hull, moving back to Leeds in 1974 where he took the Loiners to the Premiership title in 1974-75, characteristically pinning his faith in a young front row of David Ward, Steve Pitchford and Roy Dickinson. In what appears, sadly, to have been a breakdown in communications, he was not offered a renewed contract and switched to Bradford Northern, who he subsequently rescued from relegation worries.

(Keighley) and Castleford's Derek Edwards.

The signing of Risman complemented the capture, earlier in the season, of Poole, the former Hunslet loose forward who had featured for the Parksiders in the 1959 Championship Final alongside Brian Shaw before switching to Hull KR. Poole played some of his finest Rugby League at Leeds and was recognised as the Player of the Season. His form and leadership qualities were also noted by the selectors who offered him the role of Great Britain captain for

Electric Blanket

The decision of the Leeds board to instal, in April 1963, an electric blanket under the Headingley pitch was not universally popular at the time. But it proved to be inspired.
Leeds forked out £6,488 for the literally groundbreaking move, but that sum was recouped many times over.
The Rugby Football League naturally opted for Headingley rather than other venues for many of its major games, safe in the knowledge that representative games or cup finals would be certain to go ahead barring dangerous conditions on the terraces.
And the initiative benefited the Leeds side, which was free to strengthen its bid for honours while rivals were left twiddling their thumbs and watching outstanding fixtures pile up.
In addition, Headingley became a regular venue for the BBC which, like the Rugby Football League, could count on a slot in its Saturday afternoon Grandstand programme being filled.
So regularly did the Beeb visit Headingley that it was

Continued...

decided to erect a spiral staircase in the South Stand to enable easier access to the TV gantry for Eddie Waring, the commentator whose irrepressible wit and rounded northern vowels had made him a household name.

The Leeds board of the time deserve enormous credit for their vision, not least because there must have a been a strong temptation to splash the cash out on signings. The Loiners, at the time, were in a rare lull, the Championship of 1961 a distant memory as the team had slipped to the lower reaches of the First Division.

But Jack Myerscough and Alf Rutherford refused to take the easy option. Secure – and confident – in the knowledge that a raft of talented youngsters including scrum-half Barry Seabourne, stand-off Mick Shoebottom and centre Syd Hynes were coming through, Headingley bosses took the rational long-term view which must remain one of the most far-reaching, at club level, in any sport.

Says Harry Jepson, who joined the Leeds board in the early 1970s: 'Leeds were always in the forefront of initiatives like that. I remember Jack Myerscough, one season, saying to me, we'd had 14 league matches televised. I said to Jack, "is it wise, this? It's affecting our gates." And Jack said to me, "I don't care if nobody pays here. In fact we may well, in the future, just open up the gates." He pointed to the advertising hoards around the pitch and said, "this is our revenue." This was in the early days, we used to get around £1,000 for each hoarding if the game was on the telly – far bigger than the gate. "Very soon," he said, "people will be coming in without paying, so long as we've got this." Later, of course, there was an explosion of channels, it wasn't like it was when there was only the BBC. The control eventually swung more to advertisers. But Myerscough was a visionary, well ahead of anyone I ever knew, and he was certainly a visionary in his approach to TV and advertising, which was also enabled by the fact that potential advertisers knew that the game was going to be played.'

Alan Smith breaks clear against Wigan. Installing the electric blanket was continuing to pay dividends.

the 1966 tour to Australia and New Zealand. Together with Wriglesworth, who netted 11 tries in 16 games on tour, Poole was the only Headingley representative on the trip. The Lock Lane product had little luck Down Under, illness and injury causing him to become the first Lions captain not to play in an Australian Test. Significantly, Great Britain lost a record nine games in Australia, including two of the three tests, while all eight games in New Zealand were won.

The league season, meanwhile, was highlighted by an 11-match winning run between 8 January and 29 March in which Castleford, Bramley, Bradford Northern, Dewsbury, Halifax, Keighley and Hull were all disposed of. The fact that many of those games were far from easy was a cause for added satisfaction for Francis. Castleford were beaten by the odd point in 15, Halifax were toppled 12-9 at Headingley and Hull put up a solid effort after travelling west before being beaten 9-6. And while Dewsbury were comfortably beaten 18-2 a debt was owed to one man, Wriglesworth, who grabbed all of the Loiners' four touchdowns.

That run of success followed a record of 12 wins in the opening 18 games, which included an impressive 37-7 victory in late August over a Hunslet side that had performed so memorably less than four months earlier in the classic Challenge Cup final against Wigan. The prolific Wriglesworth raced over for a hat trick in the stroll, in which Dewhurst landed eight goals.

A Loiner Looks Back

John Atkinson

'I was initially a stand off with Roundhay Rugby Union and only switched to the wing after breaking my shoulder. Who knows how my career would have gone if not for that?

'My dad gave me a priceless piece of advice. He said, "when you're through the gap, don't look at the full-back. If you don't look at him he won't know what you're thinking. Many wingers go through and they do look. Once they've done that their next thought is, 'how am I going to beat him?' By the time they've made up their mind they will often have been tackled."

'My dad said, "he's in your vision, together with the posts and the tryline and the touchline, but don't focus on him." It worked perfectly, I would beat him without actually knowing I'd done it. The only problem is that people have asked me how I've scored a try and I've had to say, "I don't know, I've no idea." They've given me odd looks; it happened when I played in a country match in Australia on the 1974 tour, the press thought I was being funny. But if I analysed it I couldn't do it. In fact when you've had a bad game, when things go wrong, it's usually because you've thought about it too much.'

There was also a notable 'double' over Bradford Northern, who were settling nicely after having been reformed a year earlier and who won the Yorkshire Cup with the shock defeat of hot favourites Hunslet at Headingley.

The Loiners' league campaign finished on something of a low, however, with four successive defeats before a 12-9 victory over Dewsbury at Crown Flatt in which Risman scored a try and three goals and centre Dick Gemmell also crossed. That win was all the more commendable for having been achieved only two days after the Challenge Cup semi-final set back at the hands of Wigan. And the pressures on part-time players of the era were also illustrated by the fact that those four defeats

A Loiner Looks Back

Bev Risman

Bev Risman beats the challenge of Stan Gittins to score against Batley.

'I was frightened to death of Roy Francis when I got to Leeds but under him my career spanned another five years. I'd tried to play through a couple of serious injuries at Leigh, and I hadn't done myself any favours. I'd been on the verge of Great Britain, then Leigh started to struggle. They had a great pack when I arrived at Hilton Park but what I hadn't realised when I signed was that they were all in their thirties! I wasn't doing myself or the club justice and it was felt by both that a change of club might do me good.

'Leeds had shown interest when I was in Rugby Union but didn't want to pay the price. But Joe Warham had felt I was worth considering. I'd played stand-off, centre and full-back at Leigh but Leeds asked me to sign on the basis that they would play me at full-back. They wanted me to replace Robin Dewhurst, who had suffered a bad injury, and take over as goalkicker. That coincided with me being subjected to Roy Francis' fitness regime. Under him I became much fitter and stronger, and I only missed a dozen or so games in five seasons. My knee was never exactly right, but I put on pace. I remember Eddie Waring describing me as "deceptively slow" once. I think I know what he meant; at least I hope I do.'

Mackeson Trophy

'It looks good, it tastes good and, by golly, it does you good!'

The fondly remembered Mackeson Contest was tailor-made for a team of Leeds' qualities.

Launched as a pilot in 1961 as a means of rewarding the teams scoring most points against the touring New Zealand side – and to publicise the sweet-tasting stout – the Mackeson Contest came into its own when it was extended to League football in 1962-63.

The Mackeson Trophy and a cash prize was awarded to the side with the best scoring average throughout the season. In addition each campaign was split into five periods of six weeks each, with the winner of each period receiving the Mackeson flag, a cash prize and inscribed tankards for each of their players.

Leeds, invariably, were among the front runners and reached their apogee in 1967-68 when they not only topped the season table with a record average of 20.86, but also won three of the five periods.

That was the last season in which the Mackeson Trophy operated under the tried and tested format. In 1968-69 a 'Golden Ball' was introduced, with the ball in Warrington's possession at the start of the season and being handed on to the victor whenever the holder was defeated. The Loiners, once they secured possession, retained the Golden Ball for three games, not enough to deny Wigan who took the Trophy with 11 matches.

The following season – the last of Mackeson's sponsorship – saw another change with a 'Merit Table', which reflected the difference between points 'for' and 'against', being introduced. St Helens lifted the seasonal prize with 410 points but Leeds had the satisfaction of winning two of the four 'periods' with tallies of 117 points and 87 points respectively.

The Loiners' prowess in the competition was summed up in Oldham's programme notes for the third round Challenge Cup tie on 16 March 1968. The notes read: 'The incredible Leeds scoring spree goes on! The Headingley based club not only made it 13 League and Cup wins in a row by winning at Keighley on

Continued...

comprised games at Hunslet on 8 April (7-6), 9 April at home to Hull KR (3-0), at Wakefield (11 April) by 35-16 and at Castleford (12-10) on 16 April. A tough enough itinerary in itself, made all the more daunting by the drawn Challenge Cup quarter-final tie at Wilderspool on 6 April and the replay against Warrington on 15 April: a sequence of six important games in 11 days.

However, Football Chairman Jack Myerscough was clearly in no doubt that great days were around the corner. In his address to the Supporters' Club he insisted: 'I said last year that our immediate aim was a well-knit side capable of challenging the best. In large measure we achieved this. It was galling to see the game's honours elude us, yet at the same time we can take heart from having been semi-finalists in the Challenge Cup and having figured prominently in the League and Yorkshire Championships.

'Now we are faced with the demanding task of advancing from runners-up to winners. To do this, our immediate concern will be more forwards strength, and this means good big young forwards. The backs are relatively young and capable of reaching great heights given the lead up front.

'Our further success and your continued backing has improved the financial outlook. Despite heavy expenditure on our new lights, money will be found for men of the right calibre as they become available.'

Leeds had installed floodlights and Myerscough added: 'First acquaintance with

Saturday, but also won their third successive set of Mackeson Contest silver tankards.

'In the six-year history of the Mackeson points scoring contests no team has ever before won three consecutive period contests. After seeing Bradford Northern win period one with a 25.63 average, Leeds have now taken the next three with scores of 22.43, 24.00 and 23.22, quite remarkable consistency for well over five months.

'Leeds also look to be set for the main season-long contest prize of 200 guineas. Their average of 21.80 over 35 games puts them well clear of Hull KR (18.26) and Wakefield Trinity (17.71)

'It is interesting to note that just three years ago the Atkinson, Hynes, Langley, Smith back line were playing together in the 'A' team.

'Halves Mike Shoebottom and Barry Seabourne are one of the most dangerous combinations in the game and the Headingley side are blessed with a good pack of forwards. They have bought Bill Ramsey from Hunslet for £10,000 and another international is prop forward Mick Clark, who is playing fine football and leading the pack well.'

them will provide a pleasant thrill for all Rugby League followers. As I write, two of the four giant 110 ft pylons tower high above a Headingley turf which is as lush as it has ever been. Four gantries will top these, each carrying 36 powerful floodlights to transform night into day. With the underground heating also capable of turning Winter into Spring, the rugby world must once again recognise the pre-eminence of Headingley and it first-class amenities.

'The introduction of the lights will mean some experimentation with the fixtures. Much of this is done on a reciprocal basis with other clubs who possess lights. Our aim will always be the best possible arrangement for you, the supporters, so please bear with us during the process of finding the best formula.'

A Loiner Looks Back

Alan Smith

Alan Smith grabs a try at McLaren Field in the 14-0 Challenge Cup quarter-final victory in 1971.

'I went back to training when my broken leg had healed but once again I was surrounded by these great players they'd signed on. They'd signed Ronnie Cowan, a British Lion, while I was in hospital, for £6,000. I thought, "hell, that's my chance at Leeds finished." Then I thought, "Ah, but he's a right winger and I'm still on the left."

'Then Football Chairman Jack Myerscough said that Bramley were interested. He suggested a spell at the Barley Mow would provide valuable experience. Their chairman Doug Alton was a lovely man, and I was playing in the same side as Great Britain winger Terry Hollindrake. I could only look up to and admire these people and I loved it. I was there for four weeks; we got changed in the Barley Mow, climbing through the hatch into the pigeon loft which is where the changing rooms were based. It was a world away from having Arthur Crowther polishing your boots and having everything washed and ready for you for training. There was nothing wrong with that, I had a great four weeks, but it didn't feel right to sign for Bramley. Doug Alton said that if I wanted to go back to Leeds, Jack Myerscough would welcome me back. I was so delighted to be among my mates again that I think I scored four or five tries in my first match back.

'Then they made another big signing in John Atkinson, a left winger from Roundhay Rugby Union. It was time for an assessment and I began to look to the right wing. I don't know who was on the right wing, and it may have taken me a season, but I took the spot.'

4. THE DAWNING OF AN ERA

On 12 August 1966 Leeds travelled to Parkside for the pre-season Lazenby Cup clash with Hunslet.

The fans who gathered in south Leeds that day for the annual friendly – a misnomer, if ever there was one, for a game between these two old and often bitter neighbours – could not be aware that they were witnessing the opening page of arguably the greatest epoch in the sport's history.

The Lazenby Cup itself did not perhaps rank as a major trophy, keen as the old rivalries were, although there was obvious delight with a 28-10 win made memorable by a crunching but fair tackle in the early stages by Mick Shoebottom on Hunslet stand off Phil Morgan, a big money capture from the Valleys.

Jack Nelson who tradgically passed away at Christmas is picture back row far right, with the A team.

Leeds were to go on to win a major trophy in each of the next 14 seasons, a record almost unparalleled in the history of the game.

Significantly, the first two of those trophies, snaffled up by the summer of '67 which for Leeds was not so much the 'summer of love' as the 'summer of silver' were the ultimate reward for consistency. The Yorkshire League Championship was followed by the League Leaders trophy, arguably the one single honour which truly reflects a team's ability, against all manner of opposition and throughout the vagaries of the British climate from late summer, through autumn, into the depths of winter and back into the spring.

More importantly the Loiners assumed those mantles playing a brand of expansive football, under Roy Francis, which has perhaps never been bettered by any other side.

With his players in super-fit condition, Francis allowed men in whom he had the utmost faith to take their own options on the field of play.

The Loiners, benefiting from that approach, would finish top of the overall table, with 58 points, having sustained only five defeats in their 34 league fixtures. And of the 28 Yorkshire League fixtures included in that list, Leeds succumbed in only three.

Any side aims to turn its own home into a citadel and Leeds truly did that in league football, boasting a 100 per cent record at Headingley.

The desire to prevail on their home turf may have been fuelled by an unexpected defeat in the Yorkshire Cup when Bramley, so often a thorn in their illustrious neighbours' side, staged a stunning 20-18 victory in early September

Bev Risman

when both sides scored four tries – Leeds' going to centre Geoff Wriglesworth, with a brace, winger Ron Cowan and half-back Ken Rollin – but full-back Bev Risman's three goals weren't enough to deny the men from Barley Mow, who had gone down to Francis' men on their own patch on the opening day of the season 16-11.

Leeds had followed up that early success with two wins within the following week, 17-5 at home to Keighley and by a comfortable 23-2 margin against Castleford, with a 39-11 stroll at Mount Pleasant, Batley, wrapping up a healthy start to the campaign.

Shoebottom was in unstoppable form that day at Mount Pleasant, enjoying one of his more formidable games in the blue and gold.

The half-back, given the kicking role in the absence of Risman, landed nine goals but the youngster, now growing in stature with every game, was equally effective with the ball in hand.

Headingley Heroes

Jack Myerscough

Sport is primarily about players. They are the people who the fans pay good money to see, they are the people who youngsters place on a pedestal and hope, one day, to emulate, and they are the people who in a side such as Leeds achieve the honours and are rightly accorded the accolades.

The coaches, too, undertake a vital if more peripheral role. Men such as Dai Prosser, Joe Warham, Roy Francis, Jack Nelson – with the junior and A teams and, sadly, for an all-too brief spell with the first team – followed by Derek Turner, Eric Ashton, Francis again and Syd Hynes, all brought their individual experiences and talents to bear on the success story that is Headingley Heroes.

None of the players or the coaches, however, could have accomplished their many achievements without a solid infrastructure established and sustained by the men upstairs.

Jack Myerscough, Leeds Football Chairman for much of the period, was the mastermind behind much of the Loiners' success and together with men of the calibre of Alf Rutherford, Noel Stockdale, Norman Shuttleworth, AB Sharman and Harry Jepson, supported by Football Manager Joe Warham, created the environment in which the young talent at Headingley could blossom and flourish.

Players who joined the Loiners from other clubs were invariably struck by the benevolent and supportive management style at Leeds. Perhaps the last of the breed of 'gentlemen directors' at one time endemic in British sport, Myerscough and Rutherford were paternalist to a degree; and their coaches and players responded positively.

Myerscough's easy bon homie masked a profound resolve; a quality which was shared by his colleagues in the boardroom. As evidence, the actions of the Leeds board in 1963, under the chairmanship of Noel Stockdale, speak volumes.

As the 1962-63 season ground to a close, the

Continued...

Championship campaign of two years earlier was becoming a distant and piquant memory. From pole position in 1960-61, the Loiners had slipped to seventh in each of the following two seasons, and would finish thirteenth in 1963-64 and tenth in 1964-65.

Myerscough and his colleagues, however, were convinced that their focus on building up the junior structure at Headingley would pay off. And they were quite clearly prepared to accept, for a season or two, indifferent results in the knowledge that sustained success was around the corner

For proof, the sceptic may consider where Leeds spent their money in the spring of 1963. Not on the big money player who would have delighted the fans and perhaps brought some measure of instant success.

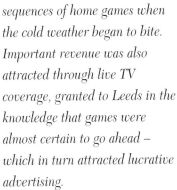

Jack Myerscough with his coach Syd Hynes.

Myerscough and his board opted to splash out £6,488 on an underground heating system. And the huge investment, while invisible, was to pay rich dividends many times over.

When the young players eventually blossomed and Francis's coaching methods took root, the 'electric blanket' proved its value on many fronts.

Leeds were able to avoid the problems caused by fixture backlogs, and also benefited from playing significant sequences of home games when the cold weather began to bite.

Important revenue was also attracted through live TV coverage, granted to Leeds in the knowledge that games were almost certain to go ahead – which in turn attracted lucrative advertising.

The Yorkshire Cup Final, controversially, was staged at Headingley for a number of years in the 1970s, giving Leeds what was undoubtedly an unfair advantage when – as was often the case – they managed to reach the decider.

That, however, was not the fault of the players or, for that matter, the directors who were merely reaping the

Continued...

Shoey raced over for four of his side's seven tries, the others going to John Sykes, John Langley and Eddie Ratcliffe.

The early-season bubble burst with Bramley but the removal of any distractions caused by the Yorkshire Cup led to seven successive victories to back up the opening quartet.

Hunslet, growing heartily sick of the sight of Leeds, were again outgunned on their own midden, going down 42-12 in the league encounter in which Risman scored a try and nine goals and Cowan had a hat trick. Centre Dick Gemmell, who raced over for two tries against the Parksiders, repeated the feat eight days later in an incredible 38-25 victory over Wigan when Shoebottom also netted two trademark touchdowns.

Risman kicked 163 goals throughout the season, landing seven in the win over Wigan and six the following week, when tries for Ratcliffe, Wriglesworth, second row Mick Clark, Rollin and Les Chamberlain steered the Loiners to a 20-point victory over Yorkshire Cup holders Bradford Northern at Odsal.

Batley, surprisingly, were of sterner mettle at Headingley than on their own patch, going down only 20-5 in the return at Headingley and Leeds went on to have a tough October, albeit in a month when they maintained their hold at the head of the table.

Three successive home victories were all hard-fought. Hull were edged 14-11 and

reward for their earlier courage and vision.
Few clubs, in any case, resented a visit to Headingley. Long-serving Leeds stalwart Billy Watts recalls that Myerscough's maxim was, 'when you win, say nothing, and when you lose, say less.' That philosophy was confirmed to the delight of St Helens players and officials when after having ended the Loiners' long unbeaten home run in January 1973 five bottles of champagne were carried into their dressing room with a congratulatory note.
That's a moving example of sportsmanship and generosity and it wasn't merely extended to the opposition.
Phil Cookson sums up the players' position: 'The management at Leeds was absolutely fabulous. If you performed for Alfred Rutherford and Jack Myerscough, if you won trophies, they would give you the world. The light training sessions and rub downs on Sunday mornings were wonderful. It didn't happen every week but very often we'd have our treatments with a bottle or two of champagne and smoked salmon. Absolute gentlemen, both millionaires in their own right. They were in Rugby League for enjoyment, not as a job. I'll never forget them as long as I live. They broke the mould and the mould's gone now with them.'
Apart from that hospitality, many an away game in Cumbria or Lancashire was broken by a stopover en route when Myerscough and Rutherford would stroll to the bar and order pints all round for the players and, of course, champagne for the directors. And it became something of a tradition, after Friday night matches in the far north west, for the players to be treated to a weekend in Blackpool.
True gentlemen directors, the like of which may not be seen again.

Doncaster – who would have only Batley to thank for avoiding the wooden spoon six months later – lost 22-14 despite matching Leeds' two tries. Risman, again, was a match winner, landing eight important goals and also scoring a try to complement Ratcliffe's touchdown.

The closeness of that season's competition was also highlighted by Dewsbury, thwarted 7-5, when a Ratcliffe try was again crucial, along with two Risman goals, and between-times the Loiners had been held to a home draw against Castleford in the BBC2 Floodlit Trophy, Drew Broatch racing over for Leeds' solitary touchdown, Risman kicking two goals and Seabourne scoring an important drop goal. St Helens ended the unbeaten run with a 16-3 victory at Knowsley Road at the end of October, Risman being denied any goal-kicking opportunities other than the conversion attempt of Gemmell's try.

Oldham, still something of a power and seeking to return to the glories of the 1950s, were overcome 21-14 at Headingley in a Bonfire Night cracker and the Loiners backed up that victory with successive away wins at Keighley, 22-15, and at Doncaster by 31-13.

Two sides in the Manchester area, however, ensured that November ended on a negative note. Oldham gained revenge for the defeat at Headingley with a 16-13 verdict at the Watersheddings, when Leeds fell just short with tries by Cowan, Rollin and Gemmell and Risman added two goals. And, four days later, Leeds had to cross the Pennines again, going down 10-4 at Swinton in the BBC2 Floodlit Trophy.

Those defeats served to galvanise the Loiners into extra effort. Bramley were brushed aside, on the return to bread-and-butter action, 34-8 when South African Lou Neumann crossed for a

A Loiner Looks Back

John Holmes

'Bradford Northern, as well as Leeds, wanted to sign me. Northern's chairman, Harry Womersley, came to see me and talked to my dad. He offered me a slightly better contract than Leeds had, with improved terms for playing so many matches, gaining representative honours and so on. And he also brought his chequebook.

Another classical pass from John Holmes.

'He wrote out a cheque, not for a massive amount, a couple of hundred quid or so, and he left it on the mantelpiece. This cheque was up there, and eventually my dad asked me what I wanted to do. I said, "I just want to play for Leeds. Tear the cheque up." So he did.

'It had been my goal, after our kid signed, to sign for Leeds too and follow in his footsteps. Leeds came down the following week and I signed. Over a bottle of whiskey, I might add, but I didn't get a glass. Jack Myerscough, my dad and, I think, Joe Warham took a bottle, as they were agreeing the deal, into another room and I was called in to sign.

'My dad wasn't a Rugby League man. He was an Irishman; he had come over here when he was 17, with his two brothers. His preferred sport was chess, and he liked crosswords. He was a very intelligent man, but the ability my brothers and I have in active sports comes from my mother's side. My uncle was Johnny Feather, who played for Leeds and then transferred to Oldham. He was killed in a motor accident going over the Pennines in about 1952.

'So it was born in us. Our Philip could play, and our Brian could play but he had mastoids in his ear when he was about 21, and he had to pack it in. In fact he was a very good backstroke swimmer; he had Yorkshire trials and he was going very well until his ear problems. We didn't have to train or practice. We were just lucky, we had it.'

try and added a rare drop goal, while winger Alan Smith netted two tries and Harry Poole scored his first try in nearly three months.

Halifax, Championship runners-up the previous season, were beaten 11-5 at Thrum Hall, and there was an equally impressive win, 19-5, against Featherstone Rovers at Post Office Road.

A tough Yuletide schedule opened with a 9-6 home win over Hull KR on Christmas Eve, and a 28-8 victory over Wakefield Trinity, also at Headingley, on Boxing Day. That schedule perhaps took its toll, the Loiners going down to Hull KR 11-9 at Craven Park the following day, although the next trip east, on New Year's Eve, was altogether more satisfactory. Leeds, who had posted a John Atkinson try and three Risman goals in the setback at Rovers, were again limited to nine points, Mick Clark crossing and Risman again adding a conversion and two penalties. But, on this occasion, Hull FC could only muster eight points as Leeds closed the year at the head of the table.

Leeds fans hoping for a relaxing festive period were again dealt no favours by their favourites who hosted Bradford for their first game of 1967 and edged Northern 10-9, Risman converting tries by Wriglesworth and Ray Batten. And it was a similar story seven days later when Featherstone came to Headingley and were pipped by the odd point in 25, tries for Atkinson, Syd Hynes and Cowan, plus two Risman goals, being enough to see Leeds through. But the watching was easier, if perhaps less exciting, in

Headingley Floodlights

The Headingley floodlights were installed in 1966, Leeds being among the first clubs to embrace a concept which met with some resistance among traditionalists.

Many of those clubs without lights of their own were reluctant to play under floodlights, insisting that their players would be at an unfair disadvantage.

By the end of the decade, however, and thanks to the popular BBC2 Floodlit Trophy, which was played on Tuesday evenings throughout the season, most Rugby League clubs had taken the idea on board.

The Loiners had actually toyed with the idea many years before. In the early days of the Northern Union, in 1896-97, Leeds had experimented with a 'new electrical system'.

Nearly 70 years later the Loiners, in common with most other clubs in the Rugby League, finally embraced floodlights, installing a high-power system, set in each corner. Football Chairman Jack Myerscough enthused: 'First acquaintance with them will provide a pleasant thrill for all Rugby League followers. As I write, two of the four giant 110 ft pylons tower high above a Headingley turf which is as lush as it has ever been. Four gantries will top these, each carrying 36 powerful floodlights to transform night into day. With the underground heating also capable of turning Winter into Spring, the Rugby world must once again recognise the pre-eminence of Headingley and its first-class amenities.

'The introduction of the lights will mean some experimentation with the fixtures. Much of this is done on a reciprocal basis with other clubs who possess lights. Our aim will always be the best possible arrangement for you, the supporters, so please bear with us during the process of finding the best formula.'

the home game against Halifax. Batten (2), Poole and Alan Lockwood netted the Loiners' tries and Risman kicked five goals in the 22-0 success which set Francis' charges up nicely for the Challenge Cup campaign.

The Loiners drew Blackpool Borough at home in what was to be a historic first round. Borough, formed in 1954, had never played Leeds before, either at Headingley or on their own Borough Park ground. Despite having occupied the nether regions of the league throughout most of their short history, Borough were not without hope at Headingley.

Only two years earlier, Blackpool had reached the quarter-finals before going down to mighty Wakefield Trinity 4-0 at Belle Vue in a match which could have gone either way.

Leeds, therefore, were 'on alert' and ground out a 15-3 victory in which tries for Gemmell, Atkinson and Cowan confirmed the Loiners' superior pace, Risman complementing the scores with three goals.

Leeds knew they were in for a tough test in the next round, at Oldham, where the home side had every right to be confident after their narrow league win over the Loiners exactly three months earlier. A crowd of over 15,000 packed the Watersheddings, many hopeful that Oldham would clear a big hurdle and go on to correct the glaring deficiency for such a great club of never having appeared at Wembley.

The Loiners were up for the task of leaving the Roughyeds with unfulfilled dreams. Atkinson netted two tries, Broatch grabbed the third, and Risman kicked two goals to help steer the club into the quarter-finals and, hopefully, improvement on the third-round defeat by Hunslet two years previously.

A Loiner Looks Back

Alan Smith

'My first recollection of even thinking I was going to be a first teamer was the Boxing Day game in 1966 against Wakefield Trinity. There was a 21,000 crowd and many fans will probably say that was the day

Alan Smith on a typically determined run. St Helens full back Geoff Pimblett has the task of attempting to halt his progress.

both John Atkinson and I forced our way into the equation. John had a mood about him, an aura of a man who was going to take the left wing spot. There was a question mark about me, they'd tried to sell me to Bramley as the story goes, I'd broken my leg, but I'd been learning my trade. I got two tries against Wakefield and I think that was the dawning of my career at Leeds, maybe the first realisation to the public, maybe to Roy Francis, maybe even to myself, that I might have a part to play.'

Swinton, another power, represented no lesser challenge in the quarter final and Leeds were glad of home advantage against a side that had been champions in successive seasons in 1962-63 and 1963-64. Many of the players who had achieved that feat were still at Station Road and it took a huge effort for Leeds to grind out a 17-15 win with tries by John Davies and Gemmell, a try and two goals for Risman and two goals by scrum-half Seabourne.

That set up a semi-final at Fartown, Huddersfield, against a Featherstone Rovers outfit which were in the last four for the seventh time in 15 years but with just one success – in their first venture, when they beat Leigh 6-2 before going down 18-10 to Workington Town at Wembley.

Leeds, having lost 7-2 to Wigan at the same venue and at the same stage in 1966, were

Headingley Hero

Barry Seabourne

A true captain courageous, the diminutive Barry Seabourne set several records during his eight-year career at Headingley and left a lasting impression with his inimitable style of football.

Yet another Hunslet lad to pursue his career 'north of the river,' Seabourne made his debut for Leeds on 25 May 1963 at Hull KR, at the age of 16 years and three months, to become the youngest Loiner in history.

And, following a suggestion by Mick Clark shortly after the Yorkshire Cup Final success against Castleford in October 1968, Seabourne became Leeds' youngest ever captain, at just 21 years of age.

The wisdom of the appointment was never in doubt but the degree of its success was nevertheless remarkable. Leeds were denied a return to Wembley after having beaten Wakefield Trinity in the 1968 Watersplash Final, Castleford edging a rousing quarter-final tie at Wheldon Road the following season. Otherwise the Loiners, guided by Seabourne and his midfield triangle partners of Ray Batten and Mick Shoebottom, carried all before them.

Seabourne was reputed to lack a yard or two of pace but with his vast armoury of skills and finely-honed leadership qualities he steered Leeds to a third

Continued...

successive League Leaders trophy, a third successive Yorkshire League title and, notably, the Championship, with the European Championship also being netted in the following autumn for good measure. The Championship semi-final win over Salford, who were toppled 22-12 at Headingley, was possibly Seabourne's finest moment and proof positive, at least, of his physical courage. Leeds' captain was forced to visit the dugout on no fewer than four occasions with a dislocated shoulder, returning to the fray in agony. But his bravery had its reward with a victory which set up a final against Castleford.

On this occasion the almost inevitable shoulder dislocation resulted in Seabourne's permanent withdrawal midway through the first half but there was to be revenge for the Challenge Cup defeat with Bev Risman's late charge leading to a try for John Atkinson, Risman's conversion sealing a 16-14 victory. Sore shoulder notwithstanding, the world appeared to be at Barry Seabourne's feet. His shrewd orchestration of his backs and his forwards, his effective kicking game, his penchant for the timely drop goal and his unique 'dummy', with arm raised, had attracted the attention of the international selectors and he was duly called up for what was to be the historic Great Britain tour of Australia and New Zealand in 1970.

Sadly, injury struck once again. This time, it was Seabourne's knee which caused the problem, limiting him to just eight games on the trip, including the First Test in New Zealand which the Lions won 19-15. Seabourne's international career, however, was over, and his time at Leeds was also running out.

The knee injury ruled the scrum-half out of all but 17

Continued...

seeking to avoid a repeat and, with the League Leadership Trophy under their belts by the time the teams met on Saturday 1 April, were viewed as strong favourites by most of the 20,052 crowd.

Featherstone, however, proved to be the hungrier – and at Wembley, too, when Barrow were beaten 17-12 – and, having had to overcome Bradford Northern, Wakefield Trinity and Castleford en route, in addition to Leeds, could certainly claim they had done it the hard way. With 19-year-old second row Jimmy Thompson coming of age, Rovers won 16-8 in a game in which Roy Francis' gamble on the fitness of Hynes, Cowan and Chamberlain didn't pay off, with only the latter lasting the pace.

There was, however, the satisfaction of having secured the Yorkshire League and League Leadership Trophies. After that big win over Halifax at the end of January, Leeds slipped at Castleford the week after the victory over Blackpool, finding themselves edged 19-15 despite a try and three goals by Bev Risman and touchdowns by Gemmell and Harry Poole, who had been raised just around the corner from Wheldon Road.

There were, though, to be no more defeats until the trip to Wakefield Trinity on 27 March, only four days before the Challenge Cup clash with Featherstone, when Trinity, perhaps understandably, won 27-9. Between those setbacks, Leeds prevailed in all five of their league fixtures, starting with a stunning 17-7 victory at Central Park over Wigan, to complete a notable 'double' which ultimately cost the Pie *games the following season; and the last was one in which he perhaps should not really have played. Barely match fit, he stepped forward following the career-ending injury to Mick Shoebottom to take a half-back spot in the 1971 Challenge Cup Final against Leigh. The day was, emphatically, to belong to the Lancastrians and a little over five months later, with Keith Hepworth having been brought to Leeds by coach Derek Turner, Barry Seabourne played his last match for the Loiners; ironically at Craven Park, Hull, where his career had begun eight years earlier.*

At 24, however, he was far from finished, joining Bradford Northern for a paltry £3,000 and serving the Odsal outfit well for six years before ending his career with a two-year stint at Keighley.

Bill Ramsey, a man able to both give and take a quality pass, remains an acolyte. He says: 'Coming on to passes was easy when Barry Seabourne was hitting you. He used to just say, "pick your gap and I'll hit you with it". He did that and off you went through. Easy enough isn't it? Well, it was with Barry Seabourne. A lot of the time I was just striding into space, he was a fine player.'

Eaters a place in the top 16 play-offs.

Hynes and Seabourne kicked a drop goal each in a resounding triumph, Risman added two goals, and the Loiners touchdowns went to Gemmell, Hynes and Cowan.

A Loiner Looks Back

John Sykes

'My best season was 1966/67. We finished top of the league and were only beaten five times. I damaged my knee in 1967 and then Leeds signed Bill Ramsey.

'I played with Lewis Jones and many other fine players. When John Holmes came I was captain of the second team. I was a local lad, from Meanwood, and I had to make way for the signings from Wales. But we were looked after, Secretary Bill Carter insisted I take expenses, even though I walked from where I lived in Meanwood. Someone once kept a programme from when we played at Halifax. Of the lads on that teamsheet, eight went on to be internationals.'

While it has to be accepted that Wigan were in something of a lull, their neighbours St Helens, emphatically, were not. The Saints, who would only be denied the Championship that season after a replay with Wakefield Trinity – Headingley providing the stage for the initial 7-7 draw – were more soundly beaten by Leeds than the 26-20 scoreline suggests, registering only two tries while Batten scampered over for a rare hat trick and Atkinson also crossed for Leeds.

York provided almost comparable opposition, also scoring two tries and shipping four, a week later, and fading Hunslet were no match for the Loiners in the Good Friday derby, going down 24-5 at Headingley when Leeds again totalled four tries, this time through Gemmell, Alan Smith, Lockwood and Hynes, with Risman adding six goals.

York were disposed of 34-16 less than 24 hours later, at Wiggington Road, when Bernard Watson bagged a brace, but with the Challenge Cup semi-final around the corner and having played two games in as many days, the Easter Monday trip to Wakefield was a step too far.

Leeds wrapped up their league season with a 38-13 victory at Dewsbury in which Ratcliffe scored four tries and Watson had another brace but Castleford were again to be Leeds' bogey side in the Championship.

Widnes were overcome 27-18 in the first round of the play-offs, through tries by Atkinson (2), Alan Smith, Langley and Chamberlain, Risman again boasting his accuracy with six

This Sporting Life

Leeds played a central role in the acclaimed film 'This Sporting Life' which starred Richard Harris.
The film, in the vanguard of the ground-breaking 'kitchen sink' dramas of the day, was based on a book by Wakefield-born David Storey, who had played for the Loiners in the 1950s. Much of the action was shot at Trinity's Belle Vue ground and featured Wakefield's stars of the day, and Leeds were again involved as the match-day crowd scenes were shot at a match between the two clubs.
Harris won an actor's award at the Cannes Film Festival for his portrayal of the hard-bitten Rugby League player Frank Machin and, impressed by the men he had met during shooting, went on to become a President of Wakefield Trinity.
Leeds, too, had their own star supporters. Diana Rigg, made world-famous by her role as Emma Peel in The Avengers, was born in Doncaster but moved to Leeds as a girl and was a regular on the Headingley terraces.

goals, but the campaign ground to a halt with the second round 13-9 defeat at the hands of the Glassblowers, who scored three tries and limited the Loiners to a solitary Drew Broatch try.

The season, though, had been a highly satisfactory prelude to a glorious era. The Loiners ended the league campaign with 704 points scored; their highest total for a decade, and a harbinger of things to come. Significantly, no player broke the 20-try barrier in all matches, Ratcliffe claiming pole position in the rankings with 16 tries. Gemmell followed on the 14 mark, Atkinson, Cowan and Shoebottom had 12 apiece and Batten and Rollin both scored 10.

Football Chairman Jack Myerscough hit the nail on the head when, in his post-season report for the Supporters' Club, he reflected: 'We were able to hold off all challengers in a record-breaking period of League Leadership which gained us the League Leaders' Trophy and the Yorkshire League Cup.

'It is not the plea of the poor loser but a statement of hard fact to claim that a series of injuries to players was the major factor in the destruction of our aspiration to Championship and Wembley glory. These injuries were not confined to first team personnel but extended to key reserves whose assistance was denied to us at the most critical period in the fight for honours.

'In the light of all this the achievement of the 'A' team in winning the Senior Competition 'double' of Championship and Challenge Cup becomes even more commendable. It is a happy augury for the future. With these youngsters maturing and a splendid team spirit permeating the dressing room, we look forward with high enthusiasm.'

Leeds, under Francis, had adapted much more quickly to the new four-tackle rule than any other side and Myerscough continued prophetically: 'The new rule has certainly injected sparkle into our game and this, coupled with the superb fitness engendered by our club coach, Mr Roy Francis, has given us some fine entertainment. Roy has worked tremendously hard and now looks forward to a season of redoubled effort to achieve that little extra which will bring us to the ultimate goal.'

5. AT THE PEAK OF GREATNESS

Leeds entered the 1967-68 campaign with the League Leadership Trophy and the Yorkshire League Championship cup safely ensconced in the Headingley trophy cabinet but determined to improve on that record and confident of their ability to do so in the first full season of the four-tackle rule after the previous year's eight-month trial.

Wakefield fans up for the cup clash with Leeds.

The Loiners arguably adapted to the change from unlimited tackles better than any other side in the competition as visionary coach Roy Francis invoked a policy of all his players being athletes. His players, in return, readily adopted an expansive approach which suited the new era. And the strategy was to reap rich rewards.

The players' fitness was important. As part-timers many were already in fine condition from work in the pit or elsewhere, others less so, but Francis moulded his side into a finely tuned unit in attack and a pragmatic machine in defence.

Leeds would eclipse the previous season's 704 points tally in league games, passing that total in the penultimate game, a 16-5 victory at Headingley over Huddersfield on 12 April when winger John Atkinson, who was to top the list with 33 touchdowns, grabbed two tries.

The Loiners were also to make another important signing with the acquisition for £9,000 of Bill Ramsey from neighbours Hunslet in the autumn.

Prior to Ramsey's arrival the Loiners had stuttered relatively unimpressively through the first third of the season.

Francis' pursuit of the international second row forward, and of others before Ramsey, had the full backing of the board and illustrated Leeds' ambitions to improve on the previous season's achievements. Those aims were perhaps fired by the side's heavy defeat at Francis' previous club, Hull FC, in the Yorkshire Cup semi-final when the Airlie Birds prevailed 31-6. Leeds had reached the penultimate stage after victories at Batley, 25-10, when Mick Shoebottom notched two tries to help haul his side back from 10-2 down at half time, and at home to Hunslet who didn't quite have enough quality to avoid an 18-14 defeat in which Loiners hooker Tony Crosby netted a brace.

League form, too, had been relatively indeterminate after the Lazenby Cup opener in

A Loiner Looks Back

Bev Risman

'Roy Francis built the team on younger players. Barry Seabourne, John Atkinson, John Holmes, Phil Cookson and Graham Eccles came through the ranks while I was there, but his trick was also to bring together a lot of good footballers and let them get on with it. He saw his role as getting us in the right frame of mind. He picked up a lot of mature players, many of whom were perhaps starting to go downhill, and he rejuvenated their careers. He was marvellous at being able to identify that kind of man. There was Harry Poole, Les Chamberlain, the South African Lou Neumann and Dick Gemmell. They were all very experienced and very good buys. He was good at bringing on men like Eddie Ratcliffe, Geoff Wriglesworth, and the likes of Alan Lockwood and Tony Crosby who weren't household names but served Leeds very well. Crosby, for example, had tremendous speed and scored a fair few tries simply by following instructions to patrol the centre channel down the pitch. Roy Francis knew the assets of his players and he allowed us to express ourselves, even if what we tried didn't always come off.

'Mick Clark was a great example, he wasn't much more than a journeyman player when he came to Leeds and he was a revelation at Headingley.'

Coach Roy Francis enjoys his first Challenge Cup success, after a series of near-misses.

which Shoebottom raced over for a hat trick in the home 34-17 win over Hunslet.

Bramley were beaten at the newly opened McLaren Field in the first league game of the season, 4,000 packing the homely arena to witness Leeds recording a 24-11 win. Four days later, however, St Helens arrived at Headingley and departed having pocketed a 13-12 win after Leeds had been 10 points ahead at half time.

Leeds, playing two games a week in a busy opening, closed August with a 17-15 home win over Featherstone Rovers, earned with tries for Dick Gemmell, Shoebottom and former Hunslet prop Ken Eyre, with full-back Bev Risman adding four goals. But there was a worrying echo of the previous game, Francis' men having to hang on at the close after having led 17-0 at the break.

Two days later, the Loiners headed to Fartown where Huddersfield were toppled 26-18 in a more classy account in which Alan Smith, in favour after several seasons in the A team, crossed. Risman, who would land 147 goals during the season, contributed a try and seven goals and the remaining two tries went to Shoebottom and Gemmell.

Five days after having beaten Batley at Headingley in the Yorkshire Cup in an unconvincing outing, Leeds travelled to Mount Pleasant for a league encounter and slumped to a stunning 13-12 defeat as the Gallant Youths, inspired by former Leeds half-back Trevor Oldroyd, played to their maximum potential.

Leeds were criticised following that defeat for a series of panic-fuelled passes, and it was with relief that the Loiners got back to winning ways three days later with a 12-10 home win over

Workington Town in which poor defence allowed the Town to dictate play and return to Cumbria as unlucky losers.

A mere four days after Gemmell, Risman and Robin Dewhurst had steered the Loiners to the narrow Yorkshire Cup win over Hunslet, Bradford Northern arrived at Headingley. Leeds were again exposed up front, and former Loiners centre Geoff Wriglesworth impressed for Northern as the visitors eased to a 20-10 victory which rammed home the message that Leeds needed to strengthen.

The supporters were, however, reminded that there was plenty of ability in the camp in the 25-8 victory at Castleford, when Dave Hick crossed twice. The Castleford programme notes, incidentally, offered a reminder of the way in which coaches, as always, will seek to get around the rules: 'From Rugby League Headquarters comes a message condemning the latest practice of teams deliberately kicking the ball dead after the third tackle in the hopes of gaining possession from the resultant drop-out. Spectators will no doubt be in agreement with Headquarters, for such tactics do not make good watching.'

Those worries led to defending sides being allowed a tap on their own 25 at the restart but Leeds supporters at the time were more

A crucial Alan Smith try in the Challenge Cup victory at Oldham in March 1968.

Headingley Hero

Ray Batten

Ray Batten was the cultured orchestrator of much that was most admirable about the Leeds sides of the era.

The loose forward possessed an almost mystical ability to prise open the most uncompromising of defences and his team-mates profited immeasurably.

Bob Haigh, the second row forward bought from Wakefield Trinity in April 1970, was a major beneficiary and broke the Rugby Football League's try-scoring record for a forward with 40 in his first full season.

Most came courtesy of Batten, as Haigh was quick to point out.

Of fine Rugby League stock – his grandfather was the immortal Billy Batten, his uncle the legendary Eric – Ray Batten carved out his own niche in the annals of the sport with his highly individual and creative game. Aided by the habit of carrying the ball in both hands, Batten's quick mind more than made up for the perceived lack of pace which put paid to his ambitions, with Heworth Under 17s, to play at stand-off half or scrum-half.Ideally suited to the loose forward role, he enjoyed a highly productive midfield partnership with scrum-half Barry Seabourne and stand-off Mick Shoebottom in the great Loiners outfit of the late 1960s and early 1970s.

Batten played for Leeds from 1963 to 1976 and also forged creative midfield links with Alan Hardisty and Keith Hepworth.

Continued...

He admits: 'I can't really explain my ball handling; I suppose it was a gift and maybe the fact that I wasn't fast enough helped me develop the rest of my game. I played from when I was four years old and I think that also helped. And I watched clever players when I was younger, such as Jeff Stevenson and Tommy Smales, and Brian McTigue.

'We scored a lot of tries from moves set up four tackles earlier, not just from free kicks. I was in charge and I'd say, 'left' or 'right' or do this or that. I'd talk to Phil Cookson or Bob Haigh and tell them where to go. Albert Eyre was another great forward. Bob Haigh and Phil Cookson got a lot of praise but Albert and Graham Eccles were just as good, and Bill Ramsey was wonderful.'

So was Batten and his long-standing team-mate Alan Smith enthuses: 'Ray was not slow. His manner seemed slow because of his handling; but he was almost mesmerising the opposition. People hardly realised that Ray was actually going forward all the time with the ball, and he looked to be doing it with so much time and so much space that everybody else seemed to be slowed down. He was absolute quality.'

When Batten enjoyed his benefit in 1973 he was honoured with eulogies from Joe Warham and the Yorkshire Evening Post's Arthur Haddock.

Wrote Warham. 'The great joy is to see the man in action – the studied handling; the casual turn and slipped pass which opens up a lane through a seeming wall of defenders. And all so simple, so easy – the ease of genius. The better one understands rugby the better one appreciates Ray Batten.'

Ray Batten as opposing defences feared him, with the ball in both hands.

Haddock enthused: 'Nobody keeps a record of these things, but it would be highly interesting to know how many men Ray Batten has sent in for tries, deceiving the opposition by sleight of hand, and then picking the right man to send haring away, using brain rather than brawn. Ray is a man who has made Leeds tick during the last decade.'

Ray Batten showed the kind of loyalty and sportsmanship that made him a deserved recipient of the Yorkshire Federation of Rugby League Supporters' Clubs' Jim Harrison Trophy in 1971 as the Fairest and Most Loyal Player in the county. He says: 'The fans, the directors, the players were all wonderful. When I finished playing I coached Wakefield Trinity and we came to Leeds and won. Even then, I was made very welcome. It's a good feeling; it's something about Leeds people, if you're successful in sport they will appreciate it.

concerned with indifferent form which was, perhaps, brought to a head with the County Cup defeat at Hull, followed by a mediocre 17-5 win over Dewsbury at Headingley.

The following week the Loiners journeyed to Odsal where a 14,469 crowd witnessed a revival with an 18-14 win, two drop goals by scrum-half Barry Seabourne providing the winning margin.

Bradford's programme revealed that Francis' hunt for talent was no secret within the game. Northern's writer, pondering on a £14,000 offer made by the Loiners to Hull KR for packmen Bill Holliday and Frank Foster, wrote: 'The answer was a quick no-sale sign but, knowing the Leeds method, one can be sure the search will be never-ending until the right man is found.'

The trawl did continue as Leeds won only five of their next nine games. Halifax sneaked a 5-5 draw at Thrum Hall in the BBC2 Floodlit Trophy, helped by a disallowed 'try' for Atkinson, the Loiners winning the replay 12-7 in a match in which winger Ron Cowan raced over for two tries before a crowd of under 4,000.

Importantly, prop Mick Clark showed his old

Hooker Tony Crosby (with the ball) and prop Ken Eyre in action at Oldham

form in the 26-10 victory over Hunslet at Parkside, when substitutes Hick and John Burke also put in creditable performances in a game described as the 'tamest derby for some time.'

Lowly Doncaster were unable to match Leeds in the first game in November, going down 45-5 in a game marred by a shoulder injury to Mick Joyce, with Hick and Atkinson grabbing two tries apiece.

But the grey atmosphere which permeated Headingley in the early part of the campaign was summed up in the game against York when a poor crowd turned up for the 32-7 win. Despite hat tricks for Atkinson and Dick Gemmell the Supporters' Club's post-season reflection was, 'poor day, poor opposition, no new signings – just over 3,000 fans. Matches such as this without personality appeal or opposition will never win back spectators.'

That was about to change – particularly the comment about 'no new signings.' A notable 13-8 win at Hull KR, when John Langley scored Leeds' only try but Risman (3) and Seabourne (2) kicked timely goals, involved displays of international class by centres Syd Hynes and Gemmell, but the Loiners were brought crashing back to earth with the 19-12 home reverse at the hands of Bramley, earned through an awesome display by the Villagers' forwards.

November closed with a grim 7-4 defeat by the Australian tourists, and a 12-9 setback at Castleford in the BBC2 Floodlit Trophy, when Langley again scored his side's only try and the departure of Robin Dewhurst following what was reported as a 'vicious tackle' was crucial.

Five reserves were drafted in for the league game, three days later, at Hull where the Loiners really upset the formbook with a 28-4 victory in which Seabourne and Shoebottom impressed.

The following Friday evening a player made his debut, in an otherwise unmemorable game against Keighley, who was to have a huge impact on Leeds' fortunes.

A Loiner Looks Back

Ray Batten

'I had 14 years at Leeds. I always said that once I'd finished I wouldn't want to play anywhere else. And I didn't. I'd played over 400 games and that was enough for me. And I hadn't had many injuries; I broke my ankle before the 1970 tour and in February 1973, which caused me to miss the 1973 Championship Final. I also missed the 1971 Challenge Cup Final with a shoulder injury.

'The only unfortunate thing was when Derek Turner was sacked. I couldn't believe they sacked him before we played Dewsbury in the 1973 Championship Final. He'd taken us to Wembley twice and we'd regularly finished top of the league.'

Only 3,445 spectators turned up on a bitterly cold night for what was to prove a seminal game as Bill Ramsey, who had been in dispute with Hunslet and out of action, put in a solid performance alongside fellow south Leeds products, brothers Albert and Ken Eyre. Ramsey got on the try-scoring list in his first game, accompanied by Ken Eyre, Hynes and loose forward Ray Batten, with Seabourne adding two goals. Albert Eyre took the man of the match award against his old club, and Leeds were only to lose three more games in the entire season.

The transformation was almost immediate. Eight days after his Keighley debut, Ramsey was in the Leeds ranks for the home fixture with Doncaster who were brushed aside 50-0 in a 12-try show in which Atkinson had a hat trick. Shoebottom, Crosby and Hynes netted two apiece and the Supporters' Club chronicler, in far happier mood, wrote, 'prospects look rosy for Leeds in the future.'

The Loiners went down at Workington the following week, 7-4, where the absent Seabourne was badly missed, the side as a whole failed to tick, and Ken Eyre was replaced by Hick after 'receiving a knock on his old trouble spot.'

But the 13,401 Boxing Day crowd witnessed what was to be the first of 18 successive wins with the 21-4 success over Wakefield Trinity. Alan Smith, Atkinson, Batten, Ramsey and Clark scored the Leeds tries on a spring-like day, Risman adding three goals.

Loiners Big Match

6 April 1968, Challenge Cup Semi-Final, Leeds 25 Wigan 4, Station Road, Swinton

A book which recounts the glory years of any club in any sport must, by definition, include accounts of many memorable successes.

Leeds supporters were, over the two decades, treated to many magnificent performances. And so, for that matter, were fans of the game in general.

It is a difficult task to pinpoint any particular game as the Loiners' finest. Moments such as the club's first Championship win, when Warrington were beaten at Odsal in 1961, spring to mind, as do the Challenge Cup Final victories over Widnes and St Helens in 1977 and 1978 respectively. There were, too, memorable successes such as the 36-9 defeat of Dewsbury in the 1972-73 Yorkshire Cup Final; a result put into perspective by Dewsbury's revenge win, several months later, in the Championship Final at Odsal.

Many supporters will have their own personal memories of superb wins, not necessarily in major matches but perhaps the kind of victories ground out in the mid-winter gloom which, come the end of the season, turn out to have been vital. Even defeats such as the 7-5 reverse at Salford in February 1976 with a weakened side which eventually cost Leeds the Championship can be seen in hindsight as glorious moments.

A side made up, as Leeds were, of thoroughbreds and high-pedigree individuals tends to respond better to the big challenge than to the run-of-the-mill, bread-and-butter fare. And one game, perhaps, stands out above the hundreds of others as the Loiners' finest hour between 1 January 1960 and 31 December 1979. And it came in a match usually viewed as one in which the result, rather than its manner, is paramount; a Challenge Cup semi-final.

The portents, unquestionably, were not promising

Continued...

when Leeds met Wigan at Station Road, Swinton, on 6 April 1968. During the previous decade the two great clubs had met five times in the competition; and Leeds had not won once.

The Pie Eaters had prevailed 14-11 in a second round clash in 1960 and, after having been held to a 5-5 draw at Headingley 12 months later in the first round, had romped home 32-7 in the Central Park replay.

There was more despondency for Leeds in 1963 with a 20-11 defeat in Wigan. And the misery was compounded when Eric Ashton's men edged the 1966 semi-final 7-2 to set up a Wembley date with St Helens.

Revenge, however, can be all the sweeter for being a long time coming and the Loiners repaid those ignominies with interest as Roy Francis' glorious young side reached its apogee.

Going, as they did, into the game on the back of a 16-match unbeaten run, Leeds hardly wanted for confidence. And nor did their hordes of fans in the packed Station Road crowd of 30,329.

That self-assurance was founded on glorious attacking skills which have perhaps never been bettered in the sport, combined with a parsimonious defence, which had led to 75 tries scored and a mere nine conceded in the lengthy unbeaten sequence.

Wigan, who were to finish eleventh in the league after having tumbled to an all-time lowest seventeenth the previous year, were in the process of rebuilding and would have to wait two more years for a reappearance at Wembley. But the Central Park men still boasted plenty of quality in their ranks, with several legendary figures hungry for one last taste of the big time.

The immortal Billy Boston was on the right flank, with his long-time partner Eric Ashton on his inside. Quality halves Cliff Hill and Frankie Parr remained effective orchestrators, and a pack comprising such as hooker Colin Clarke, second row Terry Fogerty and loose forward Doug Laughton was clearly to be respected.

Wigan also had a top quality goal kicker in their ranks in full-back Colin Tyrer, a man who came close to causing a rule change because of the inordinate length of time he took preparing for shots at goal.

Tyrer had very few opportunities, though, against Leeds on a day in which Cliff Richard came second in the Eurovision Song Contest, behind Massiel of Spain (La La La), with Congratulations.

The congratulations at Station Road were to go the way

Continued...

In a rich run of form, York were scuttled 33-0 at Wiggington Road, Atkinson and Shoebottom both crossing twice, and Hull were beaten 28-4 at Headingley when Dick Gemmell, back from injury, enjoyed himself against his former club and Atkinson and Shoebottom again had two tries each.

The pitch looks dry enough as Leeds and Wakefield walk out at Wembley. Minutes later...

The Loiners followed that win up by registering the 'double' over Hull KR when Leeds really hit the heights. Hynes grabbed two of his side's tries in the 26-13 success and the Loiners, after a relatively lacklustre showing in the 31-2 revenge win over Batley for the September defeat at Mount Pleasant, carved out a notable victory over Castleford, Alan Smith grabbing two fine tries *of a Leeds side which came as near to the pinnacle of perfection desired by coach Roy Francis as it may be possible to get.*

Francis' insistence on an expansive approach, and his determination to mould his squad into as fit a body of men as any in the sport also reaped rich dividends as his 15 players painted a masterpiece of Rugby League Football.

The tactical ploy of switching Syd Hynes from right centre to the left to monitor Wigan captain legend Eric Ashton paid off, Ashton and Boston, a man of even higher status among the immortals, being kept under wraps throughout except on one occasion, when a loose ball led to the Cherry and Whites' skipper feeding the Brown Bomber who, under heavy pressure from a host of Leeds defenders, was unable to ground the ball properly.

That was the nearest Wigan came to scoring a try in a match which Leeds dominated, other than early in the second half when one of the Loiners' relatively unsung heroes produced a moment of match-clinching class.

Centre Bernard Watson, having arguably his finest game for Leeds, turned defence into attack in stunning style when, early in the second half and trailing 7-2, Wigan looked likely scorers after a Tyrer break from deep in his own half.

The best-ever Leeds side?

The full-back, who had broken clear after collecting a deep kick by scrum-half Barry Seabourne, appeared to have created a certain try when he angled across to supporting winger Bill Francis.

But Tyrer's pass was plucked out of the air by Watson who raced away over 50 yards for a try which not only denied Wigan the chance to draw level but, with full-back Bev Risman's conversion, extended the Loiners' lead to 10 points.

Watson's score would surely have entered the annals of folklore if not for a glorious effort midway through the first half by winger John Atkinson which many supporters believe to be the best ever scored by a Leeds player.

With the sides level after Tyrer and Risman had traded early penalties, Seabourne and Parr having both been wide with drop goal attempts, Leeds' forwards were beginning to dominate. Props Mick Clark and Ken Eyre,

Continued...

in a 16-5 triumph in which the dismissal of Castleford prop Dennis Hartley for a stiff arm tackle on Hynes was helpful to the home cause.

That match was the prelude to the Challenge Cup, Leeds opening with a home game against Liverpool City, the men from Knotty Ash.

Struggling City tested Leeds, benefiting from a couple of wrong options by the home side and pulling off an interception try, before going down 23-12 before a 6,614 crowd, Atkinson netting another brace. And there was another indeterminate performance in the next game, at Dewsbury in the league, when a 13-0 win was ground out with the help of two tries for Alan Smith and an Atkinson effort.

The Loiners were still winning, though, and a pattern began to emerge of better performances against the leading sides. Halifax were put to the sword at Headingley, 35-0, in what was described as a 'wonderful exhibition of first-class football that left Halifax without a clue how to cope with this great Leeds team in which every man was of international class.' Hooker Crosby again warranted mention, 'sticking to Francis' instructions to stick to a channel down the middle of the pitch he lubricates the machinery *together with hooker Tony Crosby, linked to fine effect to give Alan Smith a chance, the winger easing past Tyrer before being brought down short of the line by Francis. And after a number of Wigan sorties inspired by the fine ball-handling of second row Terry Fogerty had been repelled, there were promising raids which led to Clark, loose forward Ray Batten, Watson and second row Albert Eyre going close.*

Wigan's defence could do nothing to deny the next attack. Second row Bill Ramsey, who breached the Pie-Eaters' rearguard throughout the game, blasted through once more and, tempting Boston into one of his trademark crash tackles on opposing centres, cut out Watson with a long pass which sent Atkinson away for a wonder score. The former Roundhay Rugby Union man glided majestically past the first, desperate, raft of cover and with Tyrer and prop Webb closing in somehow ghosted between the duo who were left sprawling and gazing at one another in consternation.

Atkinson's superlative foray had left Wigan's defence in total disarray and he touched down behind the posts to give Risman a simple conversion and his side a 7-2 lead which, after Boston's miss, was followed by Watson's vital score six minutes into the second half.

Tyrer gave Wigan some respite with a subsequent penalty but the Loiners went on to run riot, in the context of a semi-final, with three tries in the closing quarter. Free-flowing Rugby League sparked by Batten, whose ball handling skills would have done credit to a world-renowned magician, saw Ramsey, Smith and Watson carry on the charge before Ramsey popped up to race over unopposed.

Ramsey was the creator of the next score, powering through a beleaguered rearguard before feeding stand off Mick Shoebottom, who provided the final pass for Hynes' try. And in the final minutes Seabourne sold an audacious dummy, bustling over and Risman adding his third goal of the half to complete a 25-4 score-line which was a record for a Challenge Cup semi-final and a fitting statistical record of a truly wonderful performance.

Remarkably, only Risman, Hynes and Clark had featured in the 1966 last-four defeat at the hands of Wigan, Shoebottom having been sidelined by injury on that occasion. Revenge for the club, however, was sweet indeed. It has often been stated that Wakefield lost, rather than Leeds won, the subsequent Watersplash Final at Wembley. Given the roulette-wheel nature of that game, perhaps the more appropriate assessment is that Leeds won the 1967-68 Challenge Cup on 6th April 1968 at Station Road, Swinton.

Leeds: Risman; A Smith, Watson, Hynes, Atkinson; Shoebottom, Seabourne; Clark, Crosby, K Eyre, A Eyre, Ramsey, Batten. Sub: Joyce.
Wigan: Tyrer; Boston, Ashton, Rowe, Francis; Hill, Parr; Stephens, Clarke, Webb, Lyon, Fogerty, Laughton.
Referee: Mr GF Lindop (Wakefield).
Leeds: T: Atkinson, Watson, Ramsey, Hynes, Seabourne.
G: Risman 5.
Wigan: G: Tyrer 2.
Attendance: 30,329

and enables the Leeds team to blend together in this successful and spectacular way.'

Leeds crushed the opposition for the second successive game when Bramley made the short trip to Headingley for the second round Challenge Cup tie, going down 29-0 before 11,783 fans in a game in which Ramsey scored a try before being carried off with a leg injury.

Ramsey may have been forgiven for wondering whether his move to Leeds had been prudent when he was carried off in each of the next two games. The match at Halifax, won 29-10 despite the Loiners having Clark and Risman on Great Britain duty against France, involved two tries, again, for Atkinson, with Langley also bagging a brace; prior to that game, Ramsey was also forced to withdraw in the 'trial match' at Headingley against Great Britain when Leeds, after having led 7-0, finished beaten and with 11 fit players.

A Loiner Looks Back

John Langley

'Mick Joyce and I were the substitutes at Wembley in 1968. We were on £100 to win, but we didn't get on, so all we got was £60. And when we went up the steps for our medals there were only 13. It took Leeds 12 months for Mick and me to get our medals. I don't know where they were on the day; maybe Bill Fallowfield pocketed them!

'There were only two substitutes in those days, and we could only be brought on following an injury. You could only go on up to half time, and you spent a lot of nervous energy, as daft as it sounds, just sitting there, looking all over the place and wondering if players were going to get up after a tackle.

'Our kid, George, had a fiver on Leeds at 8/1. He was on the terraces and when Ken Hirst scored he threw his slip down. When Don missed the kick he was down on the floor between all the legs, trying to find his slip. They were kicking him all over the place but he found it.'

Despite having the best forward on view in Geoff Gunney old rivals Hunslet, now slipping back amongst the also-rans after losing the likes of Ramsey and Ken Eyre (to Leeds), Dennis Hartley (to Castleford) and centre Geoff Shelton (Oldham), with Fred Ward, Alan Marchant, John Griffiths and Brian Gabbitas all retiring, were brushed aside 23-4 at home in a game marred by heavy winds. Those conditions may have added to the confusion when a Hunslet 'goal' was allowed when the ball hit an upright, bounced off the crossbar towards the other post and dropped to the ground, the referee and one touchjudge allowing the effort while the other touchjudge's flag went down.

Perhaps with half an eye on the forthcoming Challenge Cup quarter-final tie at Oldham, Leeds struggled at Keighley in their worst performance for many weeks. Lacking a number of regulars, and with John Davies carried off with a suspected broken leg, the Loiners stumbled to a 10-4 win in which Alan Smith and Atkinson scored and Seabourne landed a goal and a drop goal, but Leeds rose to the occasion at the Watersheddings where 18,502 baying fans turned up, many hoping that the Roughyeds would gain revenge for the previous season's second round reverse on their own midden.

Leeds lacked Ramsey, who failed a fitness

Loiners Big Match

11 May 1968, Challenge Cup Final, Leeds 11 Wakefield Trinity 10, Wembley

Referee Mr JP Hebblethwaite awards a penalty try to John Atkinson. Wakefield's Don Fox, hands on hips, appears to be perplexed; his misery was complete 11 minutes later when he dramatically miscued his attempted conversion of Ken Hirst's try.

The 1968 Challenge Cup Final against Wakefield Trinity was, without doubt, one of the most dramatic occasions in the history of sport.

Like Foinavon's win in the Grand National in 1967, Zola Budd's success against Mary Decker in the mid-eighties and, in a more sombre arena, the charge of the Light Brigade at Balaclava, it is remembered for all the wrong reasons.

Continued...

Leeds returned north with the Challenge Cup after an epic encounter with their near neighbours but even the most die-hard Loiner had to concede that the game was lost by Wakefield rather than won by Leeds.

Don Fox is perhaps the best known Rugby League player in history, thanks to BBC commentator Eddie Waring's 'poor lad' expression of sympathy when the Trinity player collapsed to the floor after slicing his attempted last-second conversion of Ken Hirst's try. Fox, who was standing in as Trinity's kicker in the absence through injury of brother Neil, has had to live with that dreadful moment ever since and the truth is that the prop was unlucky to be involved in the very last act of an error-strewn game that, in normal circumstances, would not have been played.

Wakefield winger Ken Hirst's last-gasp try. But victory was to rest with Leeds.

A thunderstorm of epic proportions in the hour before the kick-off left the Wembley pitch covered in two inches of water. But, with over 87,000 fans milling around the Empire Stadium, and millions more settling back to watch the game on TV, Rugby League officials and referee Mr JP Hebblethwaite of York understandably opted to go ahead.

The result was a game probably unique in Rugby League history as players slithered around and generally struggled to retain their footing throughout.

Trinity went in front when Leeds winger John Atkinson slipped in attempting to tackle his opposite number Hirst, who grabbed an unlikely try. And, with football not only at a premium but virtually non-existent, the only remaining scores of a bizarre and occasionally comical first half were two penalties apiece for Leeds full-back Bev Risman and Fox.

If the authorities and Mr Hebblethwaite had a difficult decision to make before the game, they had a tougher one to consider at half time when another deluge led many to believe that the game would be abandoned.

Mr Hebblethwaite, however, again erred on the side of caution and gave the nod for the second half to continue for what became known as the 'Watersplash' final.

Atkinson, as involved as anyone in the farcical proceedings, seized a rare opportunity, kicking ahead and finding himself being brought down in the chase to the line.

Continued...

test, but the importance of having a strong squad was never better illustrated than by the display of Hick. The Loiners, again inspired by Seabourne, booked a semi-final spot with a disallowed try for Joyce, on as a substitute for the injured Mick Clark, and two tries for the redoubtable Alan Smith, to set up a semi-final with Wigan at Station Road, Swinton.

Intriguingly, Oldham had sought to laud young referee Fred Lindop in the programme notes: 'An interesting point about today's game is that it will be controlled by Wakefield referee Fred Lindop. Mr Lindop, by coincidence, also controlled the Oldham v Leeds Cup-tie last season. This game, which was a second round fixture which Leeds won, was one of Mr Lindop's first important matches.

'We are glad to see a referee of Mr Lindop's youth making the grade as a senior referee and his appointment for the three Test matches between Great Britain and Australia recently completed proves he is an outstanding and popular official.

'Mr Lindop is certainly in line for a Wembley appearance this term and, if Wakefield Trinity are not involved in the final, Mr Lindop looks a

Mr Hebblethwaite awarded a penalty try, improved by Risman. And when the full-back landed a late penalty Wakefield, with the seconds ticking away, appeared to be dead and buried.

But, in the most dramatic of finishes, Hirst was first to the kick-off, and, in desperation, twice kicked on in a frantic chase to the line.

With Leeds players sliding around in futile attempts to halt the chase, Hirst pounced by the posts to bring his side to within a point of the Loiners. And a sensational Wakefield win – and the coveted Cup and League 'double' – was a formality.

But Fox, dramatically, slipped in his run-up, and poked the ball wide of the upright. And the Leeds, players, hunched dejectedly behind their line, leapt into the air as one in disbelief and sheer joy as the prop slumped to the ground.

There was, though, massive sympathy for Fox, who ironically had already been voted the Lance Todd Trophy winner, as the man of the match, by the press. Two days later, at Featherstone's Post Office Road ground before local TV cameras, Fox kicked 10 goals out of 10, from the same position, in his carpet slippers.

Leeds: Risman; Smith, Hynes, Watson, Atkinson; Shoebottom, Seabourne; Clark, Crosby, K Eyre, Ramsey, A Eyre, Batten.
Wakefield: Cooper; Hirst, Brooke, Coetzer, Batty; Poynton, Owen; Jeanes, Shepherd, D Fox, Haigh, McLeod, Hawley.
Referee: Mr JP Hebblethwaite (York).
Leeds: T: Atkinson. G: Risman 4.
Wakefield: T: Hirst 2. G: D Fox 2.
Attendance: 87,100

firm favourite to land the job in only his second full season.'

The toffee did the Lancastrians no good, and another Red Rose outfit went down to Leeds three days later when the Loiners trekked to Knowsley Road and – despite lacking Ramsey, Alan Smith, Langley and Clark – overcame St Helens 12-4, Seabourne, again in top form, steering Leeds to a win involving tries by Albert Eyre and Shoebottom.

Francis was also without Clark, Seabourne and Smith at Featherstone, just four days later, but Leeds, despite their heavy schedule, showed few signs of tiredness as Hynes, Bernard Watson and Atkinson scored two tries each in a 25-5 success to effectively seal the League Leaders' trophy.

Following the epic Challenge Cup semi-final win over Wigan the Loiners equalled the record, set in 1957, of 18 successive wins with the victory at Headingley over Huddersfield on 12 April. The Fartowners, fresh from defeat in the replayed Challenge Cup semi-final against Wakefield on the same ground several days earlier, had been a whisker away from facing Leeds at Wembley – how different would history have been, then? – but they toiled hard in the 16-5 defeat in which Atkinson netted yet another brace. Batten was in typically enterprising form and, in those 18 games, Leeds had totalled 408 points and conceded a mere 76.

Leeds, however, were unable to break their own record. A visit to Wakefield in the final league game of the season saw Trinity, beaten by the Loiners on Boxing Day at the start of the epic run, gain revenge in their pursuit of second spot in the table. Atkinson scored a quality early try, but the 13,760 crowd saw Wakefield gain a victory that they would happily have traded for defeat, less than a month later, in one of the

A Loiner Looks Back

Bill Ramsey

'The 1968 Challenge Cup Final had been billed as a classic and that was what it should have been. But the weather ruined it. It wasn't a game of Rugby League, it was a joke. When we came out for the second half the water, in places, was above our boots. It was dangerous and I'm convinced that people could have died out there. I remember tackling Ian Brooke when he was in full flight. We skidded 15 yards through the water and over the touchline. He was under me, and he was coughing and spluttering when we got up. He could have drowned; he'd taken a lot of water in and he was really struggling.

Bill Ramsey was concerned that players were in danger of drowning.

'The referee really should have called it off. It was such a sad thing that Don Fox missed that goal. I was pleased he missed it because Leeds had won and I got my hundred quid, but it's blighted Don ever since. I felt sorry for him. If the game had been called off and played a week later I'd have had no axe to grind at all. 'I wanted us to kick to touch with the late penalty. By the time we'd had our play-the-balls we would be down at the Wakefield end and they had nobody who could go the length of the field. Mick Clark took no notice, Bev Risman kicked the goal and the fiasco happened. It shouldn't have been that way. You couldn't even catch the ball, it was really tough.'

most dramatic matches of all time...

Meanwhile Leeds, despite having finished the season seven points clear of Wakefield, were unable to secure the Championship which many felt would have been their just reward. Widnes were overcome 31-17 in the first round of the Top 16 play-offs, Shoebottom sparkling with two tries and a drop goal in a fine game. But Wigan, stung by the Challenge Cup defeat earlier in the month, turned the tables in the next round. Ramsey, in top form, didn't deserve to be on the losing side as the Pie Eaters prevailed 11-7. Crosby scored the Loiners' only try and Frank Brown, who had scored two tries and two goals against Widnes, added two goals in a clash in which Hynes and Risman were badly missed.

Leeds, a matter of days after the Watersplash Wembley, went down to Great Britain in another practice match at Headingley when Langley and

A Loiner Looks Back

Mick Clark

'Two or three weeks after the 1968 Watersplash Final, I was going to Australia for the World Cup. The Rugby League Secretary, Bill Fallowfield, said to me, "I hope you do better than you did at Wembley you didn't have a good game did you?" I said, "have you seen the rerun of it? Do you remember what Eddie Waring said five minutes before half time?" He asked "What was that?" I replied "Eddie Waring said that the teams were now going down for the 29th scrum with five minutes to go to half time. That's why I didn't have a good game; I was in the bloody scrum

Continued...

all the time."

'It was dry when we walked out. We thought it wasn't too bad but in the end we needed the lifeboats out.

'I went to the referee with 20 minutes or so to go and asked him whether he could abandon the game. He said, "I can't." I said "It's not playable." Mr Hebblethwaite just repeated, "I can't." And that was it. It came to what we thought was going to be the last kick of the game, when we'd been awarded a penalty. Bev Risman was kicking for goal and I told him to make sure it went dead. I'd asked the referee before opting to go for goal how long was left and he told me it was the last kick of the game. Anyway, Bev kicked the goal and we had to restart. Don Fox kicks off the other way, just messing about thinking that's it. It went on and on, kick, kick, kick, and Ken Hirst dived over the line and scored.

'I'd said to Bev, "don't kick the goal, kick it into touch." That kick wouldn't have happened, but you've got to go for the goal haven't you. We stood around numb, shocked, they'd to stop me swearing because I was swearing like hell at 'em for letting them get through. And Don, who was only kicking because his brother Neil was injured, went and missed it; he fell on the floor, head down and playing hell.

'I went into Wakefield's changing room after the match with the Cup to give them all a drink out of it. I said to Ken Traill, their coach, "it should have been abandoned Ken; we didn't deserve to win it and you didn't deserve to lose." I said, "look, I'll leave the Cup, have a drink out of it and then I'll take it back."'

Albert Eyre were rated as being the best two players on view.

Football Chairman Jack Myerscough had portentous words in his end-of-season review for the Supporters' Club. He wrote: 'If there is a drawback to a season as the one just completed I suppose it lies in the setting of standards by which subsequent performance might compare adversely. It is a challenge we happily accept.

'I am sure that it has not gone unremarked by the discerning among you that amid all the glamour of Wembley and League Leadership triumph, the 'A' team was efficiently lifting the Combination Cup and League double for the second year in succession. The juniors, too, secured the Championship in the Leeds & District 'B' section. It is in this promise for the future that we rejoice while basking in the light of present triumph.

'Wembley, however, was the highlight of a season rich in achievement. We would have liked to have had ideal conditions, to have played our part in a match to thrill all – adherents to the code or otherwise – and to have won conclusively on merit. In the event we found ourselves participants in a final which fiction could never have conjured up, a final which, because of the conditions in which it was played and the drama which it produced, will be talked of long after we have departed the rugby scene.'

6. TROPHIES GALORE!

The 1968-69 campaign was perhaps the least stable, behind the scenes, of the 20 seasons encapsulated in this book. As if to confirm the contrary nature of sport it was also the most successful, at least in terms of trophies earned.

The departure of Roy Francis to North Sydney in December was a serious blow, as it would have been for any club. The loss of the man seen as the leading coach in the sport was,

Barry Seabourne receives the 1968/69 Yorkshire League championship cup.

however, put in its proper perspective when A team boss Jack Nelson, who had taken over at short notice, passed away suddenly on Boxing Day.

In those dreadfully unhappy circumstances, and with the flags flying at half-mast at Headingley for that day's fixture with Castleford, the man known as Mr Reliable stepped into the breech.

Joe Warham, who had managed the Loiners to their first Championship success eight years earlier, assumed the mantle and not only held the ship steady but actually improved on Francis' record of the previous season.

Leeds atoned for the narrow miss of the previous year by lifting the Championship in a thrilling final with Castleford at Odsal. In addition to that major prize, the Headingley men retained the League Leadership Trophy – losing only three games, including the first and last matches of the campaign – and the Yorkshire League title. And, with the Yorkshire Cup added to that list on top of the Lazenby Cup, the Loiners' trophy cabinet was full to capacity.

A major new star, who would become one of the finest players and most loyal servants in the club's history, was also launched on an appreciative public.

John Holmes had already made his mark as a rising protégé with Kirkstall Boys Club, in the shadow of Headingley, and the youngster had little difficulty in opting for Leeds in the face of a tempting offer from Bradford Northern.

Holmes made his debut in the Lazenby Cup at Hunslet on 12 August 1968 and made an immediate impression with a try and 10 goals in the 47-15 victory over a south Leeds side that was becoming a shadow of its former self.

The youngster was blooded in during the season, finishing with nine goals in competitive matches, while his older brother Phil had two tries, both scored in the 'away' game at Hunslet on 28 December, which was actually played at Headingley in a successful bid to beat the heavy winter frosts.

Holmes kicked four conversions in that 35-10 victory, which enabled Leeds to turn the year

Loiners Big Match

19 October 1968, Yorkshire Cup Final, Leeds 22 Castleford 11, Belle Vue, Wakefield

Leeds' post-war drought in the Yorkshire Cup was ended in a clash with Castleford which, while not quite as brutal as so many of the matches between the old foes, was nevertheless a good example of the highly-physical genre.

The Loiners had appeared in the decider on four occasions, losing each time to Wakefield Trinity, so it was perhaps ironic that the hoodoo was broken on Trinity's own Belle Vue ground.

The folly of attempting to promote promising young players as ready-made stars was highlighted in a game in which Castleford youngster Danny Hargrave, touted by BBC TV commentator Eddie Waring as 'Rugby League's George Best' because of his dark flowing locks and good looks, discovered that that kind of focus imposes unfair pressure on players lacking talent approaching genius quality.

The Loiners' mid-field triangle of Ray Batten, Barry Seabourne and Mick Shoebottom outshone their opposites of 19-year-old Hargrave, a young Mal Reilly and Alan Hardisty and, perhaps mindful of the need to live up to his billing, it was an error by Hargrave that gave Leeds the chance to score an important try early in the match.

Castleford were very much in the game at only 5-2 adrift when the scrum-half, standing in for the injured Keith Hepworth, attempted an over-ambitious long pass which was intercepted by wily Loiners centre Bernard Watson for a gift try.

Full-back Bev Risman, who had converted a well-worked opening touchdown by winger Alan Smith after Batten and second row Albert Eyre had linked, added the goal. And Castleford, who had responded with a penalty by centre Ron Hill, looked destined for a rare defeat after having lost only one of their previous 17 fixtures.

Continued...

A south Leeds lad, Syd Hynes played for Hunslet Juniors before joining Leeds NALGO Rugby Union and then Leeds.

with only two defeats in their 22 league games.

The bread and butter campaign opened with an unfortunate 22-19 defeat at Leigh but the next game, two days later at Hull KR, saw Holmes make his league debut, impressing hugely under the Robins' 'up and unders' and kicking three goals in a 17-10 win in which scrum-half Barry Seabourne scored a try and a drop goal and centres Syd Hynes and Bernard Watson crossed.

St Helens, on big money at £25 a man to win, visited Headingley less than a week later and returned to Lancashire with their halos askew. The big bonus had little effect as the Loiners eased to an 18-0 lead and, although the Saints forced their way back into contention, tries by Ron Cowan, Hynes, Ray Batten and Bill Ramsey, with four Bev Risman goals, proved to be too much for the visitors.

It was harder at Bramley, where a 4,000 crowd packed McLaren Field and witnessed a 13-12 victory for the Loiners in a game in which the Villagers scored a last-minute interception try, converted under the posts. Leeds, though, had already done enough with touchdowns by Seabourne, winger John Atkinson and stand off

However, the men from Wheldon Road showed admirable resilience and with their forwards assuming a degree of control eased back into contention with a drop goal by Hardisty and a second Hill penalty.

A couple of successive misses by Hill, however, stemmed the revival before second row Brian Lockwood, hooker Clive Dickinson and prop Denis Hartley set up the position with a series of rampaging runs for Hardisty to land a drop goal that reduced the deficit to a mere two points. Castleford were never to overhaul Leeds, however, and their best chance vanished when Hardisty broke clear early in the second half, only to send out a wild pass to his support which went to ground.

After a promising attack involving Seabourne, Batten and Shoebottom came to nothing, it was an error by Hartley which gave Leeds the chance to put some daylight between themselves and their opponents.

Typically expansive back play by the Loiners led to the ball being moved across the line when Hartley spilled possession 15 yards from his own posts, ace winger John Atkinson sprinting over and Risman again adding the extras.

Cas never recovered, even though Hill grabbed a try after an uncharacteristic Atkinson mistake.

Risman again stretched his side's lead, with his first penalty of the contest, and when substitute David Hick raced over in the closing stages, Risman landed his fifth goal of the afternoon to add the Yorkshire Cup to a trophy cabinet already housing, from the previous season, the Challenge Cup, Yorkshire League, League Leaders Trophy and the Mackeson Trophy. Following the presentation of the cup, captain Mick Clark asked to step down, recommending that Seabourne take over in a fine example of the selfless approach which led to the Leeds unit enjoying, in 1968-69, its most successful and memorable season.

Mick Clark receives the Yorkshire Cup in 1968/69 after the 22-11 victory over Castleford at Belle Vue, Wakefield.

Leeds: Risman; A Smith, Hynes, Watson, Atkinson; Shoebottom, Seabourne; Clark, Crosby, K Eyre, Ramsey, A Eyre, Batten. Playing sub: Hick.

Castleford: Edwards; Howe, Hill, Thomas, Stephens; Hardisty, Hargrave; Hartley, Dickinson, Ward, Small, Lockwood, Reilly. Playing sub: Redfearn.

Referee: Mr J Manley (Warrington).

Leeds: T: A Smith, Watson, Atkinson, Hick. G: Risman 5.

Castleford: T: Hill. G: Hill 2. DG: Hardisty 2.

Attendance: 12,573

Mick Shoebottom, with Risman adding two goals.

It was tight, too, as September dawned with a home game against Huddersfield who looked likely winners in a rain-sodden game until second row Ramsey pulled off an interception try to help sneak a 7-4 win.

The relatively indifferent form hardly augured well for a serious assault on the Yorkshire Cup but the Loiners again illustrated their capacity for the big occasion. The Boulevard, the scene of wildly fluctuating results the previous season, was the venue for the first round and the Airlie Birds were summarily seen off in a 30-9 success, despite having led 9-4 at the interval. The high levels of fitness instilled by Francis paid off, with Risman scoring a try and five goals, supplemented by touchdowns for John Langley,

A Loiner Looks Back

Graham Eccles

'We all had blazers and when you were in the second team you could only have a small badge. When you were in the first team, after maybe 10 or 12 games, you were entitled to go to Rawcliffes for a big badge. You knew you'd arrived then!

'I got 500 quid of my contract, although I signed for £1,000. It was £150 to sign on, £100 when I was 21, and £250 after a certain number of first team games. That's as far as I got, I didn't get the £500 that I'd have been entitled to if I'd been picked for Yorkshire and Great Britain. Losing pay when I first came to Leeds, in 1968, was £6. I think winning pay was £16. But you always got a bonus on your winning pay. If we played Batley and won we'd get a small bonus, if it was St Helens or Wigan it would be a bigger one. So it was never £16, although it wouldn't be a lot more against a so-called lesser team. If you lost you just got £6, and if you didn't play you didn't get paid.'

Shoebottom and Alan Smith. And Seabourne's four drop goals made it difficult for Hull to force their way into serious contention.

The Loiners travelled to Post Office Road at the next stage – just three days after a home league game with Warrington – and denied Featherstone Rovers a try in the 18-10 victory. There were only two to Leeds in a penalty-strewn affair, one of them a glorious effort by Alan Smith close to half time. Langley also forced his way over, Risman added five goals and drop goal specialist Seabourne landed a spectacular effort from 40 yards.

Leeds' luck with the draw got no better at the semi-final stage, when Francis' side were paired with Halifax at Thrum Hall. Again, the Loiners were obliged to tough it out, especially after going five points down in the early stages, and the painful memory of the previous season's heavy defeat at the penultimate stage at Hull was assuaged with a 12-5 victory. Smith continued his record of having scored in every round with a try, fellow winger Eddie Ratcliffe also scored, and Risman landed two goals. Ramsey, adding to laurels which included power runner, ball handler and awesome tackler, landed his first drop goal for the club to help set up a final against Castleford at Belle Vue, Wakefield. And while the Loiners were reaching their first Yorkshire Cup Final for four years, progress was also being made on the league front.

Despite the absence of Atkinson (on wedding duty!) and the prospect of the Yorkshire Cup trip

Headingley Hero

Bill Ramsey

The signing of 1966 British Lion Bill Ramsey from Hunslet in the autumn of 1967 quite literally transformed the Loiners.

Leeds had begun the season in lacklustre fashion and had scoured the north for a dynamic back row man who could provide the crucial missing piece of the jigsaw.

Hull KR had erected the 'not-for-sale' signs when the Loiners offered £14,000 for international second row pair Bill Holliday and Frank Foster but a search closer to home paid dividends when Leeds snapped up Ramsey for £9,000.

Prior to Ramsey's arrival, Leeds had lost three successive games. Neighbours Bramley had won 19-12 at Headingley, the Australian tourists had prevailed 7-4 and the Loiners had slipped 12-9 at Castleford in

Continued...

to Featherstone, Leeds eased past Warrington 24-8, the prolific Alan Smith netting two tries in a superlative team display. A trip to Wakefield Trinity followed and, amazingly, in the first meeting of the sides since the Wembley watersplash of four months previously, the match was affected by torrential rain throughout the morning. The ball, as in London, squirted around like a balloon and although Leeds were generally reckoned to have been the better side and could have been at least 10 points in front, there was also a general view that a 7-7 draw, involving a Watson try, a Risman goal and yet another Seabourne drop goal was a fair result.

Young hooker Ray Handscombe, just 19, was drafted into the side for the next game, at home to Leigh, because of the suspension of Tony Crosby, and his ball-winning abilities were immediately apparent in the 32-13 win in which Langley netted two tries.

The popular BBC2 Floodlit Trophy was, once again, the vehicle for a proposed rule change, with scrum halves required to throw the ball upward into the scrum. The initiative appeared to add to the entertainment as Leeds overcame Salford 24-19 at Headingley, helped by a blistering 20-minute period in the first half in which 15 points were scored. The Loiners were deserved winners, scoring six tries to the Red Devils' three including efforts by Shoebottom, Alan Smith, Frank Brown, Dave Hick, Batten and Ratcliffe.

Just days after the win over Halifax at Thrum Hall Leeds, facing a fourth tough game in eight

the BBC2 Floodlit Trophy.
Ramsey – ball handler, copybook tackler, rangy runner and enforcer – rectified the deficiencies.
The Loiners got back to winning ways with a 26-9 success at Hull and the following week, on 8 December 1967, Ramsey made his debut on a bitterly cold night in a 16-9 home victory over Keighley.
A 7-4 defeat at Workington proved to be the last occasion on which Leeds were to lose in 18 games.
The Loiners overcame Wakefield Trinity on Boxing Day and continued unbeaten until they again met Wakefield, at Belle Vue, in the top-16 play-offs.
One man doesn't make a team but Ramsey's impact was certainly seminal as John Holmes – then a young full-back – readily attests: 'Billy Ramsey created gaps and his passing was superb. If I just said, 'I'm coming,' he'd be ready. He was one of the best second row forwards I've played with and he's one of my heroes. A top class player, a brilliant footballer and a very hard man.'
Harry Jepson shares the high esteem: 'Bill was playing the best football he ever played in 1970, and he didn't get picked for the tour. Leeds already had five men in the party but, at that time, I thought he was a better second row forward than either Jimmy Thompson or Doug Laughton. He went again in 1974; there haven't been many players who went on a tour, missed out on the next, and were then selected for the following one.'
Ramsey's call up in 1974, as a replacement for the injured John Bates, came six months after he had been the subject of a sudden transfer to Bradford Northern. He had left Headingley with a lengthy list of skills necessary in Rugby League.
The second row featured in 10 finals during his six years at Headingley, missing

Bill Ramsey charges through Phil Horrocks' challenge against his former club Hunslet.

Continued...

Ray Batten stretches out for a try in the 20-13 victory over St Helens at the beginning of the 1968/69 season.

days, entertained a Bradford Northern side destined to slip into the bottom half of the table and posted their biggest win of the campaign bar the 63-11 stroll over Batley at Easter. Poor Northern could do little to staunch the ceaseless Leeds attacks and the Headingley men finished with nine tries, including two each for Hick, Seabourne, Langley and Atkinson, and a try by Shoebottom. Atkinson, who had laid the foundations with his early brace, was stretchered off after an assault by Vaughan Thomas, no doubt to complaints from his new wife, but the epic win wasn't reproduced at St Helens the following week when little went right, other than a Ratcliffe try, in the 28-3 defeat.

Perhaps the players had Castleford on their collective mind. Seven days later the sides clashed at Wakefield to determine the destiny of the Yorkshire Cup. The Loiners made no mistake, bringing the coveted trophy back to Headingley after a decade's absence and despite having been forced to travel in every round, and to difficult opposition to boot.

Save for the defeat at Leigh in November in the Floodlit Trophy, when the Loiners lacked the likes of Shoebottom, Mick Clark, Ramsey and Hick, Leeds focused on league football until the advent of the Challenge Cup in January. There was to be only one further league defeat to add to the reverse at St Helens and that was to come on the final day of the season, at Bradford, when nearly 11,000 turned up for a game involving two below-strength sides. The highlight for Leeds in the 32-15 reverse was the debut of two young second row forwards. One, with a shock of blond hair and the style to go with it, was Phil Cookson. The other, a man who was to become the scourge of running forwards throughout the league, scored a try that day. He

out only on the Championship Finals of 1972 and 1973 – dropped by Derek Turner in 1972 and sidelined by injury 12 months later – and the John Player Final against Salford in 1972-73. He was a key figure in ensuring that the Loiners reached Wembley in 1968, his masterly pass to John Atkinson freeing the winger for the try of the era and a subsequent break leading to a touchdown for centre Syd Hynes; for good measure, Ramsey also scored a try of his own in that epic 25-4 semi-final win over Wigan. Leeds' 1969 Championship Final win over Castleford at Odsal also owed much to Ramsey's talents, a well-taken drop goal ultimately separating the sides in the 16-14 win. Cas again had reason to regret the presence of Ramsey on the Odsal pitch two years later when he spent the second half at hooker when Tony Fisher was injured, helping the Loiners to a 19-8 victory in the Challenge Cup semi-final.

The defence-breaking reverse pass which sent Syd Hynes through in the 9-5 win over St Helens in the 1970 BBC2 Floodlit Trophy Final was another cameo moment in a list which encompasses so many necessary in Rugby League. Add to those a barrel-load of physical courage and a hard-hitting approach which made him the ideal protector of his halfbacks and Bill Ramsey was very close to being the complete footballer.

A Loiner Looks Back

Steve Pitchford

'The first thing Roy Francis said to me, in 1968 just after I'd signed and just before he went to Australia was, "you'll never make a rugby player, you're too fat."'

was the one and only Graham Eccles.

Other than that defeat, the Loiners' league campaign from late October onwards was one of unadulterated success tinged with sadness over the departure of Francis and the death of Jack Nelson.

Hull KR were disposed of, to the tune of 30-12, at Headingley, with Alan Smith and Hick scoring two tries each against a quality side in a display which epitomised the Leeds style. And the trip to Fartown three days later reaped similar reward with a 32-8 victory secured with tries by Atkinson, Shoebottom, Watson, Alan Smith – with a blockbuster in which three defenders were left sprawling – Hynes and Crosby.

A quick double was registered over York, who were beaten 26-7 at Headingley after Leeds had been only four points ahead on the hour; there was no repetition in the return at Wiggington Road, when the Loiners shot into an early 10-point lead before easing to a 39-8 win.

Watson and Brown notched two tries apiece in the comfortable verdict over Hull in which Ramsey again shone and Seabourne picked up the man of the match award; and the high skills levels in the Leeds camp were in evidence in the 18-3 win at Keighley in greasy conditions.

Bramley were denied 26-0 at Headingley, with 16 points in as many minutes towards the close sealing victory, although as Francis departed for North Sydney there were signs of a possible falter in the 13-9 win at Dewsbury which was only clinched by a late Ratcliffe try.

With Nelson in charge, the Loiners carved out a 16-9 win at Wilderspool with tries for Batten and Ron Cowan, Risman kicking four goals and Shoebottom adding a drop goal against a Wire outfit fielding several reserves.

A Loiner Looks Back

Les Dyl

Les Dyl leads the way in preseason training at Boddington Hall in the hot summer of 1976. Butch Adams, David Marshall, Graham Eccles, Kevin Dick and Phil Cookson try to keep up.

'Pace was my biggest asset. I went to Castleford Boys Modern School, where I played Rugby Union on Saturday morning, then for Leeds Under 17s in the afternoon. It was too much and as my priority was to play for Leeds I asked the school not to pick me any more. It was made clear to me that if I chose not to play for the school team that life would be made difficult for me. So I had to leave school. That was a very tough decision as I wanted to become a teacher. I did go to college later, but my priority was to make it as a Rugby League player.'

Loiners Big Match

24 May 1969, Championship Final, Leeds 16 Castleford 14, Odsal Stadium, Bradford

After having endured a 65-year drought before lifting their first Championship, Leeds secured the title for the second time in a decade, overcoming fierce rivals Castleford in a match that had everything; for both the purist and the pugilist.

A dramatic finish, quality tries, narrow failures at goal with each team missing out courtesy of an upright, and superb last ditch defence by both sides were constant features; underpinned throughout by the darker side of Rugby League as the 'Swinging Sixties' eased to a close at Odsal with an array of swinging arms.

Castleford prop Dennis Hartley, the former Doncaster and Hunslet front row, typified the robust nature of the clash with an early assault which Bill Ramsey, his team-mate at Parkside, remembers ruefully.

With friendships on hold for 80 minutes it all got too much for Hartley – who was to become the scourge of Australia a little over a year later when Great Britain retrieved the Ashes Down Under – when Leeds snatched victory at the death, the abrasive pack man receiving his marching orders for a shot on Mick Shoebottom.

The tensions on the field spilled over onto the Odsal terraces where several of the 28,442 crowd were arrested as fighting broke out. The abiding memory of the match, however, is of the piece of high-quality football which won the game for Leeds, executed by two of the side's many artists.

Castleford had won the Challenge Cup seven days earlier, having overcome Salford at Wembley, and were seeking to become the first Yorkshire side since Huddersfield's 'Team of All the Talents' in 1915 to pull off the double.

With only five minutes left, Derek Turner's men appeared to be on course to complete the achievement.

Continued...

The Christmas 'double' followed over Hunslet with the under-soil heating again paying off, the Parksiders opting to stage their 'home' fixture on 28 December at Headingley.

That meant Leeds played three games on their own patch in eight days, the genuine home fixture against Hunslet resulting in a comfortable 34-14 win in which the Loiners, superior in every department, provided what was to be a fitting epitaph for Jack Nelson. As flags flew at half mast on Boxing Day at Headingley and Leeds grieved, so the team provided the best possible epitaph. Hynes scored a try and a drop goal, Cowan crossed and Risman scored three goals in the 14-5 win over Castleford.

Hunslet profited from a £1,637 gate and a £250 TV fee from their 'home' game at Headingley but Leeds took the points with a 35-10 win in which Hynes notched a hat trick, Phil Holmes and Ramsey scored two tries each and John Holmes added four goals.

Leeds completed their third unbeaten month in the league with wins in each of their four January fixtures; Halifax were also disposed of in the Challenge Cup.

An early blast in which Langley, Alan Smith and Albert Eyre crossed helped Leeds to an 11-point lead at home to Wakefield and a try for Hynes and two John Holmes goals were enough to deny a Trinity fightback for a 16-12 win. Featherstone were trounced 29-11 on their own patch, Batten's silky skills being the catalyst for a fine display in which three tries were scored in

Castleford had established a 14-11 lead and had come close to extending that advantage when a long-range penalty attempt by second row Mick Redfearn bounced out off a post.
Leeds winger Ron Cowan saved the Loiners with a try-saving tackle on Cas centre Tony Thomas, and in another attack the Glassblowers' substitute Frank Fox went close to collecting a huge Redfearn 'up and under' for what would surely have been a clinching try.
Instilled with the ethos of Roy Francis, however, the Loiners turned defence into attack in delightful and devastating fashion. Stand off Mick Shoebottom and second row Ken Eyre, adopting a brave expansive approach close to their own line, gave Bev Risman some space and, in perhaps his finest moment for Leeds, the full-back almost casually sauntered from his own danger area, past Hartley and winger Trevor Briggs, into the Castleford half.
With options limited by the pragmatic Cas defence, Risman's old Rugby Union skills as an England fly half came to the fore, his pinpoint precision kick to the corner bouncing up in pre-ordained fashion for winger John Atkinson, ahead of his opponents in mind and in body, to collect and race over for a truly sensational equalising touchdown.
It fell to Risman to land the none-too-easy conversion and put Leeds ahead for the first time since the very early stages of the match, thus gaining revenge for the 9-5 defeat almost three months earlier in the quarter-final of the Challenge Cup and leaving Castleford still seeking their first title.
Hartley, at the restart, found himself wending the long and lonely walk up the Odsal terraces for his illegal challenge on Shoebottom as joy, once more, was unconfined for the Loiners at the famous Bradford setting.
Risman, who was awarded the Harry Sunderland Trophy as the man of the match, had opened the Loiners' account with a penalty from 35 metres after Keith Hepworth had been penalised for illegal feeding. Castleford stand off Alan Hardisty – who, with

Continued...

the first 10 minutes, the loose forward, regarded as a creator rather than scorer, adding a rare brace of his own.

Batten was again on the score-sheet a week later, together with Alan Smith and Albert Eyre, as Rovers put up a better show, losing 13-3. And, after the Challenge Cup win at Thrum Hall, Castleford were accounted for in a league match at Wheldon Road, a 10,000 crowd witnessing an abrasive clash in which Clark was the man of the match and Ramsey was again to the fore. Watson's two tries were important, as were the tries for Alan Smith and Ramsey, against a Cas side still smarting from the Yorkshire Cup Final defeat.

The Challenge Cup tie at Thrum Hall, meanwhile, was another testing affair, despite

Ready for the fray! The 1969 Championship Final side.

Fax's relatively lowly league position. Halifax, still mindful of the Yorkshire Cup semi-final defeat nearly four months earlier, were determined to turn the tables but Leeds ground out a 17-12 win, Seabourne providing the vital moment with a kick from his own 25 which found touch close to the Halifax line and led to a

Hepworth, was to join Leeds a couple of years later – levelled with a drop goal, his 100th for his home town club, and then charged down what would probably have been a successful effort by Seabourne.

Leeds, however, took the lead when Thomas fumbled and the alert Syd Hynes gathered, sending Cowan over in the corner.

Risman, though, was unable to add the extras and it was their opponents' turn to take control when hooker Clive Dickinson forced his way past a posse of defenders, the conversion by Redfearn edging Cas ahead.

A war of attrition (or just a war?) Leeds pin Castleford under their own posts in the 1969 Championship Final.

The abrasive nature of proceedings continued with Leeds prop Mick Clark departing, returning with a head guard, and Hepworth being carried off with concussion before returning to the fray.

Redfearn extended Castleford's lead when Loiners' second row Mick Joyce was pulled by referee Billy Thompson for a foul tackle and, after Seabourne saw his 40-yard drop goal attempt bounce back off a post before retiring with a recurrence of a shoulder dislocation, Cas stretched their advantage to six points when Redfearn successfully converted a penalty awarded when hooker Tony Crosby became too involved at a play-the-ball.

Risman, however, kept the Loiners in touch when Hepworth was again penalised for feeding, but Leeds were contemplating an 11-7 deficit as they chewed their half time lemons.

Any doubts that the contest had been as tough as it's possible to get were dispelled when Castleford loose forward and hard man Malcolm Reilly, the Lance Todd Trophy winner the previous week, failed to

Continued...

decisive try.

Ironically, Halifax were the next visitors to Headingley and by this stage, probably sick to the eye teeth of Leeds, conceded seven tries and failed to cross the whitewash in a 29-4 defeat in the only game to go ahead, thanks to the electric blanket, on a freezing cold but sunny day. Former Rugby Union winger Mike Lamb, who had made his debut in the home game with Featherstone, scored his first try for the club while Hynes and Seabourne again came up with four-star displays for the Loiners.

The second round Challenge Cup tie at Keighley, twice-postponed because of a frozen Lawkholme Lane pitch, at last went ahead and Leeds progressed to the quarter-finals with a 17-2 victory in front of an attendance of 10,260. Keighley, inspired by full-back Brian Jefferson, offered sterling resistance and Hynes, the maestro of the interception, proved to be the match-winner with a timely example. Seabourne was awarded a penalty try and Risman scored a try and four goals, but there was to be no return to Wembley for the holders. Wheldon Road proved to be the 'end of the road' seven days later as Castleford, the eventual winners of the competition, edged a 9-5 win. Leeds, limited to a try and a goal by Risman, conceded a costly penalty for 'talking' and referee Lawrinson threatened to abandon a passionate game at one stage after missiles, including a bottle, were thrown onto the field. An early injury to Seabourne was to be seminal as 13,250 fans were treated to an epic Cup clash which exemplified

re-emerge, suffering from concussion. Leeds had a let-off when a Redfearn attempt at goal, awarded after a foul by Ramsey on Brian Lockwood, rebounded off a post and a timely Hynes interception set up the position from which Risman kicked a penalty as police waded into the seething crowd.
Hardisty, a key figure as always in the Cas camp, grabbed what many of his supporters reckoned would be the winning try when he intercepted a Joyce pass; Risman, however, again earned his spurs, forcing the stand off towards the corner and Redfearn, importantly, missing the conversion.
With Hynes hobbling around there was a suspicion that Leeds, five points adrift, were finished. But Ramsey, with other ideas, revived the Loiners' bid with a drop goal to set up one of the most memorable finales in the history of the Championship and 'that John Atkinson try'.

Leeds: Risman; Cowan, Hynes, Watson, Atkinson; Shoebottom, Seabourne; Clark, Crosby, K Eyre, Joyce, Ramsey, Batten. Subs: Langley, Hick.
Castleford: Edwards; Briggs, Howe, Thomas, Lowndes; Hardisty, Hepworth; Hartley, Dickinson, Ward, Redfearn, Lockwood, Reilly. Subs: Bedford, Fox.
Referee: Mr WH Thompson (Huddersfield)
Leeds: T: Cowan, Atkinson. G: Risman 4. DG: Ramsey.
Castleford: T: Dickinson, Hardisty. G: Redfearn 3. DG: Hardisty.
Attendance: 28,442

the tempestuous rivalry between the clubs.

Leeds eased the disappointment by retaining the League Leaders Trophy. Dewsbury were toppled 25-17 at home, thanks to a late flurry of points, with Cowan scoring two tries and Alan Smith, Shoebottom and Clark recording supporting tries. History was made on 23 March 1969 when the Loiners played their first Sunday fixture, travelling to Hull on the Sabbath at the Airlie Birds' request. 7,400 fans shared the experience and, on a bitterly cold day, saw the sides finish all-square at 11-11, Leeds scoring tries by Crosby, Clark and Hynes, with Risman adding a goal. The Loiners, despite scoring three tries to Hull's one, were reckoned to be fortunate not to lose but the loss of the 'day of rest' seemed to do Leeds no harm seven days later when the side won 20-13 at Halifax, through a try and three goals by Risman, a try and a drop goal to Hynes and touchdowns for Cowan and Clark.

Batley were overcome 25-14 at Mount Pleasant, and 63-11 in the return, when 13 tries were scored including four for Hynes and three to Atkinson, with Shoebottom (sent off at Batley) and Watson having two each and Alan Smith and Peter Fozzard also racing over. Risman, who had kicked five goals in the first game, landed 12 in the next match, and Leeds posted a twenty-third league game without defeat, and clinched the League Leaders Trophy, with the 16-2 home win over Keighley. Langley and Watson crossed and Risman added five goals despite the dismissal of Atkinson, who was sent off with his Keighley adversary.

The next stage was the Championship Play-offs and, in Joe Warham, Leeds had the man at the helm with the necessary experience having helped guide, with coach Dai Prosser, the Loiners to the title eight years earlier.

The competition had, of course, been extended from the top four system (which had prevailed from 1906-07 until 1961-62) to the top

A Loiner Looks Back

Bev Risman

When winger John Atkinson raced over in the last minute of the 1969 Championship Final, courtesy of Bev Risman's well-placed kick to the corner, the try brought the scores level. However, as Risman explains: 'Atky was forced by the covering defenders to touch down at a point which was my worst kicking position, 10 to 15 yards to the left of the posts. I had a tendency to hook the ball across the uprights with my left foot, so the kick wasn't at all easy for me. To add to the pressure, we were due to go on holiday to Cornwall the following day. If I missed the conversion the match would have to be replayed and the holiday would be off. I remember wondering as I lined up the kick what my wife would say if we couldn't go! Luckily I sneaked it over.'

Bev Risman in action in the Championship semi-final victory over Salford.

A more selfish husband, however, could have been tempted to miss deliberately as a replay could have resulted in Bev Risman entering the annals of Leeds record breakers. His four goals that day at Odsal left him with 165 for the season – just one short of the club record set by Lewis Jones in 1956/57.

Risman continues to play down his involvement in the

Continued...

16 format, which involved two more rounds. As League Leaders, Leeds were guaranteed home advantage until the final, and Oldham were accounted for 32-12 at the first stage, Langley, Crosby, Hynes, Cowan, Ramsey and Batten nipping over, Risman kicking six goals and Watson adding a drop goal.

Workington Town travelled to Headingley from Cumbria in the second round and Risman, whose father Gus had played such a huge role in Town's rise, did his 'hometown' club no favours. The full-back contributed a try and two goals in a victory in which other touchdowns went to Atkinson, Shoebottom – who put in a tremendous tackling display – and Ramsey, who had one of his best games for the Loiners, Bernard Watson landing another drop goal.

Salford – coincidentally, Gus Risman's other major club – were the next visitors to Headingley, in the semi-final, and with an appearance at Wembley against Castleford on the agenda for the following weekend were chasing the 'double'.

A crowd of 15,690 turned out to see Leeds overturn a 6-0 interval deficit to win 22-12. Second row Colin Dixon scored two brilliant long-range tries for the Red Devils but Leeds, inspired by the courageous Seabourne who ignored an incredible four-times dislocated shoulder, turned the screw in the second half and made sure of a return to Odsal, scene of their success in 1961, with two tries each for Cowan and Batten and touchdowns from Hynes and Crosby, plus a couple of goals by Risman, who saw two efforts bounce out off an upright.

That win paved the way for more glory as Leeds retrieved the Championship. Hynes finished the campaign as top tryscorer with 26, followed by Alan Smith (23), Ron Cowan (19) and Mick Shoebottom with 18 as the Loiners began to look forward to the following season

try, which he created by ghosting from deep in his own half before slide-ruling a kick which popped up perfectly for the pursuing Atkinson.
'These things happen, they really do. I didn't do anything in particular, it was just that the Castleford forwards were exhausted. I had a lucky bounce in collecting a kick and suddenly I found myself in open space, I don't really know how it happened. Atky was a bit too far wide out for me to pass, I had 50 yards to run, and pace wasn't my big asset. I drew the cover and noticed that there was no one behind and that their tryline was open. I was still too far away from Atky to try a pass so I decided to kick. I knew he would get there first, so I put in a diagonal kick and just hoped it would bounce favourably. It did, Atky took it, and ran towards the posts to make my conversion attempt easier, which I was grateful for.
'It was a brutal match. That aspect was an accepted part of the game, to an extent, as far as referees were concerned. You had to be aware that if you went into a tackle unprepared there were criminals about who, if they could do something unpleasant to you, would do. I had two incidents where the knees went in in the tackle and I was lucky to come out alive. And when I was going up for kicks I had to keep my elbows out to protect myself. The referees simply couldn't see everything.
'The game was hard. We had our own enforcer in Bill Ramsey, and we had Mick Shoebottom. The conditions were dismal on the day of the game and it was always going to be tough because there was a lot of bad feeling between the sides. Castleford were an up-and-coming team, challenging our superiority, and there was never any love lost. I was hit a few times early on, and my mouth was spread across my face. The result hinged on a few moments and happily those few moments went our way.'

under new coach Derek 'Rocky' Turner, the man who had masterminded Castleford's Challenge Cup success over Salford. The fans were understandably delighted by their side's exploits and Jack Duxbury, President of the Supporters' Club, opined: 'There is a great deal to remember of the 1968-69 season. The departure to Australia of Mr Roy Francis, the very sudden bereavement of Mr Jack Nelson and the very creditable performance of Mr Joe Warham for taking charge of the team at a critical time and winning the League Championship. We must also welcome our new coach Mr Derek 'Rocky' Turner who hardly needs any introduction to followers of Rugby League.'

Football chairman Jack Myerscough was also highly satisfied with the team's successes and reflected: 'The season past has been a memorable one, not only in the fact that we won the Rugby League Championship for the second time in our history in the game, but also by the dramatic way in which the events unfolded themselves.

'The departure of our coach Roy Francis, who went to Australia just before Christmas, left us with Jack Nelson admirably standing in as caretaker/coach. Having successfully held the team together in a manner which held our admiration and gratitude, he was tragically taken away when he died suddenly at Christmas, 1968.

'Mr Joe Warham, in spite of his other heavy and important duties, was called upon overnight to resume control of coaching. He did not flinch but stepped into the breach and by immense skill and dedication successfully steered the team to another Championship win. He thus has the unique distinction of being in command on the only two occasions on which the club has won the Championship. It is a great tribute to

Mick Shoebottom checks the score in the 1969 Championship Final.

the players, coaches and staff at this club that such success could be gained under such remarkable circumstances.

'Our loyal and vigorous support made a direct contribution to this success. Such encouragement, particularly at away matches, is greatly appreciated by the players. Testimony to this is provided by our Yorkshire Cup win despite being drawn away in every round.

'This backing up of the team home and away had also a strong bearing on the winning for the third time in succession of the Rugby League 'League Leaders' Trophy and the Yorkshire League Championship.'

Turner, meanwhile, was about to guide the Loiners into a new epoch. He said: 'Having only recently joined Leeds, and speaking therefore as an ex-outsider, I can tell you that the sportsmanship and loyalty of Leeds Rugby followers are qualities for which the club is well-known throughout the Rugby League area.

'The standards the team has attained during the past three or four years have been exceptional, and this of course means that the task facing the players and myself in maintaining those standards will be a tough and demanding one.

'However, it is a challenge which I can assure you we shall face confidently and resolutely, sparing no efforts on our part in trying to provide attractive and successful football of the type with which the Leeds club is traditionally associated.'

Those words would perhaps haunt Turner over the next four years ...

A Loiner Looks Back

Harry Jepson

'Derek Turner was one of my favourite players. We could and should have signed him when I was at Hunslet. Leeds beat Castleford in the 1969 Championship Final, when Derek was the Castleford coach. I talked to him after the match and he said, "I'm sick, Harry. I'm going to Headingley." He told me the players he was going to get rid of. One was Bev Risman, another was Barry Seabourne, another was Mick Clark. By the time I joined Leeds a year later they had gone, apart from Barry who went later.'

Scrum half Barry Seabourne enjoyed several seasons of success with Bradford Northern after departing Headingley in the autumn of 1971.

Roy Francis
A Coach Ahead of his Time?

The great Roy Francis coached Leeds from 1963 to 1968 and again in the 1974-75 season. He was often regarded as a coach ahead of his time in terms of training, man management and the expansive style of play he engendered. But what did the players who served under him think?

Alan Smith:
'The front row really benefited from Roy Francis' training techniques. Hooker Tony Crosby, Mick Clark – who he switched from second row to prop – and Kenny Eyre who was a bulky lad but who could run, all gained years from Roy.
'Roy created a spectacular footballing side which I haven't seen bettered. Such as Mick Clark, Bill Ramsey and Kenny Eyre were damn good footballers and under Roy Francis they were allowed to spin it about. The team came of age in the 1968 semi-final at Swinton, we played some football then. It was a lovely time, between 1966 and 1968, to become an established senior player. In fact it was a privilege to stand on the wing and watch it! Roy would have us standing so deep you used to almost rub against your natural feeling of wanting to take off. When you came onto the ball you got it at pace.
'His training techniques were phenomenal. Nobody had experienced training like he put us through. Other clubs used to come and watch and my business partner Brian Harrison, a former Yorkshire Schoolboy, remembers popping along to watch a session.
'Roy brought in players like Ken Rollin, Les Chamberlain, Albert Firth, lads who were towards the end of their career with Wakefield. Fine players who were good for team spirit.
'Ronnie Cowan was a finely balanced runner on the wing. His style was so relaxed and graceful. Roy would hold him up as a role model for me, he'd say, "Try and pull yourself in a bit kid, try and get your arm in motion and relax, never mind getting strain out of your neck, watch Ronnie".'

Mick Clark:
'I was surprised when Roy said he was going. I said, "What are you leaving for?" and it was a stupid thing, it was something like he wanted to be called "football manager" and not "coach". I said, "We'll call you manager, boss, we'll call you whatever you want". And he said, "No, I want them to recognise that I'm the manager". I said, "Don't be a prat – we know you're the manager". He said, "No, I want it official".
'Roy Francis transformed my career by switching me from second row to prop. I'd been struggling to get in the side and he must have been desperate when he came to me and said, "Mick I'm going to play you against Halifax on Saturday, you're at No. 8".
'I played against Kenny Roberts and I had a blinder, even though I say it myself. I thought, "No.8, you don't have to back anybody up so I'll get running and let them back me up!"'

John Holmes:
'I'd started with Leeds at full-back and Roy Francis asked me to meet him at the Queens Hotel in City Square. He didn't tell me why. So I went down to the Queens, where I'd never been before in my life, I was 18 or 19, and he comes in, sits me down and gets me a drink. And he just turned round and said, "What do you think about playing stand off?" I thought, "Is that why you've brought me down here, to ask me that?" and I just said, "I'll play anywhere". And that's how it started, with Roy Francis asking me down to the Queens Hotel. Maybe he wanted to make me feel special, perhaps he was already there, having a meal or something. I haven't a clue.
'He was very strict in his training, but fair. He'd buy you

a pint on a Saturday after the game and say, "Enjoy it because I'll run it out of you on Tuesday". And he did. He had a lot of respect for the players and it was reciprocated.

'His teams always seemed to come good in the last 20 minutes. We trained hard and were fitter than most other sides. I used to come off training on a Tuesday night so shot it took me 20 minutes to walk to the bus stop. Thursday would be easier, with the game coming up. And we all had jobs of course. Then Roy brought in Saturday morning sessions as well, when Sunday rugby started, just to go through the matches. After Saturday matches we would go up on Sunday morning for a game of touch and pass. That was voluntary but there would be 20 lads up there, then we'd have a bath to get the aches and pains out and we'd socialise again.

'Roy once said to Tony Crosby, the hooker, "All I want you to do is imagine a groove in the middle of the pitch and run up and down it. Don't go anywhere; when the ball's gone, just run up and down the middle of the pitch." I think Tony got 15 or 16 tries that season and for a hooker that was tops. That's how Roy worked, seeing something really simple.'

Roy Francis, Jack Nelson, John Atkinson and Alan Smith check out the pitch prior to the 1968 Watersplash Final. Less than eight months later Francis departed for North Sydney. Nelson, after taking over the reins at short notice, tragically passed away on the morning of the Boxing Day fixture with Castleford.

John Atkinson:

'Roy's ethos was, "If you're good enough to play for Leeds then all I have to do is get you fit. If you're fitter than everybody else, eventually it will tell." And it did, many a time, in the last 20 minutes. Everybody who played under Roy Francis, certainly in that first period, would have to say that he made them a better player because he introduced a level of fitness that they'd not been used to before, although my dad had instilled in me the ethos that you can't play rugby on just two sessions a week.

'We maybe drank a bit more than we should have done but that was the rugby culture. Roy was already talking about diets. He gave me the book "The power of positive thinking", a religious book which certainly worked as far as being on the pitch was concerned. He was quite a psychologist, long before you ever got sports psychologists, and maybe a bit of a conman as well!

'We played Featherstone at Post Office Road and I scored three tries; I had to bang my way through for one of them. Roy sat next to me on the bus coming back and he said, "How did you play today John?" I said, "Oh, not bad at all, I got three tries, I can't complain". He said, "If I see you doing that again, I'll leave you out. If somebody keeps battering your thighs and legs like that, like you've been doing it today, it'll slow you down. If it's the last minute and you've no choice, use it. But don't go looking for it."

'He was right. But he never taught us how to play rugby. His philosophy was, "If you're good enough to play for Leeds then I can't teach you how to play rugby, what I need to teach you is to be able to last for 80 minutes."

'One thing that surprises me is that he never actually

came up with the idea of players going out 10 minutes before a match to warm up. Maybe he reckoned that it would suit some people more than others. Some people, like Mick Shoebottom and Syd Hynes, you couldn't get them off the bench, and John Holmes was the same. He used to look at you and he'd be thinking, "Are you daft you lot?" He'd done his work through the week and that's how he felt he'd coped.'

Steve Pitchford:
'Roy Francis had this thing about running round the Headingley ground, we'd start off on the old bowling green, round the back of the cricket pavilion, along the road, through the middle of the press stand, round the pitch, through the centre of the south stand, up the car park, round the training ground, back into the car park, back through the middle of the south stand, round the other half of the pitch, where we used to come out in the corner – up that ramp, across the front of the pavilion, back onto the bowling green. Not once, but five times! I wasn't built for this, and when there's such as Atkinson doing it – well, there was no way I could keep up with players like that! I've spent half my life looking at 'em going forwards. It was when we got on the pitch that I used to do my business. I had the stamina obviously, because he made us have the stamina, and I never quit on the guy.
'Some coaches will swap players around if somebody's injured. Roy had no time for that. He was a great believer that if the No.10 in the first team got injured, the No.10 in the second team should be good enough to step forward. If he wasn't, then why was he at Leeds? That's how I got in, when Kenny Eyre was injured.
'He was also a great leader. He changed my style of play once; it was the era when players like Jim Mills and Phil Lowe were running down the centre spots and not through the middle. He asked me to do that, off John Holmes. I made a total mess of it, I didn't know whether I wanted to be over here or over there, I lost it all completely. After about a fortnight, the man was big enough to say, "I've made a right bollocks of your game, just go back to how you used to play." That was Roy Francis; a good man.'

Ray Batten:
'Under Roy Francis, training was harder than the game on Saturday. It lasted for two hours and it was intense, the easy part was the weekend game. He made a few bad signings and he made some very good ones. The big turnaround was when he signed Harry Poole, until then we were going nowhere. Poole was only at Leeds for two years but we all gained in confidence under his leadership. We reached the Cup semi-final in 1967 but Harry had broken his arm a month earlier. I think that's the reason we lost, and Harry then retired.'

Graham Eccles:
'Roy Francis was the first coach to use a stopwatch in everything he did. He had a lot of bluff, he used to say that you hadn't beaten your time; he always made you go quicker than the time you'd done before. He did it by encouraging you and by somehow implanting in your mind that you had sold yourself short. He was probably the best coach at motivating a team that I have played under.
'I made my first team debut in 1969 and the following season I couldn't get in the second team. They were talking about changing me to a scrum half and had me running up and down the stand, trying to change my running pattern. I went in to see Roy, to try to find out why I wasn't playing. After I came out I thought, "What have I been in there for? Why have I complained?" He was that type of bloke, he was quite intelligent, he talked you round, and you were left thinking, "Yes, I should be happy, I'm at Leeds." Then you think, "But I'm still not playing!"'

7. POINTS AND PRAGMATISM

Derek Turner was well aware that he was facing a tough task when he was appointed coach in the summer of 1969.

A real hard man of Rugby League, 'Rocky' Turner had established a fearsome reputation as a player with Oldham, Wakefield Trinity and Great Britain and his no-nonsense approach had also paid dividends as a coach with Castleford, who he had coached to Wembley success over Salford the previous spring.

Turner had moulded the Wheldon Road side into a unit capable of playing the type of football which earned them the sobriquet 'Classy Cas' and hopes were high that he would be the man to steer Leeds to even greater achievements.

In his address to the supporters, Turner had pledged to 'spare no effort' in providing 'attractive and successful football of the type with which the Leeds club is traditionally associated.'

The conundrum, during Turner's four-year reign, is that while his players scored more points than ever before, with most of the tries going to the backs, the perception was that the Loiners had lost their gift for free-flowing football.

In truth the challenge to match the feats, and the style, of the heady 1968-69 campaign was a near-impossible one. Leeds, while maintaining their status as arguably the finest side in the game, closed Turner's inaugural campaign with only two trophies – the League Leaders Trophy, and the European Club Championship, won 31-5 against Perpignan, on the back of the previous season's success.

Turner, however, retained the side's consistency and only four league games were lost, just one more than in the previous season;

A Loiner Looks Back

Les Dyl

'I signed for Leeds in 1969. My dad was Polish and didn't know much about Rugby League so my uncle Walter – Brian Lockwood's dad – went with me to Headingley and negotiated terms with the directors. He was firm and he got me a better deal. I remember Derek Turner being there, and Joe Warham. It was frowned upon for a Cas lad to sign for Leeds, though. I think 10 lads were sent to Leeds' summer school by our teacher Mr Dawson. We'd have normally gone down to Wheldon Road. The two Claughton brothers were among them, and others such as Keith Voyce who went on to Dewsbury. My mate Keith Worsley went to Castleford when I went to Leeds. Cas were determined not to lose him after they'd missed out on me and they paid him more than they usually gave to juniors, so his good deal was down to me! I played with Keith, and with Brian Lockwood, for Yorkshire at Headingley, that was a memorable moment.'

Les Dyl in action against St Helens.

Headingley Hero

Derek Turner

A striking feature of the Loiners' glory years of the 1960s and 1970s is that those involved speak, almost overwhelmingly, as one; a truth which is perhaps one of the main factors behind Leeds' successes throughout the period.

One issue, however, remains a great conundrum and the arguments continue to rage, with players, directors and fans often firmly divided into opposite camps.

The focus of the heated debate is Derek 'Rocky' Turner.

Turner, among the hardest of players during a career which encompassed Oldham and Wakefield Trinity, earned 24 Great Britain caps and although comparatively lightweight for a loose forward carved out a fearsome reputation as the scourge of the Australians.

'Rocky' Turner brought the same approach to his role as a coach. Taking over at Castleford in the mid-sixties he ensured that the Wheldon Road outfit were as hard-bitten an outfit up front as any around.

Turner steered Cas to Challenge Cup success in 1969 when his side also went agonisingly close to a first-ever Championship. Seven days after the Wembley victory over Salford Cas were denied the 'double' by Leeds.

By the beginning of the following season Turner was in charge at Headingley, seen by the Leeds board as the man equipped to steer the Loiners' successes of the 1960s into a new decade.

Turner was at the helm for four seasons, during which the Loiners twice finished top of the table and came third on the other two occasions.

Leeds were Challenge Cup runners-up in 1970-71 and 1971-72, won the Championship in the second of those seasons and were Championship runners-up in Turner's first season in charge.

The Loiners topped the Yorkshire League table in 1969-70 and the following season won the Yorkshire

Continued...

Syd Hynes and Barry Seabourne prepare for Great Britain's 1970 tour.

and Leeds extended the gap over the second-placed side (four points in 1968-69) to nine, with Castleford languishing some way behind as runners-up.

As in 1968-69, the opening league match was lost, on this occasion at Castleford, when stand off Mick Shoebottom scored his side's only points in the 11-2 defeat with a drop goal. The Loiners also went down by the odd point in 17 at Hull in November, at Wakefield in March by 30-23, and later that month at St Helens, 12-5.

Between the defeats at Castleford and Hull, however, Leeds won 15 successive league games, although there was disappointment with the 20-17 home defeat by Hull in the semi-final of the Yorkshire Cup after opening wins, also at Headingley, against Bradford Northern and Halifax.

Ironically for a side said to have lost some of its sparkle since the departure of Roy Francis, the wingers shared top billing in the try scoring tables, with left winger John Atkinson racing over for 36 tries and Alan Smith close behind with 32. Indeed, the backs led the way generally, Shoebottom netting 23, Syd Hynes posting 20,

Cup and, for the first time, the BBC2 Floodlit Trophy. In Turner's last season, 1972-73, Leeds retrieved the Yorkshire Cup, won the John Player Cup and were runners-up to Dewsbury in the Championship Final at Odsal.

But by the time Leeds played Dewsbury the announcement had already been made that Turner, despite his achievements, was on his way out and that Eric Ashton would be taking over as coach from 1 June 1973. The belief was that the football played was not in the traditional Leeds style. The statistics, however, tell a different story.

Leeds coach Derek Turner debates tactics with Alan Hardisty, another former Castleford stalwart.

In Turner's last season the Loiners scored 1,277 points, made up of 810 points in 34 league games, 158 in six Players No 6 matches, 117 in four Yorkshire Cup ties, 95 in four Championship play-off clashes, 18 in two BBC2 Floodlit Trophy matches, 11 in the Challenge Cup defeat by Wigan, 11 against New Zealand and 57 at the expense of Hunslet in the Lazenby Cup.

Most of those points, moreover, were scored by the backs. Left winger John Atkinson topped the try-scoring table with 36, stand-off Alan Hardisty and right wing Alan Smith followed with 28 each, right centre Syd Hynes was next in line with 25 and left centre Les Dyl was fifth, on the 20 mark. Full-back John Holmes had 16, together with utility back John Langley, and the first forward to appear on the list was second row Phil Cookson, one behind Langley and Holmes.

The 1972-73 season wasn't the only one during Turner's reign in which Leeds piled up the points. The Loiners' best total under Roy Francis, who strongly favoured the expansive approach, was the 972 rattled up in 1967-68, with 1,066 recorded the following year when Francis departed in the autumn. Derek Turner failed to better that only once – in 1969-70, when 1,017 points were recorded. The deficiency was, however, rectified the following season with 1,109 and Francis' best was pipped in 1971-72 with 1,071.

The figures, therefore, fail to equate with the accusation. Derek Hallas, Leeds' right centre in the 1960-61 Championship-winning side, believes simply that those behind the sacking did not understand Rugby League. Others point to Turner's penchant for a 'softening up' period in each game, with the tries flowing freely thereafter. And some lament – while others admire – his brusque manner off the field.

Following his dismissal the bruised Derek 'Rocky' Turner vowed that no one would be allowed to sack him again. And, apart from a brief spell as Wakefield Trinity coach in the early 1980s, he has not been involved in the game since.

Ron Cowan grabbing 13 and Bernard Watson notching 12 before forwards Ray Batten and Bill Ramsey featured with nine and eight respectively, to give a statistical lie to accusations that Turner's teams were forward-orientated.

Atkinson fired immediately with a hat trick in the 39-9 win over Hunslet in the Lazenby Cup, played unusually early on 1 August, and there was a hat trick for Smith, with Atkinson also crossing, as Halifax were crushed 44-6 in the second round of the Yorkshire Cup. John Langley's two tries and a touchdown from Ken Eyre, with John Holmes adding four goals, weren't enough to deny Hull in the semi-final, however, and the holders' interest in the Yorkshire Cup had been ended before August

Five 1970 tourists. Back: Alan Smith, Syd Hynes. Front: John Atkinson, Barry Seabourne, Mick Shoebottom.

was out, whereas the previous season the first round game – against Hull – had been staged on 7 September.

Leeds' winning league run kicked off with a 25-14 victory over Huddersfield at Fartown, when Bernard Watson and Atkinson raced over for two tries each and Peter Fozzard grabbed a touchdown, John Holmes adding five goals.

Cowan crossed twice in the 20-14 home win over Wakefield Trinity and the winger repeated the trick at York when the home side, who would finish 26th in the league that season, belied their lowly status by only going down 21-17.

Prop Ken Eyre used his bulk and his mighty sidestep to fine effect against his old club, charging over for a try against Hunslet at Parkside in the 20-5 success with other south Leeds men in Mick Clark and Shoebottom also crossing and yet another, Hynes, landing four goals.

The wingers simply couldn't stop scoring tries as Alan Smith raced over for a brace against Bradford in a 22-11 success, Cowan following up with a hat trick and Smith netting two more touchdowns as Huddersfield were crushed 45-4 at home. Hynes also notched a pair as Halifax again slumped to the Loiners, this time in a BBC2 Floodlit Trophy clash at Thrum Hall. And Doncaster, brave but limited, could do little to deny Leeds at Tatters Field, Cowan bagging a brace in the 30-14 success.

Leeds went down to a rare loss with the 9-8 setback at Hull, a reverse that ended a 15-match winning run in the league. The Loiners scored two tries – through Shoebottom and Atkinson – to one, but full-back Bev Risman's solitary success with the boot wasn't enough to prevent defeat.

Castleford inflicted a rare second successive reverse on Turner's men with a 9-7 win in the Floodlit Trophy at Wheldon Road but joy was unconfined in December and January as the initiative in installing the electric blanket once

A Loiner Looks Back

Phil Cookson

'It was a hell of a step coming to Leeds from Featherstone, not knowing anybody. My dad wouldn't let me play with Rovers. His brother-in-law had signed for them on a contract which took effect after six games and they kept him out for the one game. My dad said, "you're not gonna do that with my lad." And that was it.

'Leeds were totally different, they looked after their players and not just financially. So we had no complaints and we all played for one another.

'We had a good blend and I think my partnership with Graham Eccles in the second row was something special. We started at around the same time and we were probably the littlest fellas on the field although I also played at prop a bit. Scrummaging techniques were interesting; particularly with such as Tony Fisher, Terry Clawson and Mick Harrison. They were marvellous players. Fisher looked after you very, very

Continued...

well, but if he wanted the head you had to go for the head whether it was his or not. If you didn't go the right way you could break your neck, simple as that, or worse, Fisher'd do you. He was some player, he was a hard man and great to have in your side.

'By God what a great forward Terry Clawson was. You had to respect him, he could play any game you wanted, he could run, he could handle, he could kick, he could tackle, he could fight if you wanted. He was probably the complete all round forward, one of the best 8s or 10s around. Mick Harrison was another one, it was fabulous having him in your side. Not as agile as Terry but what a great forward.'

Phil Cookson.

again paid off with a regular diet of fixtures.

Dewsbury, Featherstone Rovers and, on Boxing Day, Castleford, were all accounted for at Headingley, by scorelines of 40-7, 11-7 and 8-0 respectively, while the Loiners triumphed over Bradford Northern 12-10 at Odsal when Ramsey's drop goal provided the winning margin.

January, too, was circumvented without defeat. The seventies opened with a revenge 22-9 victory over Hull at Headingley in which Batten, Shoebottom, Atkinson and Alan Smith crossed, Holmes landing five goals. Bramley, obliged to switch their 'home' game from McLaren Field because of the weather, went down 20-9. Atkinson, irrepressible, raced over for a hat trick with Hynes, Alan Smith and Trevor Briggs – who was to earn lasting glory a little over three years later for the Villagers with

Loiners Big Match

16 May 1970, Championship Final, Leeds 12 St Helens 24, Odsal Stadium, Bradford

Leeds had high hopes of retaining the Championship when they travelled to Odsal for the second time in 12 months for the title decider.

The Loiners had staged an imposing victory over Castleford at Bradford a year earlier and their ambitions were also fuelled by the fact that St Helens had struggled to beat Castleford's second string in the other semi-final. Cup Finalists Castleford, held to a 9-9 draw in the first game, were angry at being forced to stage the replay at Knowsley Road a mere five days before their Wembley date with Wigan. The Wheldon Road men sent their A team over the Pennines but, incredibly, the young Cas side were 12-10 up with seven minutes remaining.

It needed two late tries for Saints to secure a 21-12 win and, maybe stung by that escape, St Helens were thoroughly focussed for their meeting with Leeds.

A notable casualty of the narrow win over Castleford was Frank Wilson, who was dropped with second row Eric Prescott taking the Welshman's place on the wing in a tactic aimed at thwarting the threat of Alan Smith. And with Great Britain stand off and captain Frank Myler in the sensational form which would help Great Britain retrieve the Ashes Down Under that summer, Leeds were forced to concede second best.

Not that it looked that way in the early stages. Coach Cliff Evans' 'Prescott ploy' appeared to backfire when the Loiners took an early lead with a try for none other than Smith, who charged over from a long pass. St Helens, though, soon recovered from that setback, a tap-penalty move involving second row pair John Mantle and Eric Chisnall paving the way for Myler to send hooker Bill Sayer over for a touchdown which was converted by loose forward Kel Coslett.

The Loiners replied with arguably the try of the game. Having exerted heavy pressure, Leeds forced a drop

Continued...

out which Ron Cowan, playing in the centre, collected 40 yards from the St Helens line. The Scotsman had no right to score from that position, but score he did with arguably his finest try for the club. Seven defenders were left stunned, sprawling and simply spectators as Cowan swerved and shimmied his way past half the St Helens side for a sensational try which, with full-back John Holmes' goal, put Leeds three points in front.

With Mick Shoebottom in fine form at stand off, Leeds had their opponents under the cosh and any lesser side than St Helens would surely have buckled. The Lancastrians, however, not only held out during the crucial period until half time. Leeds were denied any further try, and the Saints were only a point adrift at the break following a Coslett penalty.

Centre John Walsh landed a 25-yard drop goal six minutes into the second period to retrieve a lead which St Helens were not to lose and as the Saints pack began to get on top a six-man move led to Prescott racing over off Myler's reverse pass.

Coslett hit a post with his conversion attempt but the momentum was maintained when Walsh kicked another drop goal and followed up with a try.

As the Odsal bowl was swept by heavy rain, Coslett and Holmes traded two penalties each before Prescott again justified his shock selection out wide by scooping up a loose ball to touch down five minutes from time.

Loiners skipper Barry Seabourne could only watch on as St Helens counterpart Cliff Watson lifted the Championship Cup and Myler, the Harry Sunderland man of the match, collected his first Championship medal after a lengthy career with Widnes and Saints.

Messrs Atkinson, Hynes, Myler, Seabourne, Shoebottom, Smith and Watson were to join forces during the summer in the Great Britain cause with the memorable series victory over Australia.

Leeds: Holmes; A Smith, Hynes, Cowan, Atkinson; Shoebottom, Seabourne; Burke, Crosby, A Eyre, Ramsey, Eccles, Batten. Subs: Hick, Langley.
St Helens: Barrow; Jones, Benyon, Walsh, Prescott; Myler, Heaton; Halsall, Sayer, Watson, Mantle, Chisnall, Coslett. Subs: Whittle, Rees.
Referee: Mr WH Thompson (Huddersfield).
Leeds: T: Smith, Cowan. G: Holmes 3.
St Helens: T: Prescott 2, Sayer, Walsh. G: Coslett 4. DG: Walsh 2.
Attendance: 26,358

Five Saints corner Mick Shoebottom in the 1970 Championship Final.

the magnificent BBC2 Floodlit Trophy victory – grabbing the other Leeds tries and Risman adding a goal.

Alan Smith emulated Atkinson in the next game, at Dewsbury, with a hat trick in the 26-10 victory and the signal was sent out that Leeds were in serious mood when Wigan were toppled 23-14 at Central Park. Young second row Phil Cookson proved he could turn on the talent in a tough arena with a try, with the backs scoring the remaining touchdowns through Shoebottom, Atkinson, Hynes and Risman, who added four goals.

The focus switched to the Challenge Cup in February. The Loiners were tested by Batley before easing through to the second round with a 17-5 victory earned with tries by Cookson, Dave Hick and Hynes. Warrington posed what appeared to be an altogether greater threat at the next stage at Wilderspool but the Wire, in the middle of a lull which was to lead to the involvement of Alex Murphy a little over a year later, could not match the Loiners and succumbed to tries by Shoebottom, Atkinson and Hynes in the 11-5 reverse.

That game was to be Risman's last, the full-back being carried off with a leg injury which was to end his career. And Wembley hopes were to come to an end in the next round, at Hull KR, when the Robins ground out a 7-2 victory in which Leeds were limited to a Holmes penalty.

That defeat heralded an indifferent spell in which two of the other four games played in March were lost. Wakefield Trinity won a high-scoring 30-23 thriller at Belle Vue and Knowsley Road again proved to be a less than happy hunting ground, the Loiners recording an Atkinson try and a Hynes goal in the 12-5 reverse.

Between those games Bramley were brushed aside 24-2 at Headingley, when Batten and Atkinson scored two tries each, Cookson scored a try and a goal, and hooker Peter Dunn, signed from Hunslet, nipped over. Intriguingly the three Leeds goals that day were scored by different players, Holmes and Hynes joining Cookson on the score-sheet.

Batley slipped at Headingley as April approached, Watson scoring two tries and Hynes adding a try and six goals with Ramsey also touching down in the 24-7 success.

Leeds went on to seal the League Leaders trophy and the Yorkshire League with three wins in six days as the league programme was wrapped up by Easter. Atkinson crossed, and Seabourne landed two goals, as Halifax were edged 7-5 at Thrum Hall, Hunslet weren't

Leeds Sevens

Seven-a-sides was a popular version of the sport throughout the 1960s and 1970s.
Wigan had launched their own tournament in 1959 after previous contests in 1923 and 1949. Leeds followed suit in 1964 and five-figure crowds regularly flocked to the end-of-season festival, which generally involved eight teams and was sponsored for many years by WD & HO Wills.
Despite boasting many star players, however, Leeds rarely had much success on their own patch, winning the Wills Embassy competition on only one occasion, in 1973.
That triumph was, however, followed by consecutive successes in Wigan's pre-season tournament, in 1974 and 1975.

No luck for Leeds this time! Miss World presents the 1969 Wigan Sevens Trophy to Salford's David Watkins.

Leeds 'Sevens' winners:

1964 Bradford Northern	*1972 Halifax*
1965 St Helens	*1973 Leeds*
1966 Bradford Northern	*1974 Salford*
1967 Huddersfield	*1975 Wigan*
1968 Salford	*1976 Castleford*
1969 Salford	*1977 No competition*
1970 Salford	*1978 Widnes*
1971 Wakefield Trinity	

Tony Wainwright clears the Leeds line against Barrow in the 1971 Headingley Sevens.

strong enough to prevent an 18-0 defeat at Headingley which involved two tries and three goals for Hynes and touchdowns by Briggs and Alan Smith, and an 18-10 victory at Featherstone Rovers was achieved through two touchdowns for Watson, a try and three goals by Hynes, and a Batten try.

That finish, leaving Leeds at the top of the table and well clear of the chasing pack, led to a general belief that the Loiners were by some distance the best side in the competition and worthy of the Championship.

Leeds, indeed, looked on course to retain a trophy which they had taken so long to collect in the first place as Turners men cantered through the early play-off rounds.

Halifax could do nothing to prevent a 24-4 victory in the first round when Alan Smith grabbed two tries and Shoebottom, Graham Eccles, Langley and Hick touched down, Holmes kicking three goals. The gallant Cumbrians of Whitehaven travelled south at the next stage, determined – as Whitehaven tend to be – to assuage the bitter memory of the late defeat, through Jeff Stevenson's drop goal, in the Challenge Cup semi-final at Odsal in 1957.

Haven did not lack confidence, having toppled Wigan at the first round stage, drawing 20-20 at Central Park and winning the replay at the Recreation Grounds 9-4.

Another giant-killing act, however, was never on the agenda as the Loiners strolled to a 45-10 victory. Four players – Hynes, Langley, Atkinson and Shoebottom – scored two tries each, Watson, Alan Smith and Batten also crossed the whitewash and Holmes added six goals.

Leeds should have expected a difficult encounter with Hull KR, who had finished fifth, in the semi-final. The Robins, though, crumbled as Shoebottom registered four tries in the 47-5 stroll. Other tries went to Albert Eyre, Alan Smith, Atkinson and Seabourne, with Hynes scoring a try and three goals and Holmes netting seven goals in a stunning victory which left Leeds' hordes of fans confident of accounting for St Helens in the Odsal decider a fortnight later.

Leeds, though, could only muster tries for Ron Cowan and Alan Smith in the 24-12 defeat, Holmes kicking three goals.

With the League Leaders Trophy and the Yorkshire League Cup in the cabinet, however, the campaign had been without question a success and the quality of the squad was confirmed when five players – Atkinson, Hynes,

Seabourne, Shoebottom and Alan Smith – were selected for the Great Britain touring party to Australia and New Zealand. The quintet and their fellow-Lions were to return with the Ashes, which had been lost three years earlier.

The strength of the British side was illustrated by the fact that Ramsey, arguably in the finest form of his career, and Batten were overlooked and given that strength it was no real surprise that the Lions also whitewashed New Zealand, all 26 players in the party appearing in at least one Test. Atkinson, with 18 appearances from which he scored 15 tries, was the busiest man on the tour. Smith also totalled 15 tries while Hynes outdid his club colleagues, topping the list with 19 touchdowns.

On the Leeds front, Atkinson resumed pole position from Hynes in the try-scoring list, closing the campaign with 36. Smith recorded 32 tries, Shoebottom had 23 and Hynes 20. Remarkably, eight players shared the goal kicking duties. Risman headed the list with 89, Holmes landed 57 and the others comprised Hynes (25), Seabourne (4), Watson (3), Ramsey and Shoebottom with two each, and Cookson with his solitary success against Bramley.

A Loiner Looks Back

Bill Ramsey

'I had a bad game in the 1971 Challenge Cup Final against Leigh. We were unfortunate, we lost three vital players and the players who came in weren't good enough to replace them. That particular game, though, was dictated by one man and he got away with everything. What surprised me was Billy Thompson, who I always thought of as a fair referee. He certainly wasn't on that occasion; he was completely dictated to, not only by Alex Murphy but also by Kevin Ashcroft and by Jim Fiddler. They were just chat, chat, chat all the time and we got off to a bad start and got worse. There were times when we could have got back into the game but every time we started to show anything we got penalised so we were on the back foot again. Of all the times Billy has refereed at Wembley I'm sure he seen worse incidents than what happened in that game.'

Nearly 12 months later and John Atkinson, Keith Hepworth, Les Dyl and Bill Ramsey enjoy the 1972 Challenge Cup semi-final win over Halifax at Odsal. Leeds, however, were to experience another disappointing defeat at Wembley.

8. TRIUMPH AND TRAGEDY

The 1970-71 season will be remembered for many varied reasons.

Several exciting new talents emerged, including a young centre from the Castleford area by the name of Les Dyl who opened his account with two tries in the Floodlit Trophy win in October at Craven Park, Barrow.

John Holmes escaped the semi-shadow of Bev Risman, who had retired at the end of the 1969-70 campaign, and broke the 300-point barrier.

Second row Bob Haigh, a £6,500 close season buy from Wakefield Trinity, hit the headlines with 40 tries, shattering the previous record for tries in a season by a forward of 36, set by Hull second row Bob Taylor in 1926.

Half back Tony Wainwright fires out a pass in the 4-0 Challenge Cup second round victory over St Helens.

Haigh's feat, which he readily admitted owed much to the creative abilities of loose forward Ray Batten, helped Leeds to a massive 856 points haul in League football, but despite having registered that total the Loiners slipped from top to third in the League.

Leeds made up for that disappointment by winning the BBC2 Floodlit Trophy for the first time and also lifted the Yorkshire Cup with a 23-7 success over Featherstone Rovers at Odsal.

The season as a whole, however, was

Loiners Big Match

21 November 1970, Yorkshire Cup Final, Leeds 23 Featherstone Rovers 7, Odsal Stadium, Bradford

Leeds, hot favourites to overcome Rovers in the first meeting of the sides in the Yorkshire Cup Final since 1928, when the Loiners had won 5-0, were rarely in difficulties as they recovered the trophy after a gap of two years.

Featherstone went into the game with their worst 'points against' record in many seasons and lacked several players, notably prop forward Charlie Stone and full-back Harold Box.

The Post Office Road outfit's lack of pace was another factor which concerned their fans in the build-up to the game and against that background it was no surprise that Rovers adopted a highly physical approach in the early stages, when Leeds hooker Peter Dunn complained to his former Hunslet colleague Bill Ramsey that his Featherstone counterpart Arnie Morgan was repeatedly hitting him in the scrums.

The fact that Morgan was sent off after only 12 minutes would suggest that he had been very active during his short stay on the field.

A touch judge had, indeed, found it necessary to enter the field of play twice prior to Morgan's dismissal; and this after a scrum had erupted in a brawl within the first five minutes.

The Loiners, firmly focussed on football, opened the scoring after 10 minutes when centre Syd Hynes, the Yorkshire Federation of Rugby League Supporters' Clubs White Rose Trophy Man of the Match, essayed an astute grubber, winger Alan Smith beating the defence to the touchdown.

Any preconceptions Rovers may have harboured that

Continued...

they could overcome the loss of Morgan were shattered within a minute, Loiners full-back John Holmes making intelligent use of the blind side to send Smith over for his second try.

Featherstone, however, with Vince Farrar switched to hooker from loose forward, kept Leeds at bay for the remainder of the half, other than the concession of a late penalty by Hynes. John Atkinson went close for the Loiners, only to be denied by full-back Cyril Kellett, while the underdogs threatened twice, through centre Ken Cotton and second row Jimmy Thompson, after Kellett had opened their account with a 25th minute penalty.

Les Dyl stretches the Featherstone defence in a league match in 1974.

Leeds extended their lead early in the second half when Ramsey bored over from close range after Phil Cookson – the opening bowler for Featherstone in the Yorkshire Council League – and Bob Haigh had combined. Rovers, better served by opting for football, could have narrowed the gap but missed out when scrum-half Terry Hudson was unable to collect Austin Rhodes' pass and when Cotton was unable to pull off an interception.

Ramsey, meanwhile, was thwarted on a rampaging run by Kellett but Featherstone's solid defensive work came to nothing when Atkinson crossed for a controversial try, every player having stopped expecting the referee to blow for an infringement.

Two Hynes conversions put Leeds in an unassailable position. And although Rovers grabbed their first try in the closing stages through Hartley, with Kellett's goal bouncing over off an upright, the Loiners deservedly had the last word when Dunn burrowed through in the last minute for a converted touchdown.

Leeds: Holmes; A Smith, Hynes, Cowan, Atkinson; Wainwright, Shoebottom; J Burke, Dunn, Cookson, Ramsey, Haigh, Batten. Subs: Langley.
Featherstone: C Kellett; M smith, Cotton, Newlove, Hartley; Harding, Hudson; Windmill, D Morgan, Lyons, Rhodes, Thompson, Farrar.
Referee: Mr DS Brown (Preston).
Leeds: T: A Smith 2, Ramsey, Atkinson, Dunn.
G: Hynes 4.
Featherstone: T: Hartley. G: C Kellett 3.
Attendance: 6,753

overshadowed by sadness and controversy.

Mick Shoebottom, one of the greatest half-backs to have played the game, had his career cut short by an injury sustained while scoring a try in the 37-22 Championship play-off round two victory over Salford at Headingley on 1 May 1971. The initial prognosis of a fractured jaw and concussion suggested that the main consequence of the incident would be Shoey's absence from the Challenge Cup Final line up against Leigh a fortnight later. The episode, though, was to have far more serious repercussions.

Unaware at that stage of what the future would hold for one of its favourite sons, Leeds were also bereft when centre Syd Hynes became the first man to be sent off at Wembley after a 'did he, didn't he?' alleged head butt on Leigh player/coach Alex Murphy.

Leigh, in fact, provided interesting opposition throughout the season, finishing fourth in the table to earn a rating as serious Championship contenders, and inflicting a 38-8 defeat on Leeds in early September at Hilton Park.

Murphy's men were no doubt helped in that result by the fact that Leeds had had a tough opening to the campaign in which league wins over Featherstone and Widnes were followed by a testing Yorkshire Cup first round tie at Wakefield Trinity. The Loiners came through

Massed defence denies St Helens at Knowsley Road.

20-10 with the help of tries by winger Alan Smith, second row pair Bill Ramsey and Phil Cookson and, on his first return to Belle Vue, Haigh.

The daunting opening to the season continued with trips, within four days, to Hull KR and Bradford Northern. Northern, heading for a slump which would see them drop from twelfth to twenty-seventh in the table, were scuttled 49-10, winger John Atkinson scoring a hat trick, Dave Hick bagging a brace and Holmes netting a try and eight goals.

The journey to Castleford two days later took its toll, however. Leeds came away with a 14-7 victory – and a semi-final trip to Hull as the 'reward' – courtesy of tries by hooker Peter Dunn and Shoebottom, with Holmes kicking three goals and Hynes contributing a drop goal. But five games in 12 days had its inevitable effect at Leigh, where Turner's men were limited to tries by Shoebottom and Ron Cowan, plus a Holmes goal, in the heavy reverse.

Leeds quickly got their season back into gear with successive victories over Swinton, Bramley and Halifax, scoring over 20 points in each game and conceding a mere 20 in total in response, with Haigh sharpening his partnership with Batten.

A Loiner Looks Back

Steve Pitchford

'Dennis Hartley knocked my teeth out at Castleford in my second game. He taught me a very fast lesson – don't mess with the older boys who know what they're doing. My first game was at Featherstone, who had Arnie Morgan and Vince Farrar in the front row. I got a slap off Vince, then one from Morgan.

I was a young Buck, I had no idea of anybody's reputations. The following season Great Britain came back from Australia with the Ashes, thanks to props like Cliff Watson and Dennis Hartley. 'My next game was away to St Helens and I propped against Watson; he was a big powerful man. When I toured in 1977 Cliff was already over there and we went out for a meal and it was fabulous. He taught me a lot.

'I used to rule the world when I started, I was 18 years of age and full of everything. I had to swap over in that game against Dennis Hartley, I couldn't handle him. I was a blind side prop and Dennis was open side but for some reason they played me at No. 8 and Alan Bence at No. 10, which was totally the wrong way round. They said to me, "get underneath Hartley and hold him up," and I was pinned down. Anyway we swapped over and it worked a lot better.

'I did one of my bolstering runs and knocked Dennis on his arse, because he didn't know what was coming at him did he? But he did the second time. He knocked my frigging teeth out! Bop! Thank you.

'But there was no malice in it. We both used to live in Crossgates and we'd bump into each other in the paper shop and we'd be "alright Dennis?" and "OK, Steve?" That's how it was, there was nothing malicious, if you got hit, you got hit. I've had some cracks and they'd wish you, "Merry Christmas, thank you."'

September ended with victory at the Boulevard, by 12-11, in the Yorkshire Cup semi-final. Winger Barry Parker and Cookson scored the tries and the epic nature of the clash was vividly illustrated by the fact that Hynes and

And when Saints do break free the touch judge seems ready to help...

Shoebottom kicked a drop goal each to supplement Holmes' single goal.

Parker went on to score a hat trick in the next fixture, a 12-5 win at Halifax, the fourth game on the trot in which he had crossed the opposition's whitewash.

But Leeds slipped at Wigan two days later, Haigh crossing with Hynes and Shoebottom in the 30-17 defeat.

Another trip, this time to Barrow in the Floodlit Trophy, saw Dyl netting two tries in a 15-6 win which set in motion an 18-match unbeaten run. Haigh scored a hat trick in the 50-13 romp against Featherstone at Headingley, Parker and the promising Tony Wainwright crossed as Huddersfield were beaten 20-3, and there was another try for Wainwright, plus two by Alan Smith, as Leeds continued to progress in the BBC2 Floodlit Trophy with a 16-6 win at Widnes.

Hynes scored a try and four goals and Atkinson, Alan Smith, John Langley, Batten and Wainwright nipped over as the Loiners warmed up for the Yorkshire Cup Final at Odsal with a 26-10 success over Warrington at Wilderspool.

Loiners Big Match

15 December 1970, BBC2 Floodlit Trophy Final, Leeds 9 St Helens 5, Headingley

Leeds' first win in the popular Floodlit Trophy was notable for several reasons, the first of which was that the final wasn't played under floodlights.

As Bramley also experienced three years later, outside influences could play havoc with the central theme of the competition, which was staged on Tuesday evenings throughout the autumn with the sole match of the night televised live.

Bramley were to win at Widnes in a game played in the afternoon because of a power strike. Leeds' game at Headingley went ahead as scheduled in the evening, with the floodlights switched off because of a power shortage and light provided by a host of BBC generators.

St Helens, who had beaten Leeds in the previous season's Championship Final, were nevertheless underdogs when they headed east for a clash between two of the most attractive sides in the game. The Saints were facing their third game in four days, while the Loiners had enjoyed a comfortable 23-0 win the previous Saturday at Whitehaven, with their only concern a cheek injury sustained by half-back Mick Shoebottom in Cumbria.

Shoebottom recovered from that knock to take the scrum-half berth as the Loiners, who rested centre Les Dyl, drafting in Ron Cowan, set about lifting the only available trophy thus far denied them.

Prop Ted Barnard, a product of the Heworth club in York, had perhaps his finest game in the Leeds colours while second row Bill Ramsey was at his cultured best.

Both needed to be in top form as the Saints belied their wearying schedule to take a surprise early lead against a side which had won its previous 10 games, netting 276 points in the process.

Eric Chisnall, moved up from second row to prop in

Continued...

the injury absence of Cliff Watson and Albert Halsall, stunned the big Leeds contingent in the 7,756 crowd with a powerful early run, slipping the ball after his 40-yard surge to centre Billy Benyon. Benyon linked in classic fashion with his winger Les Jones who held off the cover to touch down in the corner for a try which called into question the wisdom of Loiners' chairman Jack Myerscough's assertion that this was Leeds' finest opportunity to lift what had proved to be an elusive trophy.

Leeds, however, bounced back when centre Syd Hynes kicked a penalty, and the Loiners took the lead as half time approached when a moment of magic by Ramsey, who worked an inside pass for Hynes, saw the centre scampering over despite the attentions of St Helens second row John Mantle, full-back John Holmes adding the goal.

Hynes came close to notching a repeat, again off Ramsey, the Saints' defence holding firm on this occasion. When Holmes kicked a penalty to extend the lead to six points, St Helens' prospects looked limited and although loose forward Kel Coslett responded in kind, Leeds were not going to be denied their second trophy in a month, having lifted the Yorkshire Cup in November with a victory over Featherstone Rovers.

The success meant that the Loiners, who had never even reached the semi-final of the competition before, had won every trophy in the game over a four-year period; a remarkable achievement by a team at the peak of its powers.

Leeds: Holmes; A Smith, Hynes, Cowan, Atkinson; Wainwright, Shoebottom; Burke, Fisher, Barnard, Haigh, Ramsey, Batten.
St Helens: Barrow; Jones, Benyon, Walsh, Wilson; Whittle, Heaton; Rees, Karalius, Chisnall, Mantle, Prescott, Coslett.
Referee: Mr E Lawrinson (Warrington)
Leeds: T: Hynes. G: Holmes 2, Hynes.
St Helens: T: Jones. G: Coslett.
Attendance: 7,756

Featherstone Rovers were comprehensively outflanked in the White Rose decider 23-7. Alan Smith led the way with two tries, Ramsey and Dunn crossed, and there was a try for Atkinson, with Hynes kicking four goals in a comfortable win.

Cowan and Haigh each scored two tries in the subsequent 31-16 league win at home to Hull, and the Airlie Birds' neighbours, Kingston Rovers, were the next visitors to Headingley, three days later, for the semi-final of the Floodlit Trophy; a competition in which Leeds had enjoyed scant success since its launch in 1965.

Leeds, who welcomed former hooker Tony Crosby – transferred to Craven Park several weeks earlier – back to Headingley for the game, could point to a sequence of 10 away games out of 13 in the competition as a factor in their failure. It was to be a different story this time as the Loiners secured a first appearance in the final with a 24-2 victory involving two tries apiece for Atkinson and Batten, with Hynes and Alan Smith also crossing and Holmes and Hynes adding a goal each in addition to Wainwright's

Syd Hynes crosses off Cliff Watson's pass, with Mick Shoebottom and Alan Smith and a packed South Stand sharing his delight, in Great Britain's 11-4 World Cup victory over Australia. The Kangaroos, however, went on to beat the Lions 12-7 in a torrid final between the top two at Headingley.

Tony Wainwright and Barry Seabourne prepare to pair up at half-back against Leigh.

drop goal.

Warrington, again, were easy meat in the build-up. Alan Smith crashed over for four tries as the Wire were beaten 48-8 at home and Haigh, who had also crossed in the spree, had two tries in the following week's 23-0 win at Whitehaven.

The Saints travelled to Headingley for the decider eager to improve on their status as runners-up the previous season but the Knowsley Road outfit were to be denied 9-5. Hynes, the epitome of the big match player, scored a try and a goal and Holmes landed two goals in a hard fought encounter which was to be repeated in the Challenge Cup two months later.

Leeds continued their rich vein of league form with Christmas victories over Bradford Northern and, on Boxing Day, Castleford. And there was revenge at the turn of the year for the heavy defeat at Hilton Park when Leigh conceded their highest total of the season so far, going down 28-10 at Headingley. Shoebottom, selected at scrum-half, outplayed Alex Murphy and collected the man of the match award.

Haigh, a scorer against Leigh, cruised over for four more in the 30-8 win over Huddersfield at Fartown and grabbed at least one try in each of the next seven league games. And the superb Challenge Cup first round win over Oldham ratified Leeds' rating as 7/2 competition favourites. The 49-2 victory, a margin which eclipsed Leeds' previous Challenge Cup best of 44-12 against Hull KR in 1951-52, was achieved despite a lack of possession from the scrum.

By this stage of the season, Atkinson and Haigh were vying to be the top scorer yet in an

A Loiner Looks Back

David Ward

'There's no finer moment than signing on, than being a professional Rugby League player. And you're talking about Leeds Rugby League club. As soon as you put pen to paper you've gone beyond being the average kid in the street. You're wearing that status on your shoulders, you're representing the club, you're representing the game, and it's a great honour.

'It was always at the back of my mind that Wakefield would be my club. But I knew Derek Turner very well, through my uncle Ken, and when he came round there was only one club I was going to sign for. He didn't have to pull me round, really, because I didn't speak much. It was "be here, or don't be here." I signed on the Thursday evening when the squad were training out on the main field the night before setting off to play Leigh in the 1971 Challenge Cup Final.'

A youthful David Ward offers support in the Challenge Cup quarter final tie against Wakefield Trinity in 1972.

A Loiner Looks Back

Harry Jepson

Harry Jepson presents John Holmes with a silver salver to mark 550 appearances, achieved in 1984.

'I went to Leeds in 1970 and it was the best thing I've ever done in my life. Jack Myerscough was a great bloke, the football chairman for 19 years. He said to me, "I don't know anything about this game, Harry, but I talk to people who do." He was a very shrewd operator.

'The first player I ever signed for Leeds was Brian Hughes. We used to get together on Sundays at Headingley, champers and everything. I was coming down Dewsbury Road and I saw a match taking place on Cross Flatts Park, so I thought I'd watch it. Cutsyke were playing and one of their players took my eye. I spoke to somebody who said his name was Brian Hughes. So when I got to Headingley I was late and Jack said, "where have you been?" I said I saw a match. He asked if I'd seen anybody interesting, I said yes there was a lad down there who was very impressive. Jack said, "do you want to sign him?" I said "I think he could do us a lot of good, Jack." Jack said, "well go and sign him." I said, "shouldn't we have a meeting?" Jack said, "no we're having a meeting now, you and me, go and sign him, if he wants more than £800 have another word with me." I said, "£800!" I nearly fell through the floor.

'I went to sign Brian for £250. We sold him to Halifax for about three or four thousand. Many years later I was walking in Castleford and I bumped into Brian and his wife. He introduced us and he said, "this is the gentleman that gave me two hundred and fifty quid, and we bought our first house." So I told him the tale. He said, "you never told me you could have gone to £800!" We had a good laugh about it.'

example of the fine team spirit at the club Atkinson, who had touched down to level with Haigh on 24 tries, ignored a chance to add another, waving Les Dyl over for the centre's first try in the Challenge Cup. And Haigh, to rapturous applause, edged ahead again with his twenty-fifth try of the campaign later in the game.

Any doubts over Leeds' right to be classed as one of the top sides around were laid to rest when the Loiners visited Salford for their first league game at the Willows for almost 13 years. In their programme notes the Red Devils speculated: 'Many Lancastrians in recent seasons, seeing this evening's guests almost continually at the top of the League table, have pointed disparagingly at Leeds' fixture lists which have included the less well-endowed Yorkshire clubs. A look at this season's record shows that they have taken on Widnes, Leigh (twice), Swinton, Wigan, Warrington (twice), Whitehaven and St Helens in League games and lost only two of those – both away – to Leigh, and Wigan. They have also won at Barrow and at home to St Helens in winning the Floodlit Trophy and have slated Oldham in the Challenge Cup.' To add weight to that supportive assessment, Leeds went on to beat Salford 42-4, scoring eight tries including two for Haigh and one for Atkinson. Only once before, since the Second World War, had Leeds topped 40 points in Lancashire, when Warrington were beaten 42-7 in 1957. The only black spot was the dismissal in injury time of

Headingley Hero
Mick Shoebottom

It was Phil Morgan's misfortune, when Hunslet signed the Welsh stand-off half in 1967, to play opposite Mick Shoebottom in his very first match.
Morgan was rated with the likes of Barry John and David Watkins but he was given a rude awakening as to the requirements of the professional game when Hunslet hosted Leeds in the pre-season Lazenby Cup clash.

Mick Shoebottom races over for one of his four tries in Leeds' 47-5 Championship play-off semi-final win over Hull KR on May 2 1970.

Shoebottom clearly aimed to impress upon Morgan that defence is an integral part of the league code and shook the Welshman with a perfectly legitimate diving tackle at the very first scrum.
To his credit, Morgan retained possession – and his composure – and probably was never again on the receiving end of such a forceful yet legitimate assault. The incident, however, perhaps summed up what set Shoebottom apart from most other stand-off halves. As silky-skilled as any around, 'Shoey' also boasted a hard-hitting approach envied by many a back row forward.
Mick Shoebottom was a mainstay of the Loiners side until the 1970-71 season, when he sustained a head injury in an incident with Salford's Colin Dixon. The blow ended his career as a brilliant half-back who collected 12 caps, including two on the Ashes-winning tour to Australia in 1970.

Continued...

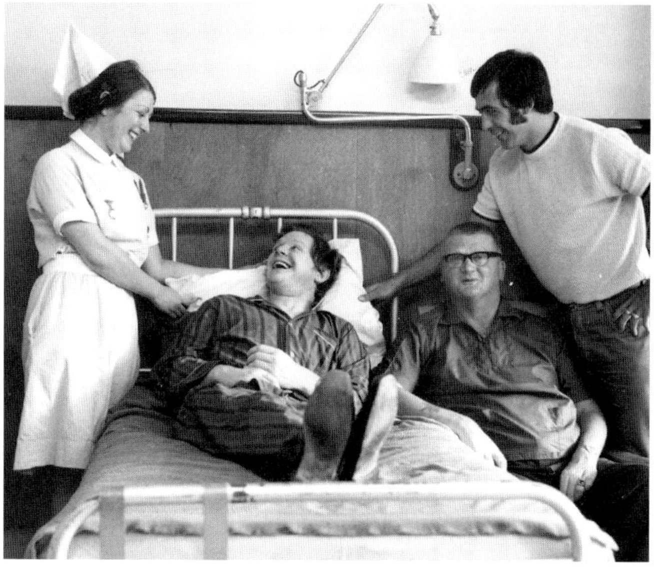

Peter Dunn, Leeds' hooker in the 1970 Yorkshire Cup final, visits Mick Shoebottom in hospital.

Alan Smith for a crash tackle. In his report for the Yorkshire Evening Post, Arthur Haddock commented: 'To be fair there was some tackling to do, particularly on Dixon, and invariably it was Shoebottom who did it.'

That win ensured that Leeds equalled the 18-match winning run established in 1967-68. That kind of record inevitably threw the players into the international spotlight. Six players were selected for Great Britain's match against France at Toulouse with Hynes emulating Barry Seabourne's role as captain the previous year. Shoebottom, hooker Tony Fisher, Alan Smith, Haigh and Atkinson were also in the side that beat France 16-8 but the exercise wasn't without cost, Fisher sustaining ligament damage when a scrum collapsed and Smith having to depart with a groin strain.

Those injures hardly helped the Leeds cause as the long winning run came to an end with the 14-9 midweek defeat at Hull – Haigh scoring the only try – but it was business as usual when Whitehaven came south and succumbed to Holmes' two tries and seven goals, and a brace apiece for Haigh and Wainwright, in a 44-5

A lively figure in the dressing room, Mick Shoebottom made his debut for Leeds on 24 February 1962, at the age of 17, scoring a try from scrum-half in the 34-8 victory over Doncaster.

The former Hunslet Boys Club and Bison protégé also played for Leeds at full-back and centre but his forte was the stand-off berth, where his all-action style quickly endeared him to not only the fans but also to his colleagues.

Bev Risman, the Loiners full-back from 1966 to 1970, joined Leeds after an injury-blighted spell at Leigh. He insists he owed Shoebottom a debt and pays homage: 'Mick Shoebottom was an aggressive stand-off, which is a fairly rare thing. He had the opposition frightened. He was like an extra full-back and I could count the number of tackles I had to make on one hand when he was around. Invariably a move broke down, because of him, before the opposition reached me. That was one reason I was able to steer clear of injuries – he extended my career. I used to say that I wasn't at full-back to defend, and that I didn't expect anybody to come through. Mick Shoebottom made certain they didn't.'

Shoebottom featured in each of Leeds' finals between 1964 and 1970, collecting winners' medals in the Challenge Cup in 1968, in the Championship (1969) in the Yorkshire Cup in 1968 and 1970, and in the BBC2 Floodlit Trophy in 1970, appearing at scrum-half in the last two games. His only runners-up medals were in the 1970 Championship Final against St Helens and in the 1964 Yorkshire Cup Final at the hands of Wakefield Trinity.

His international caps would surely have totalled far more than the 12 gained between 1968 and 1971 but for his injury and his high point for Great Britain was undoubtedly the Ashes-securing victory over Australia in the Third Test in 1970 when he played at full-back. Shoebottom was alongside Leeds team-mates Alan Smith, Syd Hynes and John Atkinson that day and Smith recalls of the tragic moment less than a year later: 'Shoey was probably Derek Turner's ultimate player. Derek was near to tears when he carried him off the pitch. Mick had everything. He was a great footballer, he could kick goals, he could pass and he could mix it. Whatever mode you wanted, Shoey could come up with it.'

It all came to an end at 3.25pm on Saturday 1 May 1971. Harry Jepson accompanied Shoebottom to hospital and the immediate fear was that the star stand-off could miss the Challenge Cup Final against Leigh a fortnight later with a broken jaw. Says Jepson: 'Colin Dixon wasn't a dirty player, but it was certainly late. I asked the surgeon how long he was going to be out, because we were worried about Michael's jaw. There was a silence. He could tell straight away. He must have been very perspicacious. He said: "No, he won't be fit for Wembley. There's something more." That's when he had to get the neuro-surgeon Miles Gibson to the job. It was diagnosed an hour or too later. Bloody awful thing. I'd known Michael from the age of 11. There are some real heartaches in this game of Rugby League you know, and Leeds have had their share of it.'

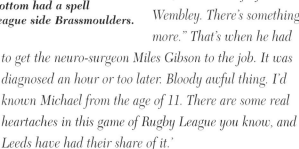

Now out of the game, Shoebottom had a spell coaching Hunslet Sunday League side Brassmoulders.

crushing.

It was going to be tougher – much, much tougher – in the following week's second round Challenge Cup tie against St Helens at Headingley. Much debate, in the build up, centred on the selection at half-back, with Seabourne, Shoebottom and Wainwright vying for the two slots. Derek Turner, perhaps mindful that Seabourne had been struggling for much of the season with a shoulder injury, eventually plumped for Wainwright at stand off and Shoebottom at scrum-half as two of the greatest sides in the game met in the greatest competition in the game for the first time in over 40 years. The pair, indeed, had not met in the Challenge Cup since St Helens won a second round clash at Headingley 18-5 in 1929-30 en route to a shock defeat by underdogs Widnes at Wembley.

The crowd of 16,500 witnessed a thriller, although not the kind of thriller usually associated with two of the pedigree breeds of Rugby League in a match in which fists flew in the early stages. Leeds toppled the Saints with the help of two drop goals, the only scores of the match, which earned the Loiners a 4-0 victory. Shoebottom scored the first, after 57 minutes and Holmes, not for the last time in a Challenge Cup tie against St Helens, kicked the other (with his wrong, left foot) five minutes from time.

Seabourne remained out of the reckoning for the quarter-final, a hugely attractive derby tie with Bramley at McLaren Field, with Wainwright retaining his spot after having scored 14 tries in 24 games since his elevation in October. A cold March put the game in some danger and Leeds applied some pressure for a switch to Headingley where the electric blanket would ensure play. Bramley chairman Bill Norfolk was having none of it. 'I would be shot at dawn if we gave up home advantage,' he said, and he was probably right. And the man holding the pistol could well have been any of Robin Dewhurst, Tom Higginbottom, Peter Astbury and Trevor Briggs, all former Leeds players now in the Bramley ranks. A tricky hurdle was surmounted by a gritty display in which the squad as a whole showed a huge appetite for hard work, none more so than Shoebottom who, according to Haddock, 'once went in so hard that besides flooring the opponent he also knocked himself out. He also went a bit too far with one tackle and was booked.' Shoebottom also scored the try which put the game beyond gallant Bramley for a 14-0 win; Ray Batten, meanwhile, sparked the move which led to Alan Smith's first half touchdown, one which will have given the former Brookhouse man special satisfaction, having been on loan to the Villagers several seasons earlier.

Leeds, who had beaten Salford 24-13 in a

A Loiner Looks Back

Billy Watts

Billy Watts, the long-serving member of the backroom staff recalls Mick Shoebottom's injury: 'Mick Shoebottom's bad injury went through the whole club; everybody was just heads down. It was at the far end of the ground, after 37 minutes, 22 seconds. 3.00 pm kick off, and a beautiful day. Shoey went right across the field with Colin Dixon after him, he went over with the ball and Dixon followed on, and bum-bum-bum, that was it.

'I can see Mick now, stretched out on the floor. Derek Turner ran on with Eric Lewis, the Physio, and they carried him off, arms round his shoulders. At the time you saw him, with his head rolling over to one side, you didn't realise it was going to be as bad as it turned out. It didn't just end Mick's rugby career, he was never the same person again. He was a bubbly person, a real joker in the dressing rooms, everybody was happy with him around. He could turn a loss into a good performance and as a player, well! In broken ground play, Mick was absolutely marvellous. He could all of a sudden punch a hole in the defence, and he was away. And he had a very aggressive defence.'

Loiners Big Match

15 May 1971, Challenge Cup Final, Leeds 7 Leigh 24, Wembley

Perhaps only two men can really tell the tale of what actually happened on a blade of grass in north London at approximately five minutes past four on the afternoon of Saturday 15 May 1971.

Despite the presence of 85,514 potential witnesses the truth remains unclear and the arguments will rage for as long as Rugby League is played over the culpability or otherwise of Syd Hynes, the Leeds captain, and his opposite number Alex Murphy.

What is certain is that with underdogs Leigh 17-2 ahead with only 15 minutes remaining Hynes was tackled by Murphy and that, as play progressed, the legendary Leigh scrum-half was seen to be lying, comatose – or apparently comatose, according to most Leeds fans – with no hint as to the cause.

Huddersfield referee Billy Thompson had been described, on his appointment as Cup Final referee, as a 'disciplinarian and a man who is always on the spot ready to stamp out trouble before it starts.' After a brief consultation with his touch judge he opted to send Hynes off, thus condemning the Loiners centre to the ignominy of being the first man to be dismissed at Wembley.

Leeds, down to 12 men and already in lacklustre mood, were in no shape to rescue the situation. But there was consternation when Murphy returned to the field in time to lead his victorious troops up the steps to the Royal Box to receive the Challenge Cup and their medals.

For Hynes, it was a miserable finale to a game that Leeds, who had not conceded a single try on the way to Wembley, had been expected to win with ease. Although quite why the Loiners were red hot favourites to prevail is hard to fathom, given that Leigh had finished fourth in the table that season, only four points behind third-placed Leeds.

Continued...

Mick Shoebottom responds to the fans as Leeds are given a civic reception following the Wembley defeat.

league game prior to the Bramley clash – Haigh again netting two tries – overcame Widnes and Hull KR in league fixtures and were then forced to travel to St Helens on the Monday evening prior to the Challenge Cup semi-final against Castleford. Wainwright scored the Loiners' only try, Seabourne adding a goal and two drop goals, as Saints won 30-9, and there was another tough match two days after the semi when Wigan came to Headingley, beating a tired outfit 10-8.

The main game, however, went Leeds' way, Turner firing up his troops against his former side and getting the desired response when Cowan and Hynes crossed in the first 10 minutes, Holmes adding a goal, to put Leeds in control and put paid to Cas' hopes of a third successive final. Cowan's second try ended Castleford's prospects, Holmes kicked four goals in all and Hynes added a drop goal. Equally satisfyingly, Castleford were denied a try in the 19-8 victory. Leeds had reached Wembley without having their tryline breached.

Just six days after that victory, and with the game against Wigan also under their belts, Leeds made the short trip to Wheldon Road in pursuit of a win which would help secure second spot in the table. The Loiners pulled it off,

And the fact that the Headingley men were without ball-handling maestro Ray Batten and winger Alan Smith, and had lost stand off Mick Shoebottom only two weeks earlier – never to return to Rugby League after his tragic injury against Salford – hardly helped the Leeds cause.
Hynes himself had been fortunate – or possibly, as it turned out, unfortunate – to play, the Leeds victory over Salford being important in allowing him to serve a one-match ban in the Championship semi-final against St Helens.
Leigh, meanwhile, had been inspired by the willingness of most pundits to dismiss their prospects. Murphy, the motivational master, used one newspaper report to rouse his players, insisting that they all read on the trip down to London of how they had been written off.
Suitably riled, the Lancastrians blasted into a 13-point half-time lead with a try for centre Stan Dorrington, three goals by the metronomic Stuart Ferguson, and an early and inspiring drop goal by prop Jim Fiddler and a drop goal from, yes, that man Murphy.
Leeds hit back with a penalty by 19-year-old full-back John Holmes but a second Murphy drop goal and another penalty for Ferguson added to Yorkshire woes before Hynes' sorry dismissal put paid to any hopes of a fight-back.
Half-back Tony Wainwright grabbed a late consolation try, awarded when Mr Thompson ruled obstruction, but Leigh were on a roll and went into ecstasy with a try and a drop goal for full-back David Eckersley.
Arguments have raged ever since. Murphy, quoted years later in Ray French's book 'The Match Of My Life', said: 'The tales of Syd Hynes and myself are now more far-fetched than those of Jesse James. The stories get worse as the years go by. I've heard tales of me getting off the stretcher and stories of me winking at Syd as he was walking off. Syd is one of my best friends in rugby, but I must say he took a chance and got caught.
'I was sat in the bath in the dressing room, still dazed, and the Wembley doctor had said that I could take no further part in the game when the message came that the Leigh players wanted me to go up to receive the cup. They had struggled

Simply not Leeds' day. No way through a determined Kevin Ashcroft for the flyer John Atkinson.

Continued...

winning 15-2 with the help of tries for Batten, hooker Ray Handscombe and Atkinson, to record a fourth win of the season over their rivals, but the Headingley management was given a worry when Hynes, a key figure in Turner's plans against the other finalists Leigh, was sent off.

All that was temporarily forgotten as Haigh set about overhauling Bob Taylor's old record. An 8,000 crowd turned up for the home game with Bramley, when the popular second row drew level with Taylor's 36 tries, burrowing over from acting half after a Hick run despite having been withdrawn earlier in the game after catching an elbow on the nose.

Leeds won 32-0 and it was simple, too, three days later against Batley when Haigh passed Taylor's total with a try in the 25-2 success.

The Championship season closed at Swinton, Atkinson racing over for two tries and Holmes scoring the clinching try, plus three goals, in the 21-14 win, passing the 300-point mark in the process.

Leeds embarked on the assault on the Championship with a 28-0 first round win over Batley in which former Loiners man Phil Holmes, now a Gallant Youth, played opposite brother John. The victory led to a second round clash with Salford which was viewed as important not only for its own sake but because *long and hard to win the cup and I wasn't going to disappoint them.'*

John Atkinson recalls: 'Things didn't go particularly well but we'd lost Mick Shoebottom, we'd lost Alan Smith and we'd lost Ray Batten. I don't think people realised what a big loss Mick was, not only to us as a team but as mates of his. We knew that he'd never play again and I think it had a profound effect on us.'

Two mysteries, then. The first: what exactly DID happen when Hynes and Murphy clashed on that little patch of grass in northwest London? And why were Leigh, who when all is said and done had finished fourth in the league, four points behind third-placed Leeds, ranked as out-and-out underdogs? Particularly when the Loiners lacked Batten, Smith and, of course, Shoebottom. And a final point. A score-line of 24-7 looks comprehensive enough. But Leigh only scored two tries to Leeds' one.

Leeds: Holmes; Langley, Hynes, Cowan, Atkinson; Wainwright, Seabourne; Burke, Fisher, Barnard, Hick, Haigh, Ramsey. Subs: Dyl, Cookson (did not play).

Leigh: Eckersley; Ferguson, Dorrington, Collins, Walsh; Barrow, Murphy; Watts, Ashcroft, Fiddler, Grimes, Clarkson, Smethurst. Subs: Chisnall, Lester (did not play).

Referee: Mr WH Thompson (Huddersfield).

Leeds: T: Wainwright. G: Holmes 2.

Leigh: T: Dorrington, Eckersley. G: Ferguson 5. DG: Murphy 2, Fiddler, Eckersley.

Attendance: 85,514

success would ensure that Hynes could serve his one-match suspension, incurred following his dismissal at Castleford, prior to the Challenge Cup Final. Leeds did win, and Hynes was allowed his big day – a fact he would, perhaps, come to regret – but the game was to be remembered for altogether more sombre reasons.

Arthur Haddock, in his report for the Yorkshire Evening Post's Green Final, which was on the streets within an hour or two of the final whistle, reported: 'From a fine pass by Ramsey came their fourth try, by Shoebottom, who went in gamely for the touchdown in the corner, almost in the spot where Smith scored and similarly got hurt in doing so. He was carried to the trainers' bench and Cookson went on.' Haddock continued: 'Leeds had to meet a Salford rally in which Holmes stopped Hesketh as Shoebottom was carried to the dressing room on a stretcher.'

The seriousness of Shoebottom's injury, caused when Salford second row Colin Dixon followed through in an attempted try-saving tackle, wasn't immediately apparent to everyone. A broken jaw certainly put him out of the Leigh game, but the long-term damage was to be more far-reaching and that try was to be the half-back's last act on a Rugby League pitch. Focused on Wembley, Leeds were hit by a shoulder injury to Batten, their only try scorer, in the 22-7 Championship semi-final defeat at St Helens, which would leave the Loiners unable to contemplate the 'double' and without two of their main play-makers for the Leigh clash.

A Loiner Looks Back

John Sykes

'When Syd Hynes was sent off in 1971 he took his shirt off and threw it onto the floor. It then went missing. Syd didn't like to make a fuss about it because it was his fault. We had a do some years later and Eric Lewis, the physio, came. He made a presentation to Syd that night; it was the shirt. He'd picked it up and put it in his bag, and he'd looked after it for all those years.'

A Mystery Solved?

On Saturday 15 May 1971, Syd Hynes became the first man to be sent off at Wembley. The Leeds centre, dismissed for an alleged head-butt on Leigh captain Alex Murphy 15 minutes from time, served a six-match ban and was fined £2 for his misdemeanour.

No appeal was mounted but Hynes, who has accepted his infamy with grace and good humour, continues to protest his innocence. Murphy, also with good humour, insists that his long-standing friend deserved to walk.

Referee Billy Thompson, in common with the other players, 85,514 fans and millions of TV viewers, missed an incident which carries as much mystery as do the assassinations of President Kennedy and Martin Luther King and dismissed Hynes on the evidence of Widnes touchjudge TC Clayton.

The key witnesses deliver their submissions:

Syd Hynes:

'Billy Thompson was being tipped all week long in the press to send one of us off. Either Spud would go, or me. Unfortunately it was me and I didn't deserve to go, because I missed him! There's an old film of the game somewhere which shows me running across the park, towards the Royal Box. I let the ball go to Smithy and Spud came in and tried to smack me. I bounced away from it, went back and tried to nut him. I missed him and he just fell away, but that was part and parcel of the game.

'He wrote his book, did Murph, and he got it all cocked up. I think he must have forgotten what happened. He asked me to do an after-dinner job with him for the fire bobbies around Huddersfield and West Yorkshire. We were on the stage and all night we were being asked did you, didn't you? Murph was just signing the books and selling 'em. "You'll have to buy a book and read about it," was all he'd say! There were about 450 fire bobbies there that night; he made a few quid out of it did the lad!'

Syd Hynes covers, pending the unexpected, as Les Dyl has Featherstone centre Steve Quinn sized up.

Alex Murphy:

'It was just one of those things that happen. I think it stemmed from frustration on Syd's part more than anything. Leeds were 5/1 on favourites to beat us, while I had a lot of good kids in my side, lads like David Eckersley, Kevin Ashcroft, Les Chisnall and Mike Collins, who weren't going to be great but were going to be above average. No one fancied us, in fact we were 66/1 before the first round with a local bookie, Bert Hulme, who was also a Leigh Director. He lost more money, when we won at Wembley, than at any time in his career.

'Leeds were packed with internationals and I think they totally underestimated us. I knew what we were going to do and what they would do; no one was going to run 100 yards at Wembley so we adopted a kicking game aimed at keeping them on the back foot. And I picked winger Stuart Ferguson solely for his goal kicking. We didn't drop much ball, and we took our chances. Leeds hadn't conceded a try in the whole competition but there was no way we were going to lose.

'Syd's one of my best mates, and he did butt me. I think

he'd got very frustrated, the Leeds lads had got it into their heads that all they had to do was turn up to collect the Cup. They were a great side, many of them are big mates of mine. All the tales about me winking at people from the stretcher are rubbish. People forget that the doctor in charge at Wembley is employed by the stadium, not by the Rugby League or by the clubs. I didn't wake up until I was in the bath, when I got the call from the players to go up to receive the cup.

'People forget that Leeds stand off Tony Wainwright was awarded an obstruction try that should not have been given. The rules state that the ball must be over the try line and that a try would certainly have been scored. The ball was actually still in the field of play and there were two men between Tony and the ball.'

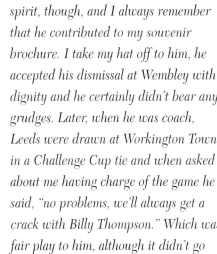

Alex Murphy.

Billy Thompson:

'I didn't see it but I always used to say to my touch-judges that if they came onto the field of play I wanted to know exactly what had happened. The touch judge in question was Terry Clayton of Widnes. He came on, with his flag high, and told me that Syd Hynes had head-butted Alex Murphy. So I walked Syd. I didn't want to. The Challenge Cup Final is the referee's day as well as the players' and it wrecked it for me. I was subdued for a week, but I had no choice. There's been controversy ever since but it's interesting that Syd got a six-match suspension and there was no appeal.

'That night, the three match officials and their wives were invited to the Leeds celebrations at the Park Lane Hotel. I went, with my wife, but the touch-judges didn't turn up. We sat with Joe Warham, Jack Myerscough, Arthur Clues, and Alf Rutherford. No one said anything unpleasant to me at all. The only reference to the game was by the club chairman Alf Sharman who said in his speech that Leeds had been well beaten on the day.

'Amazingly I was one of the referees at the Wills Sevens at Headingley later that month. And would you believe it, I was allocated to the first game, which involved Leeds, and Syd Hynes was playing. I said, "Be a good lad, Syd." And he was. But I think I was a jinx for Syd Hynes, I remember a Premiership Final when they were playing St Helens at Wigan when Syd crossed for a try, pulled a hamstring in the act of scoring, and had to go off.

'Syd always took everything in good spirit, though, and I always remember that he contributed to my souvenir brochure. I take my hat off to him, he accepted his dismissal at Wembley with dignity and he certainly didn't bear any grudges. Later, when he was coach, Leeds were drawn at Workington Town in a Challenge Cup tie and when asked about me having charge of the game he said, "no problems, we'll always get a crack with Billy Thompson." Which was fair play to him, although it didn't go down too well with the Workington fans.

'It worked both ways, though. I sent Aussie Billy Smith off, against Leeds, in a tour match in 1967.

'I used to enjoy going to Headingley. I could count on football chairman Jack Myerscough coming into my changing room before a game asking for a time check. He did it every single game. Eventually I took to saying that he must have the worst watch around. He was a real Champagne Charlie, was Jack. And there was Arthur Crowther, who sold programmes. He always used to cadge a lift from me for his sister and himself back into Leeds after a game. He was another character. He used to sell programmes to Jack Myerscough and the rest for a quid; he must have ended up with more money than them!'

And a witness for the defence – former Leeds player Peter Astbury:

'The week before the final, Billy Thompson had sent Leigh's Dave Chisnall off against Hull KR. As he walked off, Chisnall said, "I hope you've got the guts to send somebody off at Wembley." Billy said, "I have." That was like a red rag to a bull. That just did it for me; I knew Syd would walk, and sure enough Billy walked him.'

9. THE H BOMBS ARRIVE

The disappointing end to the 1970-71 season led to swift action by the pro-active Leeds board. One issue, tragically, was forced on them but dame fortune opted to lend a helping hand when, as it became clear that Mick Shoebottom would never play again, another great stand-off half became available.

Alan Hardisty, a man with black and amber running through his veins, had been a fixture at

Leeds' commitment to defence under Derek Turner was impressive. Eight defenders monitor the lack of progress of Widnes second row George Nicholls.

Castleford since his debut for his home-town club in 1958. Now coach of the side, he had fallen out with a notoriously autocratic board which, several years earlier, had managed to part company with legendary coach Harry Street over a dispute involving parking spaces.

Incredibly, Castleford offered Hardisty a free transfer and the Loiners stepped in quickly before anyone had the chance to change their minds.

To add to the chagrin among the Wheldon Road faithful, Leeds didn't just pick up a stand off from Cas. They also enticed his long-term partner, scrum-half Keith Hepworth, and full-back Derek Edwards, both of whom had been key figures in Castleford's success story of the late 60s and early 70s.

The 'H bombs' of Hardisty and Hepworth quickly settled at Headingley. The duo became firm favourites with a crowd which had been limited to grudging admiration in previous years, helped haul the Loiners back to the top of the table, and almost guided the club to the coveted League and Cup 'double' in their first season.

Leeds also snapped up another strong character in Terry Clawson and the prop was to become a seminal figure in the Challenge Cup and Championship Finals in May.

Hardisty made his debut in the Lazenby Cup win over Hunslet, scoring a try in the 48-3 rout of the fading Parksiders who had appointed loyal servant Geoff Gunney as coach. An often overlooked factor which was to be central to the return to the two-division formula two years later was referred to in the programme notes which stated: 'Pennine Motorway: With the opening of the latest section of the M62 two weeks ago, all supporters will find the travelling into Lancashire nowadays a more pleasant and easier journey than in previous years. It is now possible, for instance, to reach Wigan from Leeds in under two hours, and without the delays which often occurred in Oldham and in the outer suburbs of Manchester.'

Leeds also welcomed the Players No 6 Challenge Trophy, launched that season, which

A Loiner Looks Back

David Ward

'I played my first game for Leeds in the A team on a Friday night, subbing at Castleford. I was to be travelling reserve for the first team the next day, at Bramley, but Derek Turner phoned to say I would be playing because of injuries. Our prop, John Burke, was picking me up at the Bull Ring in Wakefield so I went along, got in his car and never told John I was playing.

'We got to the gates at McLaren Field and, like all other Rugby League clubs, Bramley had these old timers on the gates who wouldn't let anybody in without a ticket. John had one; I hadn't. John had a few choice words to this old chap on the Bramley gates and we drove straight through. I got in the dressing room and started to take my shirt off and John said, "what are you doing?" "I'm playing," I said. He said, "why didn't you tell me in the car, why didn't you tell me at the gate? We wouldn't have had that altercation with the gateman!"

'I got a lot of protection on the field as well as off it from John and the other prop, Ted Barnard. Billy Ramsey, Bob Haigh and Ray Batten were the back three, with Barry Seabourne at scrum-half. Barry said, "every time I move my right leg up, you come across." I'd just come out of Shaw Cross, and I hadn't heard this one before. So I just did what I was told. He moves his right leg, I come across, boom he drops it in. Little scrummaging tactics. I was learning.'

was explained as a knockout competition 'on similar lines to the Rugby League Challenge Cup' including 'all Senior clubs plus the two Amateur clubs which won through to the First Round Proper of the RL Challenge Cup Competition last season.'

Controversially, however, Leeds – the holders – opted out of the Yorkshire Cup which had been played in early August. The league campaign opened with a 36-2 hammering at Wigan, before St Helens were beaten 20-13 and Oldham edged 16-12, centre Les Dyl crossing twice against the Saints. A 23-2 win at Bramley was notable chiefly for the selection, for the first time, of a young hooker by the name of David Ward who stepped in when Tony Fisher went down with a stomach upset.

Ward scored his first try for the club, winger Alan Smith and stand off Tony Wainwright had two tries each, Bob Haigh nipped over and John Holmes netted a try and three goals in the comfortable 27-10 victory at Halifax. And Ward was again to the fore three days later with two tries in the 49-12 Headingley romp over Oldham.

The Loiners went down at Salford 27-2 before overcoming Dewsbury 33-5 at home when there was controversy following the dismissal of Fisher and opposing hooker Mick Stephenson, who appeared to have an uncertain understanding of the rules of the game. In the Leeds programme for the next home game, against Hull KR in the BBC2 Floodlit Cup, the Supporters' Club scribe reflected: 'The strict interpretation of the Laws of the Game by the referee puzzled many spectators. This occurred after the dismissal of Fisher and Stephenson, after which the Dewsbury man returned to the trainer's bench, to be again instructed by Mr R Wood to leave the official party on the touchline. This was correct. In Section 16, the Rugby League Law says: "A dismissed player can take no further part in the match, nor shall he be permitted to take up a position near the playing area where

A Loiner Looks Back

Graham Eccles

'You'd go to Featherstone and there'd be Malcolm Dixon, Les Tonks and Vince Farrar in the front row. You thought there'd been an eclipse playing against massive fellahs like that. They were three bonny lads as well!

'Everybody wanted to beat Leeds, all the Yorkshire teams. Bramley used to give us a tough game; we'd pick the team sheet up and Billy Ramsey and the like would say, "Oh, Dave Horne's playing!" He was a big, rough lad with a penchant for nipping opposing props under the armpits in the scrum. I remember losing to them once at Headingley when Ronnie Cowan should have scored but dropped the ball over the line celebrating prematurely.

'You never had an easy game, at Castleford, Featherstone or Wakefield or anywhere else for that matter. They are all derbies and the lads I played against were lads I'd been brought up playing against as an amateur, there was always that personal rivalry. And it was just as hard elsewhere. Phil Cookson and I once played against Frank Foster, at Barrow, when we were raw kids, and he absolutely battered us. I'd got a swollen mouth, Phil's teeth had gone through his lip, we were cut all over. Foster said to us, "you're the best second row forwards I've seen for a long time, you two." So Phil said, "why did you keep hitting us then!" But Frank would have gone through the same thing himself.'

Graham Eccles didn't have to worry much about the opposition's bruisers when Tony Fisher and Terry Clawson were around.

his presence is likely to provoke further incident."'

Holmes, meanwhile, had forced his way into the thoughts of the international selectors. He had to wait until the third test of the series with New Zealand before donning the red, white and blue for the first of his 20 caps. Playing at centre, Holmes scored two goals and two drop goals to complement John Atkinson's brace in the 12-3 Headingley victory as Great Britain avoided a whitewash.

Only Bob Haigh of the Leeds side had featured in the first two tests, breaking his arm in the game at Castleford which was lost 17-14. Haigh and his colleagues had been at Wheldon Road two weeks earlier, when Hardisty made his first appearance against his old club. The Loiners, who had won all four games against Castleford the previous season, were unable to extend that sequence but still managed to deny their hosts, Holmes scoring a try and three goals and David Barham nipping over in the 12-12 draw.

Dyl crossed twice as the Loiners toppled Huddersfield 20-12 at home, and Atkinson raced over for a hat trick in the 33-6 romp over Widnes, brushing aside the concession of an early interception try to celebrate his return to action after a month on the sidelines with a mysterious back injury that had also ruled him out of the Tests.

A 16-13 victory at Keighley, who gave Leeds a scare in fighting back from 13 points down to within striking distance in the closing quarter, was followed by a 12-6 defeat at Hull KR before the Loiners hosted Salford, for the first time since that fateful match in May.

It had become increasingly obvious that Mick Shoebottom's recovery from his injury five

Headingley Hero

Syd Hynes

One moment of magic perhaps captures the rare, if not unique, player that was Syd Hynes. It came in a game at Headingley against St Helens, who featured international centre pairing Billy Benyon and John Walsh.

Pragmatic defenders of their quality were not easy to bypass but Hynes was another matter. The centre drifted apparently aimlessly towards the gap between the duo, the ball resting on his palm in the manner of a French waiter. Beguiled, mesmerised or simply bamboozled by a circular motion of Hynes' ball-carrying hand, Messrs Walsh and Benyon incredibly parted.

Syd Hynes eased through the gap, drew full-back Geoff Pimblett and fired out a try-scoring pass for left-winger John Atkinson.

Not a trick to be tried at home or anywhere else for that matter, as the author discovered when he attempted the routine the following week in a Leeds & District Amateur game only to end up in a pile of blood and snot.

Hynes, a master with the ball in hand, treated the fans and his colleagues to similar cameos throughout his 11-year playing career at Headingley and the only unusual feature of that incident was that the try scorer was Atkinson and not Hynes' right-wing partner Alan Smith.

Syd Hynes enjoyed a host of attributes, including a sharp turn of pace, a solid defensive game and a hard-edged temperament.

His work with Smith, in particular, was a joy to behold and Smith himself happily admits that very often he himself did not know if he had the ball, such was Hynes' sleight of hand.

'Sometimes even I thought I had the ball! And there would be Syd scampering to the corner, nobody with him. Full-backs would just stand looking at me, realising I hadn't got it and that it was too late.

'We also worked well in defence. I'd crash tackle the

Continued...

Alan Hardisty outpaces full back John Risman in the 59-5 league victory over Workington Town on 25 March 1972.

months earlier would, if ever achieved, be slow and uncertain and it was perhaps unfortunate that Leeds chose the occasion of the Red Devils' first return to Headingley since that fateful day in May to parade the former hero around the ground. The debut of scrum-half Keith Hepworth, signed from Castleford to join his old colleague Alan Hardisty, was overshadowed by the presence of Shoebottom in the stands and, on the pitch, Salford's Colin Dixon was greeted with boos and jeers whenever he touched the ball in a grim atmosphere.

The Great Britain second row was escorted off the field by police officers at the end of the game, one Leeds supporter almost breaking the cordon in an attempt to punch him.

Leeds were to remain unbeaten in the league until April and attention returned to football and, specifically, the Floodlit Trophy and the John Player Cup throughout November. The first round BBC2 Floodlit Trophy win over Hull KR, in which Hardisty had scored a hat trick, was backed up by a second round verdict against Halifax when Hardisty was again on the score-sheet with a brace. St Helens, however, brought an end to the run with a 17-0 success at Headingley against a side which ran out of

The John Player Special Trophy proved to be a popular competition, helped by a bevy of marketing beauties.

centre and Syd would move out for my winger. It was confusing for referees and I remember Billy Thompson sending Syd off at Headingley, just after he'd dismissed him at Wembley, when it should have been me. Fortunately the referee Eric Clay was in the stand and confirmed that Billy had got the wrong man.'

Many of Hynes' qualities were more usually associated with that of a scrum-half and that, indeed, was his original position with Hunslet Juniors and subsequently Leeds NALGO Rugby Union.

Incredibly he was a very late developer, not signing for Leeds until three months after his 21st birthday. But he more than made up for lost time after making his debut in the 20-7 defeat at Wakefield on 19 April 1965 when he scored a drop goal.

Leeds, partly through his contribution, began to carry all before them, winning the League Leaders Trophy five times between 1966-67 and 1971-72 and featuring in 14 finals of which Hynes missed only one, the 1972 Championship Final victory over St Helens.

Continued...

substitutes following the departure of Hardisty in the second half and which ended up being nilled for the first time in almost six years.

There was progress on the league front, Widnes being disposed of through a try, three goals and a drop goal by Holmes and tries by Atkinson and Hardisty. And there was some form of revenge against Leigh for that Wembley defeat when the Hilton Park outfit were toppled 18-8 in the John Player Trophy – Ray Batten (the Yorkshire Federation of Rugby League Supporters' Clubs' James Harrison trophy winner as the 'Fairest and Most Loyal Player' in the county) and Leigh's Mooney being sent off – Dyl bagging a brace in the success.

Helped by a narrow miss by Mick Redfearn, whose touchline conversion attempt bounced back off the cross bar when Castleford were 11-5 ahead, Leeds ground out a 13-11 win at Wheldon Road in the second round, courtesy of a try and two goals for Holmes and touchdowns by John Burke and Ron Cowan. But the shadow of Shoebottom's serious head injury continued to add a sombre note. The assessment, now, was that Shoey would never be able to again play Rugby League, or indeed follow his normal employment, and Leeds formally opened a Testimonial Fund for the 26-year-old with a donation of £5,000 after ruling out the option of making the home game with Wigan on 1 January his official benefit match. The call went out for help and the close relationship between club and supporters was illustrated when the Leeds team coach stopped and picked up fans when the Headingley Grounds branch of the Supporters' Club were left stranded on the East Lancashire Road on the way back from Widnes.

Syd Hynes found himself on the wrong side of the referee again in the early December home fixture with Halifax, being controversially sent off – by Wembley whistler Billy Thompson – in an incident with the visitors' full-back Tony Hepworth which involved winger Alan Smith rather than the centre and was witnessed by thousands, including whistler Eric 'Sergeant

His form secured him a place, alongside Mick Shoebottom, John Atkinson, Barry Seabourne and Alan Smith, in the 1970 Great Britain squad which returned from Australia with the Ashes, Hynes scoring a vital try in the 21-17 victory in the Third Test which clinched the series.

Less than 12 months later, Hynes suffered the biggest blow of his career with his controversial dismissal, on the intervention of a touch judge, in the 1971 Challenge Cup Final against Leigh.

His qualities as a winner, however, shone through when he became coach following the departure of Roy Francis at the end of the 1974-75 season.

Yet another trophy for the man who never lost a final as a coach. Graham Eccles looks down with admiration at Syd Hynes.

Initially operating as player-coach – the first in Leeds' history – Hynes oversaw a side which tended towards indifferent form in the league but which was always capable of rising to the big occasion.

Hynes, aping the approach of Francis and working closely with his captain David Ward, allowed his players to impose their own tactics as they saw fit on the field of play.

The policy worked. Of the seven finals in which Leeds featured during his reign, none were lost; a remarkable record which reflected the big match temperament of one of Leeds' finest servants.

Major' Clay who was sitting in the stands.

The next match, the home game with Wigan on 11 December in the John Player competition, was used to support Mick Shoebottom's Testimonial Fund with a £565 collection taken before kick-off. Clawson, a recent signing from Hull KR, the third international to move to Headingley in six months, was cup tied and Leeds finished all-square when Wigan full-back Colin Tyrer landed a 45-yard goal towards the end. The Loiners, with second row Graham Eccles coming of age with the kind of tackling stint which was to become his trademark, won their first cup tie at Central Park since 1947 in the replay. Despite the dismissal of Fred Pickup and the departure of prop Steve Pitchford with concussion, and a low scrum count, the Loiners forced a 12-5 win with tries for Hepworth and Alan Smith and three goals by Hynes. Leeds fans were handed a glowing tribute in the programme notes, former Wigan full-back Martin Ryan enthusing: 'The Leeds crowd have a lesson for us in the way they yell on their team much like an enthusiastic soccer crowd, except that they are never slow to compliment the visitors when they deserve it. After things I have read about the alleged behaviour of the Leeds crowd, I was most impressed by their sportsmanship.'

Clawson made his debut against Leigh in the build up to Christmas as Leeds sought to resolve a problem at prop which had seen nine players packing down at 8 and 10 at various times comprising John Burke, Alan Bence, Pitchford, Ted Barnard, Phil Cookson, Ward, Handscombe, Bill Ramsey and Haigh. Early evidence was that Clawson's acquisition would be a success as Leigh, who had not conceded a try in the previous three games, shipped touchdowns to Alan Smith, Hardisty, Atkinson, John Langley and Dave Hick with Clawson (4) and Holmes adding goals in the 25-8 win.

Loiners Big Match

13 May 1972, Challenge Cup Final, Leeds 13 St Helens 16, Wembley

The fates occasionally conspire to thwart the best-laid plans of mice and men and the Loiners discovered, as have so many sides throughout the history of the game, that there are times when Rugby League teams simply have to shrug their collective shoulders and get on with it.

Little went right for coach Derek Turner and his players as injury-ravaged St Helens made a mockery of the Loiners' rating as 2 to 1 on favourites in the first clash between two of the code's greatest clubs at the Twin Towers.

The Saints lacked hooker Tony Karalius and powerhouse second row Eric Prescott, both of whom were hurt in the Championship play-off victory the previous week against Bradford Northern.

There were further scares for the Lancastrians during the week as forwards Eric Chisnall and John Stephens pulled up in training, together with scrum-half Jeff Heaton. And to add to St Helens' troubles, former Welsh Rugby Union second row John Mantle was hurt in a car accident four days before the final. The schoolteacher, however, confirmed his fitness on the day, playing in a scrumcap to protect his 12 (he refused 13) stitches, while Heaton, Stephens and Chisnall all made the starting line-up.

Leeds' injury worries, considered relatively unimportant during the build-up, turned out to be far more crucial. Full-back John Holmes, who had been carrying an ankle injury, was considered fit to play but not in good enough shape to take on the field-kicking role. With second row Phil Cookson and prop Terry Clawson both eminently capable of handling clearance kicks on the last tackle the Loiners were spoilt for choice.

That turned out be all too literally true. Heavy pressure by St Helens at the kick-off resulted in Leeds

Continued...

Alan Hardisty and Keith Hepworth achieved notable success at Headingley after a sustained period of glory with hometown club Castleford where they earned the soubriquet the 'H Bombs.' Hardisty is pictured lifting the John Player Trophy in March 1973.

The speedy Dyl grabbed two vital tries in the 16-12 victory at the Boulevard, and the biggest crowd of the season – 15,342 – turned up on Boxing Day for the derby clash with a Wakefield Trinity side that was to finish ninth in the table.

The 13-2 win helped hoist Leeds into top spot for the first time, ahead of Castleford and Swinton on points difference, with Hardisty netting two tries, Atkinson touching down and Clawson kicking a couple of goals to put Leeds in fine shape, at the turn of the year, for an assault on the John Player Cup, the Challenge Cup, the Championship and the League Leaders Trophy.

Ambitions in the John Player Trophy were quickly thwarted by Halifax who, encouraged by a winning bonus of £68, beat Leeds 15-7 at Headingley on 8 January in the semi-final to end a run of 17 successive defeats against the Loiners stretching back to October 1967. On the *being camped on their own line when the fourth and last tackle beckoned. Hooker Tony Fisher, at acting half-back, was flung into confusion when both Clawson and Cookson – the only players in the Leeds side without any previous Wembley experience – called for the ball.*

Fisher's pass went to neither, scuttling along the ground. With St Helens' evergreen Welsh prop Graham Rees bearing down, scrum-half Keith Hepworth opted to fly kick the loose ball which simply rebounded off Rees who followed up for one of the most astonishing – and, at 35 seconds, early – tries ever scored at Wembley.

Hooker Tony Fisher keeps a watching brief as prop Bill Ramsey battles to progress.

The Loiners never fully recovered, although fate was to take another hand in the shape of a serious attack of the gremlins on Clawson. The former Featherstone Rovers and Hull KR prop, a mid-season signing, finished the campaign with 88 goals and managed five at Wembley. But the form which he had enjoyed in practice at the stadium the previous day deserted him, four attempts going astray including three from in front of the sticks and one effort, the conversion attempt of Cookson's try shortly after half time, failing to get off the ground.

Kel Coslett, by contrast, landed four goals and a drop goal for the Saints, including one massive effort from inside his own half shortly after he had been wide with a touchline attempt of winger Les Jones' try.

His first goal, the conversion of Rees' try, was simple enough, before Clawson reduced the deficit with an 11th minute penalty after his first shot had rebounded off an upright.

Jones' touchdown, following approach work by Mantle and Chisnall, and Coslett's penalty stretched Saints' lead to a mighty eight points and it stayed that way until shortly before the break as the Welshman and Clawson traded penalties.

Clawson, however, reduced the arrears to six points at the interval with a goal on the stroke of half time and Leeds were, amazingly, back in the contest within a minute of the restart when Fisher and loose forward Ray Batten combined to fine effect to send Cookson charging over.

Clawson's nightmare, however, resurfaced with his stumbling kick, leaving Leeds still three points adrift.

Coslett extended St Helens' lead to seven points with a penalty and a 35-yard drop goal. And although Clawson at last found his kicking boots, reducing the gap to three points with a couple of goals in the closing quarter, the damage had been done.

Fate, however, was to take more kindly to Clawson seven days later, against the same opposition, in the Championship Final at Swinton...

Leeds: Holmes; A Smith, Hynes, Dyl, Atkinson; Hardisty, Hepworth; Clawson, Fisher, Ramsey, Cookson, Haigh, Batten.

St Helens: Pimblett; Jones, Benyon, Walsh, Wilson; Kelly, Heaton; Rees, Greenall, Stephenson, Mantle, Chisnall, Coslett.

Referee: Mr E Lawrinson (Warrington)

Leeds: T: Cookson. G: Clawson 5.

St Helens: T: Rees, Jones. G: Coslett 4. DG: Coslett.

Attendance: 89,495

same day the Loiners sold Barry Seabourne, who had been staying away following the signing of Hepworth, to Bradford Northern; Leeds, however, were to lose only one more game, other than the Challenge Cup Final, and that came at Dewsbury in early April when the Crown Flatt men won 14-4, limiting the Loiners to two Holmes goals.

Otherwise the Loiners enjoyed a run of unbroken success, starting with the New Year's Day league win over Wigan when Holmes scored a try and four goals and Hynes, Dyl and

A Loiner Looks Back

John Holmes

'When I first joined Leeds at 16, the senior players took me under their wing. I'd get off the bus after an away match and say I was going home and they'd say, "no you're not, you're coming with us." I'd drink orange juice, at that time, but they'd still take me. Players like Billy Ramsey, Mick Shoebottom and Mick Clark. They were absolutely brilliant to me. They used to have an end-of-season trip to Blackpool and I thought, "God, a 16-year-old kid going to Blackpool with these players." They looked after me, and they looked after Phil Cookson when he joined a season or so later. I hadn't dared walk into the first team dressing room. I'd been in the A team and if you wanted to go for some treatment you had to wait until they'd gone out, and hide round a wall so they wouldn't see you. But when you got your own peg in the first team dressing room you'd made it; only so far, though, you'd still to prove yourself.'

Batten nipped over in a 20-11 win.

Leeds' strength in depth was illustrated by the fact that both Cookson and Haigh were sidelined for lengthy periods through injury, and Dyl missed a month with a broken finger, but the handicap was brushed aside – even in a testimonial game for Mick Shoebottom against Great Britain which finished 12-12 and raised another £1,765 for the stricken star. The fund was to close at the end of the season at £20,326.

Turner's side ground out a 19-7 win in a niggling game at Batley which served evidence of the game's ills which had persuaded the Rugby Football to engage a firm of marketing consultants. The Loiners then drew 15-15 at St Helens after having allowed a seven-point lead to slip and subsequently looking set for defeat in a thriller which lived up to the billing by TA Owen who wrote in the Saints programme: 'Nobody wants snow, or rain, for the Leeds visit. A nice dry day? I need not say that the best 'gate' of the season is expected – and perhaps the best game.' As George Chambers wrote: 'If Rugby League could be played like this every week the marketing consultants advising the League would not be necessary.'

The display against their near challengers for the League Leadership set Leeds up nicely for the Wembley trail. Evidence that the sporting public preferred a switch to Sunday rugby was provided by gates for the first round, which totalled 47,803 for the six Sunday ties, with only 23,174 turning up for the nine Saturday games which included Leeds' home clash with Widnes.

Leeds were unconvincing in the 17-8 win, benefiting from a marginal offside decision which ruled out a Chemics' try and making sure of progress with a late Wainwright touchdown. In an example of concerns over the Loiners' style Arthur Haddock of the Evening Post lamented: 'It baffles me, as it must puzzle other people, that slow Leeds forwards will try to get in on the handling act when the situation cries

A Loiner Looks Back

Billy Watts

'David Barham carved out a niche in Leeds' history in the 1972 Championship Final. Saints were pressing on our line, John Stephens had the ball, and Barham went to tackle him, put his hands underneath and took the ball away from him. Stephens just looked and, I'm sure, he went with his arms as if "I'm going to crack you one!" And that won us the game.'

Loiners Big Match

20 May 1972, Championship Final, Leeds 9 St Helens 5, Station Road, Swinton

John Atkinson and Alan Hardisty, adversaries in the 1969 Leeds V Castleford Championship Final were united three years later. It was smiles all round as St Helens were beaten 9-5 at Swinton as revenge was gained for the previous week's defeat at Wembley.

That was the story of the 1971-72 Championship Final as Leeds, beaten seven days earlier by the Saints in the Challenge Cup Final at Wembley, exacted retribution in amazing style with a weakened side. Scrum-half David Barham, drafted into the side when Keith Hepworth fell ill on the morning of the game, had his best game for Leeds and was the undoubted match-winner with an astonishing 'steal' from St Helens second row John Mantle.

That single act denied Mantle what would have been a certain try, beneath the posts, which could well have led to St Helens becoming the first side to win the title for three successive seasons and only the third team since the Second World War to achieve the 'double.' Barham, a bustling beacon of energy throughout, both in attack and defence, was the man of the match in the opinion of many but was denied the Harry Sunderland Trophy by Terry Clawson. The prop, who had had a miserable time at Wembley, missing three simple goal-kicks in the 16-13 defeat, overcame the pressure in phlegmatic fashion, kicking three crucial goals, including two from the touchline, despite constant barracking from a section of the St Helens

Continued...

out for swift, crisp passing to the speed merchants, of which Leeds have more than most sides.'

The Loiners, struggling for possession, were alternating between Tony Fisher and David Ward at hooker, and a wide permutation of props. Leeds hosted Hull without Hynes – who missed out for the second time on captaining Great Britain, this time with a hamstring injury – and Holmes who had been called up as his replacement in France, in an hors d'oeuvre for the second round Challenge Cup tie at the Boulevard. The Airlie Birds, who had hooker Tony Duke and Paul Ibbertson sent off, could not match the Loiners while Holmes was the match-winner for Britain, kicking the late penalty which ensured a 10-9 win over France in Toulouse, the Lions' first success over the water for four years.

Leeds' preparation for the Cup trip to the Boulevard could hardly have been better, with a six-try win over Wakefield in which Atkinson and Alan Smith both scored hat tricks and Clawson kicked four goals. Atkinson's feat, though, failed to impress the Great Britain selectors, who promptly dropped him, along with Holmes, for the home game with France. There was some solace Headingley way, however, with the recall of Hynes and Smith while hooker Mick Stephenson became the first Dewsbury player to be recognised since his predecessor at number 9, Harry Bradshaw, 20 years earlier. And Atkinson became a late call up for the Odsal international when Smith sustained a knee *crowd.*

The win ended Leeds' season in style but the victory owed much to sheer cussednesss and a willingness to work. The so-called 'fringe' players rose to the occasion admirably, with centre John Langley, in the starting line-up for the injured Syd Hynes, another serious contender for the Harry Sunderland Trophy and young hooker David Ward, named as substitute in the Wembley programme the previous week but missing out to Graham Eccles, also outstanding.

There was nothing better than Langley's long pass, which missed out Les Dyl, courtesy of an equally impressive ball by Fred Pickup, a veteran of the 1961 success, which sent winger John Atkinson over for the Loiners' only try.

David Barham – star of the 1972 Championship Final.

That score, registered shortly after Langley should have been awarded a penalty try after being hauled down by Saints centre John Walsh in chasing a kick by young hooker David Ward, was converted from the whitewash by Clawson who had earlier landed a penalty from a similar position. Added to the prop's first half goal, the Loiners were now six points ahead. St Helens, who had opened with a try for hooker Greenall, who burrowed over from acting half-back with Kel Coslett missing the simple conversion in a reversal of fortunes from Wembley, were unable to close the gap, despite a long range drop goal by Walsh, as an energetic defence exemplified by second row Graham Eccles – called up in place of the injured Bob Haigh – held firm.

Alan Hardisty and John Holmes had been unable to convert drop goal attempts of their own in the first half, but it didn't matter as Leeds won the Championship for the second time in three years with, remarkably, the same scoreline as in the BBC2 Floodlit Trophy final win over Saints the previous December.

Barham, a former Leeds junior, was unable in subsequent years to quite repeat the form he showed that day at Odsal. The youngster made six appearances for Leeds the following season, scoring a try and a goal in the 22-16 league defeat in February at Castleford.

Leeds: Holmes; A Smith, Langley, Dyl, Atkinson; Hardisty, Barham; Clawson, Ward, Fisher, Cookson, Eccles, Batten. Subs: Hick, Pickup.
St Helens: Pimblett; Jones, Benyon, Walsh, Wilson; Kelly, Heaton; Rees, Greenall, Stephens, Mantle, Chisnall, Coslett. Subs: Whittle, Earl.
Referee: Mr S Shepherd (Oldham).
Leeds: T: Atkinson. G: Clawson 3.
St Helens: T: Greenall. DG: Walsh.
Attendance: 24,055

injury.

The accolade of joint-favourite status sat well with Leeds in the 15-6 win at the Boulevard, where Eccles, Ramsey and Pickup set the platform before a 14,500 crowd for classy tries for Alan Smith, Hardisty, Dyl and Atkinson, Clawson and Holmes sharing the goals.

The heady Headingley mood improved with a 19-3 win at Workington, despite again losing the scrums, involving two Hardisty tries and touchdowns by Alan Smith, Holmes and Dyl which helped establish a four-point lead over Salford, Wigan and Bradford Northern and was the fifth game in succession in which the tries had all been scored by backs. Town's only try was a controversial affair, scored from a quick tap while Atkinson was off the field retrieving the other ball.

Leeds, meanwhile, appeared to be settling on Ward at hooker. A disgruntled Fisher joined Peter Dunn and Handscombe on the transfer list, with Fisher not turning up for the trip to Workington or for the following Monday's training session. Said chairman Jack

Myerscough: 'He is reported to have written a letter to the club but we have not got it yet. Candidly, we are more interested now in players who want to play for Leeds, and in the Cup game with Wakefield Trinity.'

Interest in the quarter-final tie was high. 20,855 – a 5,000 increase on the previous best of the season, also against Trinity, on Boxing Day, and the best home gate for six years – turned up for the first Sunday game to be played at Headingley. Leeds reached the semi-finals despite the dismissal of Ramsey for a foul on Wakefield half-back Dave Topliss, while a Hardisty try, three goals by Clawson and a Holmes drop goal were enough to see Leeds through in the first cup meeting of the two clubs since the watersplash final in 1968.

The league momentum was maintained with a one-point win over Castleford in which Hepworth grabbed two tries against his old club, the Loiners crushed Keighley, and Leeds went a step nearer to retrieving the League Leaders trophy with a 27-2 win over Hull KR.

Haigh, back in action after five months on the sidelines with a broken arm, raced over for two tries in his first match back, a 59-5 stroll over Workington Town in which Alan Smith and Atkinson each notched a hat trick.

The subsequent 28-6 win at Huddersfield was Leeds' 169th in 200 league games spread over six seasons – easily the most successful period in the club's history, leaving the Loiners needing to win at home to Bramley and then at Dewsbury to clinch the League Leader's trophy.

Mick Stephenson, a fine hooker, touches down for Dewsbury in the 1973 Championship Final despite the attentions of Les Dyl.

Atkinson raced over for a hat trick – each of the three tries from a Batten pass – in a hard-fought 18-9 win over Bramley in which youngster Chris Sanderson also crossed. But Leeds, with the Challenge Cup semi-final against Halifax at Odsal around the corner, could only muster two Holmes goals in the 14-4 defeat by emerging Dewsbury who added the Loiners to the scalps of Salford, Castleford and Wigan as Crown Flatt victims.

Fisher, selected for the Challenge Cup semi-final in place of Ward, who sustained an eye injury against Bramley, showed just how fortunes can change in Rugby League. Less than a month after being in danger of drifting back to South Wales he turned in an epic performance, blotting Halifax danger man Terry Fogerty out of the game with a masterful defensive display and ending Halifax's hopes of forcing their way back into the game with six successive heels in the second half. Clawson landed five goals, two from over 50 yards, despite a strong wind, in the 16-3 win and Atkinson and Alan Smith crossed to book a date with St Helens at Wembley and take a step nearer the coveted 'double.'

A 22-10 victory over Leigh sealed the League

Leadership Trophy for the fifth time in six years, which was awarded to Hardisty by RFL Secretary Bill Fallowfield prior to the last league game of the season, a 39-7 win against Batley.

Leigh, now sick and tired of the sight of Leeds after the Wembley upset 12 months earlier, were beaten for the fourth time in the season, 40-2, in the first round of the Championship play-offs, eight Loiners men crossing.

Turner was forced to read the riot act to his players at half time in the second round game against Widnes, who eventually went down 20-9 to tries by Alan Smith, Haigh, Dyl and Cookson, and a 10-0 win over Salford in the semi-final set up a decider against St Helens, with both sides set to go for the 'double' at Wembley and Swinton.

Leeds had quietly gone about their business through the rounds but voiced a long-standing worry when the Championship finalists were known. As League Leaders, the Loiners were dismayed to have to travel into Lancashire to face Lancashire opposition and with a Lancashire referee at the helm.

Proposals from both clubs to play the game at either Knowsley Road or Headingley on the toss of a coin fell on deaf ears, however. It didn't matter, though, as Leeds retrieved the title for the third time in 11 seasons, thanks largely to Clawson who landed three wonderful goals in the 9-5 Championship Final win over St Helens in a vivid example, following his misses at Wembley seven days earlier, of the fluctuating fortunes of sport.

Atkinson topped Leeds' try-scoring table with 33, sharing top billing in the full RFL list with Bradford's Mike Lamb, who had been his next-door neighbour in Ireland Wood, Leeds, during childhood. Hardisty was next behind Atkinson on 27; Alan Smith crashed over for 21 tries and Les Dyl and John Holmes had 20 tries each. Holmes and Clawson landed 88 goals apiece.

A Loiner Looks Back

Graham Eccles

'I've so many wonderful memories. The best is probably the 1972 Championship Final when we beat St Helens at Swinton. The worst was being beaten by Blackpool at home in 1980 but I've no bad memories of the 70s. I enjoyed scoring a try against Dewsbury in the 1972 Yorkshire Cup Final and I also scored against them in the Championship Final later in the season. And I can't forget scoring a hat trick against Blackpool in the John Player in 1972/3. We were on the front afterwards and somebody had one of those silly papers made up. They said, "look at this Graham, you've made headlines in the Blackpool paper!"'

Games involving Leeds and St Helens were always closely fought.

10. MAESTRO OR MUG?

Harry Jepson remains as perplexed, after the event, over the sacking of Leeds coach Derek 'Rocky' Turner as he was at the time.

Jepson, formerly a long-serving Secretary at Hunslet, had crossed the river to take on a similar role at Headingley and wasn't party to the decision to dismiss Turner, who was felt not to have served up quite the brand of football with which Leeds are traditionally associated.

The facts, however, suggest otherwise. During the 1972-73 season, Leeds set a new record of 1,220 points, made up of 810 points in 34 league games, 158 in six Players No 6 matches, 117 in four Yorkshire Cup ties, 95 in four Championship play-off clashes, 18 in two BBC2 Floodlit Trophy matches, 11 in the Challenge Cup defeat by Wigan and 11 against New Zealand.

Ray Batten, Alan Preece and Chris Sanderson support Alan Smith as Leeds hold a practice match in 1972 following the introduction of the six-tackle rule.

Says Mr Jepson: 'We won two trophies – the Yorkshire Cup and the John Player Cup – and we reached the Championship Final, where admittedly we were beaten by Dewsbury. It was an amazing decision, supposedly because of our style. I hadn't been at Leeds long then, so I wasn't as involved as I was later, but I did hear that there was too much forward-orientated play. But if you look at the records you'll find that Alan Smith, John Atkinson, Les Dyl, Syd Hynes and Alan Hardisty scored well over 100 tries between them, which tells you that the assessment was completely wrong. Hardisty played more games that season, over 40, than he had ever played before, and he scored 28 tries. Atkinson scored 36, Smith got 28, Hynes scored 25, Dyl scored 20, John Holmes totalled 16 and John Langley scored 16 before Phil Cookson appeared as the first forward on the list with 15. And Derek got the sack.'

Hardisty had been looking forward to the new season and fancied his side's chances under the new six-tackle rule; the four-tackle rule, which had been introduced six years earlier, having been extended.

The former Castleford captain was also focusing on the Yorkshire Cup, the only trophy in the game to have eluded him and a competition in which Leeds were again involved after having pulled out the previous season. After scoring five tries against Hunslet in the Lazenby Cup Hardisty said: 'I found I can still give the forwards 10 to 15 yards and get up with them for a pass. I think this new six-tackle rule is going to be a great improvement. I never did like four tackles, it was supposed to be made for the backs but the trouble was that after you'd beaten the opposing half-back the forwards were always

A Loiner Looks Back

John Langley

'I missed getting on at Wembley in 1968, my day came in 1971 against Leigh. I wasn't even in the programme but Alan Smith cried off on the Friday with a knee injury so they drafted me in. I was the nearest player to the incident involving Syd Hynes and Alex Murphy but I didn't see it. I don't know whether he hit him or not, the ball had gone away and although the game is on the telly you can't tell. Old Alex was stretchered off, but he came back later on to the cheers of the crowd.

'That defeat was soul destroying, but the worst one was the following year when St Helens beat us, when I was on the bench. The following week, we beat them in the Championship Final, with David Barham at scrum half and Fred Pickup and me in the centres. We beat them 9-5, Terry Clawson kicked three goals and that's one of the best results I've been involved in, because we were lacking several players and Saints were expected to win.'

The 1972 Championship Final was a highlight for John Langley. The 1973 decider was a less happy experience. Here he can only chase as Dewsbury centre Nigel Stephenson glides over for a clinching try.

coming across to cover. Now there should be more tackling for the forwards and it should make it better for the backs. It should also cut out a lot of panic kicking.'

Leeds opened the season with the thumping 57-0 win over Hunslet in what was to be the last of the traditional Lazenby Cup openers against their old rivals, and the reigning champions opened the defence of their title confidently, winning their first six games while simultaneously progressing to the Yorkshire Cup Final.

The Loiners rattled up the points on the way to an Odsal pairing with Dewsbury. Hynes, loose forward Ray Batten and second row Bob Haigh raced over in the 19-8 first round win at Hull, and there was a hat trick for Alan Smith and two tries for Atkinson in the eight-try 36-5 romp over a Featherstone Rovers side that had dominated the opening quarter at Headingley.

It was Dyl's turn to grab a hat trick in the semi-final, Huddersfield having no answer to the centre's pace in the 26-13 victory in which Hardisty bagged a brace and Atkinson crossed,

A Loiner Looks Back

Bill Ramsey

'Alf Rutherford was the manager both of Yorkshire Cricket and of the rugby side. At first, he wasn't interested in Rugby League at all but within two years of his arrival at Headingley he was very much into it. After our voluntary Sunday sessions the champagne would come out at 12 o'clock. There'd be such as Kenny Eyre, Syd Hynes, John Atkinson and Alan Smith there, we used to have some interesting afternoons. It was good, really good. After the final in 1968 Alf, who was also a big racing man, took me, Kenny Eyre and Syd Hynes down to Epsom to the Derby. We stayed overnight, went racing the following day and came home and it cost us nothing. That was absolutely superb. I remember old Alf putting £1,000 on this horse to win the Derby and it didn't win. And he just took it on his chin.'

to set up what would be the first of two meetings that season with Dewsbury at Bradford.

Just four days after the semi-final win over Huddersfield, Leeds were at Borough Park, Blackpool, in the first round of the John Player Trophy, where second row Graham Eccles crashed over for a hat trick, each try off a Bill Ramsey pass, in the 51-9 victory that sent Leeds on their way to their second trophy of the campaign.

Salford (twice), Hull KR, Huddersfield, Doncaster and Bramley all succumbed to the power and the pace of Turner's Leeds in the bread and butter arena of league football. The Loiners would have won by a bigger margin than 15-5 at the Willows if not for lack of possession at the scrums, and while the 'double' was completed in the return less than three weeks later the 19-10 victory provided ammunition for the anti-Turner element on the Headingley terraces who insisted that his tactics involved too much one-man, forward-dominated football.

Hardisty guided the Loiners to the 21-5 home win over Hull KR in which Atkinson had a brace, and Leeds had to work harder than the scoreline would suggest for the 28-2 verdict over Huddersfield.

It was more straightforward, though, when previously unbeaten Doncaster travelled to Headingley and had their 100 per cent record smashed, the half century being breached with hat tricks for Haigh and Atkinson.

Alan Smith scored his customary two tries against Bramley to remind the Villagers that

Loiners Big Match

7 October 1972, Yorkshire Cup Final, Leeds 36 Dewsbury 9, Odsal Stadium, Bradford

An oddity of the 1972-73 Yorkshire Cup Final was that Dewsbury were – for Rugby League purposes at any rate – a 'Lancashire' team.

In an era in which all professional sides played in a single league, fixtures comprised Lancashire and Yorkshire League games, with (in 1972-73) three opponents from across the Pennies providing six more games.

It's all under control as Graham Eccles watches Dewsbury prop 'Dick' Lowe run into trouble in the Yorkshire Cup Final.

With 16 of the 30 clubs hailing from the county of the broad acres, a financial incentive was given for a Yorkshire team to switch; and, for several years, Dewsbury jumped at the chance.

So the Crown Flatt outfit reached the 1972 Yorkshire Cup Final – and were, later in the season, to win the Championship, also at Odsal and also against Leeds – as 'foreigners' and only met fellow countymen Huddersfield, Hull and York in domestic football during the campaign.

Not that Tommy Smales' men were unknown quantities as far as Leeds were concerned. The Loiners had, in fact, slipped at Crown Flatt the previous April, going down to one of only four defeats as they seized the League Leaders' Trophy with a 14-4 reverse after a run of five games in fourteen days; and only five days prior to the Challenge Cup semi-final against Halifax.

Leeds had to contend with similar distractions as they prepared for the Yorkshire Cup Final. They had a tough trip to Wakefield Trinity six days earlier, losing

Continued...

13-12, and they went into the Odsal clash aware that three days later St Helens were to provide the opposition at Knowsley Road in the First Round of the BBC2 Floodlit Trophy.

There was, however, no sign of harassment as Leeds, after a hesitant start, set about disposing of their opponents by the highest score registered in a final to that date.

Early promise by Dewsbury in which a bewildering array of moves involving hooker Mick Stephenson, prop Dick Lowe and scrum-half Alan Bates came to nothing, a Leeds defence in which second row Graham Eccles was prominent standing firm.

The Loiners could also draw satisfaction from winning so comfortably despite being starved of possession. Alfred Drewry of the Yorkshire Post calculated that Leeds scored two tries for each scrum won, gaining two heels in the first half, when three tries were recorded, and five in the second, from two scrums.

Full-back John Holmes, celebrating his selection for Great Britain's World Cup squad, scored a hat trick with the help of a series of judicious passes by stand off Alan Hardisty, to collect the Yorkshire Federation of Rugby League Supporters' White Rose Trophy as man of the match.

Hardisty and Holmes were also prominent in a move which sent centre Les Dyl over for a first half try which helped tilt the balance after Dewsbury's promising opening.

Apart from being involved in each of Holmes' touchdowns and the Dyl try, Hardisty also crossed for a try of his own to push his full-back hard for the individual award. But he was happy simply to collect, together with his former Castleford colleague Keith Hepworth, his first Yorkshire Cup medal.

Prop Terry Clawson landed five goals from as many attempts to confirm his liking for the swirling Odsal bowl winds after his success in the Championship Final a few months earlier, while Dewsbury sorely missed the goal-kicking skills of injured centre Nigel Stephenson, Lowe failing with three first half attempts at goal which could have kept his side in contention.

Stand off Allan Agar went on to kick three, while Mick Stephenson was at the hub of everything positive in the Dewsbury side, but Leeds simply held too many aces. Eccles topped his customary big tackle count with a try, ploughing over off one of Ray Batten's many smart passes, Dyl finished with a brace, and John Atkinson used the touchline admirably for a solo scorcher. Syd Hynes also kicked a goal and, despite their plethora of elaborate and exciting pre-planned moves, Dewsbury could only muster a try for Welsh winger Greg Ashcroft, a speedster from Pontypridd, to supplement Agar's goals.

As Hardisty reflected afterwards on Dewsbury's approach: 'They were perhaps too clever for their own good. These moves might pay off in the league but you need the straight-forward hard stuff for cup football.'

Leeds: Holmes; A Smith, Hynes, Dyl, Atkinson; Hardisty, Hepworth; Clawson, Ward, Ramsey, Eccles, Cookson, Batten. Subs: Langley, Fisher.

Dewsbury: Rushton; Ashcroft, Childe, Day, Yoward; Agar, A Bates; Bell, Mick Stephenson, Lowe, Grayshon, J Bates, Hankin. Subs: Lee, Beverley.

Leeds: T: Holmes 3, Dyl 2, Eccles, Hardisty, Atkinson. G: Clawson 5, Hynes.

Dewsbury: T: Ashcroft. G: Agar 3.

Referee: Mr MJ Naughton (Widnes)

Attendance: 7,406

they had been unfortunate to have missed out on his services several years earlier, before the Loiners went down to their first defeat of the campaign with the 13-12 reverse at Wakefield Trinity. Leeds could have won, if Holmes had managed to convert a late Les Dyl try from the touchline, but the consensus was that they deserved little from the game.

There were, however, to be no more league defeats until the turn of the year, while further progress was made in the John Player Cup, although the side went out of the BBC2 Floodlit

Cup 9-4 at Widnes after having won 14-6 at St Helens in the first round.

A weakened Wigan side which was to sneak into the top 16 play-offs suffered the biggest defeat in its history with the 58-3 reverse at Headingley, which followed defeats at Central Park by Wakefield Trinity, Dewsbury and Whitehaven. Alan Smith scored a hat trick in the rout, and only three days later Leeds were demolishing Halifax 34-0, also at Headingley, with Holmes scoring 25 points with three tries and eight goals.

Bradford Northern, beaten 29-11 in an abrasive affair at Odsal, Hull (23-17 at home) Castleford (20-5 at Headingley) and Northern again, also at home, were the next league victims while Atkinson scored a hat trick in the second round John Player victory over Leigh. Hull, after a replay, were disposed of in the quarter-finals, Hynes scoring two tries and seven goals in the 37-5 Headingley success.

Leeds finished the year with four successive league wins, Hunslet, Featherstone (under the cosh from a Hardisty hat trick) Wakefield and Halifax all succumbing to the Loiners' lash, and a second final of the season was booked when St Helens were beaten 19-0 in mid-January in the semi-final of the John Player Trophy.

That victory, earned with tries for Hynes, Cookson and John Hay plus three Terry Clawson goals and two Hardisty drop goals, was needed. Leeds had lost their two opening games of the year, at Wigan (11-8) and at Hull KR (26-16) and questions were being asked about Turner's

Headingley Hero

John Atkinson

It was said of the immortal Brian Bevan that if he had only the full-back to beat, he had no one to beat. Much the same could be said of John Atkinson. One of the most thrilling sights at Headingley during the 60s and 70s was of Atkinson taking possession in his own 25, with less than half an opening in front of him, and with eyes firmly focused on the opposition try-line. In those circumstances the flyer was invariably a certain scorer.

Fleet of foot, with the ability to sidestep or swerve off either pin, the charismatic former Roundhay Rugby Union winger was a firm favourite with the fans and derived equal enjoyment from tripping back to his position, waving to a packed South Stand or North Stand, as from the act of scoring.

Plying his trade in an era in which wingers were perhaps given fewer opportunities than their predecessors, who had often netted 50 or 60 tries in a season, Atkinson still achieved highly-creditable totals and became the first Englishman since St Helens' Alf Ellaby in the late 1920s to top the try-scoring tables in successive seasons when he netted 36 in 1971-72 and 39 in 1972-73.

His abilities were recognised by the international selectors, who called him to the colours on 26 occasions between 1968 and 1980; a total that made him the most capped man, as a Leeds player, in the club's history.

Significantly, he was a member of the Great Britain sides that won the Ashes Down Under in 1970, and two years later lifted the World Cup.

Atkinson was prominent in the 1970 triumph, grabbing two tries in the decisive 21-17 Third Test win in Sydney, and he also had a penchant for netting important touchdowns in the Loiners' cause; something of a family trait as his uncle, George Broughton, had netted two vital tries when Leeds beat Whitehaven in the 1957 Challenge Cup semi-final. Atkinson's first try at Wembley was certainly the most

Continued...

John Holmes congratulates Clive Sullivan on scoring the winning try in the 1972 World Cup Final.

recruitment and selection policies, and about the nature of Leeds' ambitions.

Whereas Wigan's heavy defeat at Headingley in October had been attributed to the horrendous injury list at Central Park, there was comparatively little understanding shown when similar troubles hit Derek Turner. Leslie Temlett, after the St Helens defeat, had opined: 'It is time for questions at Headingley. And fans hope the answer will come before the Challenge Cup visit to Wigan towards the end of January.

'That league defeat at Central Park was the starting gun for all kinds of criticism of the Leeds line-up.'

Temlett pondered: 'Why wasn't young David Barham retained at number seven? Or, at least, why wasn't he brought on from substitute after Syd Hynes had made such a hash of the position?

'Why was John Hay, normally 'A' team centre or wing, playing full-back when the Loiners have a recognised number one, Geoff Nichols, on their books? That question arises not because Hay did not play well – in fact he put on a fair show – but that it was a strange role for him. And the natural follow-up question: what happens to Nichols, formerly of Hunslet and Barrow? Since he came from Barrow earlier this season he has had one first team outing, a nightmare match at Wakefield. Is he to be discarded after one poor match? The answer to that could be Yes now that Leeds have bought Derek Edwards.

'Another grouse from Leeds fans is the lack of first team wingers on the club's books. With World Cup men Alan Smith and John Atkinson there has been no need to look elsewhere. But now both are injured and there is just no one to step up.

'Barry Parker will always get tries through sheer grit and determination, but he is lacking in pace. And to put forward Phil Cookson out near the touchline is a criminal waste of talent. So there are problems at Leeds. They have been there for a while, but Wigan lit them up with a defeat which could cost the side plenty. Defeat

controversial, York referee Mr JP Hebblethwaite awarding him an obstruction try in the infamous Watersplash Final against Wakefield Trinity, in 1968. Disappointment followed in 1971 and 1972 before Atkinson renewed acquaintance with a winners medal in 1977, when he grabbed the try that brought Leeds back into contention after Widnes had established a 7-2 lead. And it was a similar story for Atky 12 months later when, in his 400th game for the club, he finished off a move sparked by centre Les Dyl to beat two defenders in a 30-yard sprint for a touchdown which restored Leeds' hopes after the Saints had blasted into a 10-point lead.

There was also the tremendous touchdown against Salford at Fartown, Huddersfield, in the 1973 John Player Final when his raised arm alerted full-back John Holmes to the possibility that a score was 'on'. Few players would have had the ability to fling out

Continued...

the long, one-handed pass which Holmes utilised on that occasion but it's also true that the difficult pass had to be taken.
Atkinson, typically, took it with aplomb before striding over the whitewash in the majestic style which was his trademark.
The long range try against Wigan in the 1968 Challenge Cup semi-final rates, for most fans, as Atkinson's best but he pinpoints a night a little over two years later as his most memorable game. Widnes were the opposition, at Headingley, and he recalls: 'We'd just come back from Australia and paraded the Ashes. I made an early mistake which gave them a try. Ray Dutton was playing at full-back for Widnes, he'd just come back off tour with us. My dad said that two of the tries I scored in that game were the best he'd seen at Headingley, and he'd followed Leeds through the 1930s, in the Eric Harris era. I scored three down the touchline and I went inside and outside, for two of them, on Ray Dutton, who was a very good full-back. I was very pleased with how things went that night and having come back with the Ashes, well, I was on top of the world.'

put Leeds into a position where Warrington must slip up if the League Leaders trophy is to go to Headingley for the sixth time in seven seasons. And Leeds, like most top clubs, prefer the ball to be in their court.'

Arthur Haddock, in the Evening Post, made the point that the Headingley men had gained little financial reward for having won all but 28 of their previous 220 league games and that they were perhaps understandably turning into the 'Prizefighters' in focusing on sponsored competitions such as the Challenge Cup and the Players' Trophy.

He also debated whether the £8,000 paid for Jeanes, combined with a total of £7,750 forked out for Derek Edwards (Castleford) and Geoff Clarkson (Warrington) could have been used to entice a real 'big money' signing in the old Leeds tradition.

The John Player victory over St Helens was followed by a home defeat, seven days later, by the Saints in the league. It was the first reverse at Headingley since the 10-8 defeat by Wigan in March 1971 and led to more stinging criticisms.

Holmes came in for rebuke following a defeat in which Fisher won nine of the first 10 second-half scrums, Alfred Drewry of the Yorkshire Post reflecting: 'If Hardisty had been playing the theme of my piece would probably have been how the return of Fisher had eased the task of the Leeds attack. There is no point in reflecting on the damage Hardisty might have done; the fact is that poor Holmes found the position and the conditions so patently beyond his scope that it would have been both a mercy to him and a blessing to his three-quarters had the signs been read right and Holmes moved to his rightful

A Loiner Looks Back

Steve Pitchford

'Our winger Barry Parker was a little tinker, he lived off his wits more than he did by working. He'd lost his money at three-card brag when we stayed over in Blackpool once so he bet everybody – and there would have been 25 of us – a fiver for the first one to find a crab. I don't know if you've ever seen 25 Rugby League players running up and down a beach trying to find a crab at 4 O'clock in the morning! Anyway, we're all looking for crabs and all Barry did was go to the first rock. Sure enough, a crab was there and he got all his money back.'

position at full-back at half time, with either Hynes or Langley at stand off half.'

Drewry would surely have been obliged to review that assessment several years later, when Holmes had carved out a reputation as one of the best – possibly the best – stand off halves in the club's history.

Leeds, typically, accepted the defeat in a sportsmanlike manner and sent five bottles of champagne and a congratulatory note to the St Helens dressing room.

But a 25-11 Challenge Cup defeat at the hands of Wigan, Leeds' first first-round exit since 1964, added to Turner's problems as Bill Ashurst arose from his sick bed and, although still ill with a chest complaint, landed four drop goals for the Pie Eaters who were on a reported £100 a man to win.

One writer to the 'Green Final' lamented: 'I suggest Leeds drop John Atkinson and John Langley, who never get a pass anyway, and play two forwards on the wings. This will provide two extra forwards for bashing and barging up the middle of the field. They could also release Ray Batten and Bob Haigh, who seem to expect someone to back up their breaks, as all followers of the team realise that 'backing up' is no longer part of the Leeds play. The introduction of these measures will allow myself and the other faithful fans who turn up hoping to see football to stay away with clear consciences.'

However the knockers were given short shrift by another supporter, who wrote: 'They should learn that they have to take the rough with the

Loiners Big Match

24 March 1973, John Player Final, Leeds 12 Salford 7, Fartown, Huddersfield

Much has been made, and rightly so, of the high skills levels of leading Australian players. However, few – if any – have been able to better the peerless talents of several of the Leeds squad in an era made glorious by both style and success.

Ray Batten, the magician in the number 13 shirt, and Syd Hynes, conjurer supreme either at centre or, if need be, at scrum-half, were just two men who lit up the winter gloom, week after week, at Headingley and beyond.

Bestriding the sport, from 1967 until his retirement in the late 80s, was John Holmes, a glittering star whether at full-back, centre or in what many view as his best position, stand off half. A real natural, Holmes won many a match for Leeds with his vision and, equally importantly, the ability to turn that vision into reality.

There was no finer illustration of this than in the John Player Final of 1973. The man of the match award went to scrum-half Keith Hepworth for a hard-working, strong-tackling display but it's hard to figure how Holmes' mercurial input could have been overlooked.

The former Kirkstall Boys Club star overcame an edgy start in which he collected, with difficulty, a couple of testing high kicks by Salford centre David Watkins. The Red Devils had already opened their account with a try after only three minutes by loose forward Colin Dixon, who strolled over after a break by second row Bill Kirkbride to give Watkins a simple conversion. Leeds, though, hit back with a penalty for prop Terry Clawson, who put his side ahead with a fine conversion when winger John Atkinson squeezed in at the corner.

Then came the moment that will remain rooted, forever, in the minds of the fans privileged to bear

Continued...

witness.

Vision, again, was crucial, the first example revolving around winger Alan Smith who, hemmed in by the Salford cover, turned the ball inside to his centre Les Dyl. Dyl, in turn, fed Holmes who, in a cameo classic, sidestepped past two defenders before catching winger Atkinson, arm raised, in the corner of his eye. An incredible one-handed pass, from centre field to the Fartown touchline, left stranded Salford defenders gaping as Atkinson collected with typical aplomb and raced over unopposed.

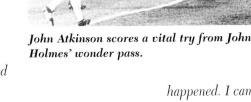

John Atkinson scores a vital try from John Holmes' wonder pass.

One of the greatest of tries and, to show that he was not one to rest on his laurels, Holmes was in brilliant action a minute or two later.

This time the full-back sparked a move from behind his own line, collecting a difficult kick by Salford prop Johnny Ward who was left sprawling before another defender became the victim of a well-timed hand off. Hynes was on hand to take up the running, linking in trademark style with Alan Smith, the move finishing 15 yards short of the Salford tryline.

Watkins, however, reduced the deficit in the first minute of the second half with a penalty, which sparked a couple of abortive drop goal attempts by Alan Hardisty. The Loiners had a real let off when, in the windy conditions, the ball fell over as Watkins was attempting a penalty from 35 yards in front of the posts. The centre, committed, was unable to withdraw and his kick was wayward; as were the Red Devils' tactics in generally spurning a strong supporting wind in the second period. The only further score was a Holmes penalty, the full-back having taken over the duties from the impressive Clawson who had been substituted by David Ward, with Tony Fisher moving to prop. In another highly satisfactory note for Leeds, Ward won each of the last three scrums, the Loiners closing with an 8-5 tally in their favour as Salford, who had prepared for the game with a three-day sojourn to Majorca, and who were on over £100 per man to win, finished second best after having looked likely winners in the opening quarter.

Holmes reflects modestly on that magical moment: 'It just happened. I came from full-back, sidestepped, saw Atky with his arm up and I just let him have it. I could throw a rugby ball a long way through messing about before training. I used to do it with Neil Hague, he'd be at one end of the pitch and we'd sling it to each other, just messing about for something to do. But those 15 minutes or so we spent before training started were invaluable once or twice in match situations. We'd only been messing about in practice but if it came off in a game, you were there.'

Leeds: Holmes; A Smith, Hynes, Dyl, Atkinson; Hardisty, Hepworth; Clawson, Fisher, Jeanes, Haigh, Cookson, Eccles. Subs: Ward, Pickup.
Salford: Charlton; Colloby, Watkins, Hesketh, Richards; Gill, Banner; Ramshaw, J Ward, Mackay, Grice, Kirkbride, Dixon. Subs: P Ward, Davies.
Referee: Mr WH Thompson (Huddersfield)
Leeds: T: Atkinson 2. G: Clawson 2, Holmes.
Salford: T: Dixon. G: Watkins 2.
Attendance: 9,952

smooth. Leeds have struck a bad patch but they have had their share of bad decisions. Have these so-called supporters forgotten how long Leeds were without Atkinson and Smith? There have also been injuries to other key players.

'Another point to remember is that Leeds thrashed Featherstone with 12 men and beat St Helens in the semi-final of the Players' Trophy in one of the finest games seen at Headingley in recent years. We have the best of everything at Headingley, management, committee, chairman, coach, team and ground. It all adds up to the fact that we are the champions, and I believe we still will be at the end of the season.'

The general mood, though, wasn't helped when Leeds went down 22-16 at Castleford, the Loiners battling back in vain from 22-6 adrift despite the dismissal of Clarkson. Amid reports of discontent in the camp, with Ramsey 'seeking a showdown' after being dropped from the Challenge Cup team (Keighley were reported to the Rugby League for an alleged illegal approach to the former Hunslet man) and skipper Alan Hardisty publicly calling for a halt to the habit of swapping players from position to position, a midweek home game against Batley was timely.

A run of four league defeats was ended with the 22-7 win, built on an opening quarter in which 15 points were scored without reply, but many home fans in the 4,247 crowd were less than happy as the Gallant Youths, on their own assessment, had the better of the rest of the game.

The hoodoo, however, was broken. Huddersfield were beaten at home three days later by 22-8 and the visit to Tattersfield saw the Loiners run riot, Atkinson and Hardisty netting four tries each in the 51-0 win.

With the odd pundit pointing out that the vast majority of Leeds' tries were being scored by the backs, and others such as Arthur Haddock lamenting the tendency of forwards to try to play like centres, reaction to Turner's style continued to be mixed.

The tries kept on coming, though, particularly

Loiners Big Match

19 May 1973, Championship Final, Leeds 13 Dewsbury 22, Odsal Stadium, Bradford

1973 was a memorable year for Rugby League. There was sadness at the demise, after 90 years, of Hunslet, although the gloom was lightened by the launch, within days, of New Hunslet as former Parkside 'great' Geoff Gunney and a few friends sought to continue the south Leeds tradition.

On the field, the year was notable for the successes of the so-called 'smaller' clubs. Featherstone Rovers, long a thorn in the side of the allegedly bigger names, won the Challenge Cup with a thumping win over Bradford Northern at Wembley, and later in the year one of the most romantic victories in the history of the code was registered when Bramley lifted their only trophy with a wonderful win over Widnes on the Chemics' own ground in the BBC2 Floodlit Trophy Final.

Against that background it was hardly surprising, perhaps, that Leeds should succumb to Dewsbury in the 1972-73 Championship Final. Dewsbury were then at their apogee and boasted a fine side which included the heady talents of the unrelated Stephensons, Nigel and Mick, singularly effective at centre and hooker respectively. Mick Stephenson had played a central part, a few months earlier, in Great Britain's World Cup win in France, Nigel Stephenson possessed some of the most silky skills in Rugby League, and Allan Agar and Alan Bates were as intelligent a half-back pairing as they come. A pack comprising the likes of props Trevor (Dick) Lowe and former Leeds man Harry Beverley up front, second row pair Geoff Grayshon and John Bates, and Joe Whittington as last man down were not going to be anybody's pushovers and with Adrian Rushton in fine attacking form at full-back Dewsbury posed a real threat to any side.

This was proved by the assault on the Challenge Cup and the Championship by the men from Crown Flatt.

Continued...

Defeat in the Cup semi-final at Headingley at the hands of Bradford Northern was hard to swallow for a side that had yet to return to Wembley after having appeared in the first final at the Empire Stadium, back in 1929, but coach Tommy Smales quickly got his men back on track in the top 16 play-offs.

There were murmurings about the right of a club which had finished eighth in the league to feature in one of the most important games of the season, but players can only deal with what is presented to them and Dewsbury carried all before them en route to the Odsal meeting with Leeds with a 29-14 win over Oldham at Crown Flatt, followed by victories at Featherstone (26-7) and Warrington (12-7). Leeds, who had finished third, had beaten Bramley 45-8, Castleford 30-5 and St Helens (7-2) on their way to Bradford. The Loiners were well aware that they had a challenge on their hands, even if Dewsbury had been beaten 36-9 at the same venue six months earlier in the Yorkshire Cup Final.

In the event fate, which was clearly conspiring in favour of the underdog that year – Leeds United also went down, famously, to Second Division Sunderland in the FA Cup Final – was in control throughout, as were Dewsbury, on a day on which little went right for the Loiners. Other than hooker Tony Fisher's 7-3 pull in the scrums, Leeds players generally had little to be pleased about and there was anguish for stand off Alan Hardisty who was sent off for the first time in his career in the 25th minute for a high tackle on John Bates. Leeds, at that stage, were 7-2 down and as Hardisty relates in Paul Hardisty's book 'Alan

The end is nigh as Hardisty walks.

Continued...

for the backs and Langley raced over for four as Hunslet were disposed of 39-5 at Headingley. And, despite the doom-mongers, Leeds actually rose back to the top of the table, a point ahead of Warrington who admittedly had three games in hand, with a 13-5 victory at Hull which owed much to a typically glorious Atkinson try in which the flyer collected a loose ball 50 yards out, beat two men with a scorching burst and held off two others on the touchline before touching down behind the posts. Hynes inexplicably failed with the simple conversion but the score put Leeds in front in a game in which Langley, at full-back, shone with a series of takes and his courage in pouncing on the loose ball.

Keighley, and former Loiner Albert Eyre in particular, posed problems before going down 19-12 at Lawkholme Lane, but York were unable to match the Loiners despite going 2-0 ahead when Steve Quinn kicked an early goal after Hardisty's kick off failed to travel 10 yards.

The 32-4 win in which Alan Smith and Atkinson scored two tries each was ideal preparation for the John Player Final against Salford at Fartown, Huddersfield. Keith Hepworth was the man of the match but the game will be remembered for a try by Atkinson, the only player to have taken part in each of Leeds' 10 finals of the previous five years, who raced in at the corner from a majestic long ball by Holmes.

Turner, despite the critics, now had two trophies under his belt but a visit to St Helens

Hardisty – Rugby League Maestro': 'We were getting beat, and you can sense it, Dewsbury were going very well. I thought to myself that I had to do something. Then they did a move, which I'd seen, a 'tap penalty-three run round thing,' finishing with a pass to John Bates, running out wide. I thought if I could get there and take an interception it could turn the game.

'I set off, I'm going like a train and I miss it by about a yard. I stick my hand out and we both went up in the air. It must have looked shocking but if I'd curled my fist I'd have killed him. The referee just went, 'off!' The changing rooms, then, were right at the top of the Odsal bowl so I had to walk right through the crowd, with a copper on each side, and as I walked up they were all spitting on me and calling me all the names under the sun. That was a hell of a do.'

The Loiners momentarily brushed aside the loss of Hardisty, Syd Hynes landing a drop goal, but a touchdown for Agar and, with only four minutes of the second half gone, a second try for Mick Stephenson, presented coach Derek Turner with real problems.

And the end has already been announced for coach Derek Turner who exhorts his troops to end his reign in a blaze of glory.

There was a brief rally when second row pair Graham Eccles and Phil Cookson crossed within three minutes of each other but the task became almost impossible when Nigel Stephenson ghosted over midway through the second period, adding his fourth conversion of the afternoon. And Les Dyl's late try was scant consolation for Leeds, leaving Turner, who had gone into the game aware that his services would not be required at Headingley the following season, cutting a forlorn figure.

Leeds: Holmes; A Smith, Hynes, Dyl, Atkinson; Hardisty, Hepworth; Clawson, Fisher, Clarkson, Cookson, Eccles, Haigh. Subs: Langley, Ward.
Dewsbury: Rushton; Ashcroft, Clark, N Stephenson, Day; Agar, A Bates; Beverley, M Stephenson, Lowe, Grayshon, J Bates, Whittington.
Leeds: T: Eccles, Cookson, Dyl. G: Clawson. DG: Hynes.
Dewsbury: T: M Stephenson (2), Agar, N Stephenson. G: N Stephenson 4. DG: N Stephenson.
Referee: Mr H Hunt (Prestbury)
Attendance: 18,889

just three days after the victory over Salford was asking too much and the Loiners went down 19-12, the dismissal of Fred Pickup on the half hour and the absence of Hepworth after seven minutes with a head injury effectively ending the Loiners' hopes of retaining the League Leaders trophy.

Keighley and Batley were both dispensed with, Keighley again battling hard against a side lacking Hardisty and Hynes but struggling to contain Atkinson, who netted two tries. Batley, meanwhile, couldn't prevent Langley – rated the best 'stand in' in the game – scoring another hat trick,

As Lewis Jones confirmed that he would play in a friendly at Headingley in May in aid of the Alan Smith Testimonial – £4,500 was raised for the popular winger – and Leeds pulled out of a proposed tour of Australia claiming uncertainty over financial guarantees, the league campaign closed with a 30-17 defeat at Featherstone, a 21-10 win over Bramley and a 10-10 draw at York, before Leeds announced their intent on retaining the Championship with a 45-8 hammering of Bramley in the first round of the play-offs in which Atkinson and Smith scored two tries each.

The mid-season tremors, however, had had their effect and, prior to the second round game against Castleford (a mere four days after the Bramley fixture) Leeds announced the appointment of Eric Ashton as coach. The former Wigan captain and coach was due to take over on 1 June and Turner agreed to remain at the helm for the rest of the season, adding that he would then focus his attentions on his removal business in Ossett.

Another ex-Cas man, Hardisty, ensured that the men from Wheldon Road's interest in the title ended there and then with a superlative performance, scoring a try and creating several others in the 30-5 verdict. And a huge defensive effort, plus a Hepworth try and goals by Hynes and Clawson, helped Leeds reach their second successive Championship Final with a 7-2 semi-final win over St Helens.

Atkinson, meanwhile, finished the season with 39 tries in all games, including 36 for Leeds, to become the first UK-born player since the war to top the try scoring list in successive seasons.

It had been a strange season in which a coach lost his job for adopting a forward-based style of rugby, the general opinion being that the backs were starved of the ball. Yet the statistics show a record points haul by the Loiners; with the backs boasting the lions' share of the tries. Rugby League can often be an impossible game to understand.

A Loiner Looks Back

Phil Cookson

'They wanted me running wide off such as John Holmes and Ray Batten, and getting about. It was absolutely marvellous, they were wonderful ball handlers.

'Obviously your timing had to be good, one of us would call it or I'd call it from the back and see what was in front of us. We called one move "the joker." At Wembley, in 1978, St Helens had blanked me out a little bit. I just bowed out of the game for 10 minutes or so, just did a bit of tackling up front and then, when the time was right, I shouts to Holmesy again, "John, Joker," and that was it, it was on. We got things like that right in training but you have to put it on at the right time.

'Billy Ramsey had a move with Ray Batten where he came up on the blind side, 10 or 15 yards inside the touchline, after Ray had sold a couple of dummies. These things were practiced, they didn't just happen, and the positioning had to be exactly right. And John and Ray were so good that they could slip a ball from any position. They were clever players. Holmesy would see a weakness in the defence and he'd say, "come a yard from me" or "come inside on this one" and it was just a thing you did after a while, you followed him. You had to position yourself right because you could either get him killed or kill yourself, but that's how it used to be. We worked at it and it paid off big time.'

Phil Cookson strives to make headway against the Dewsbury defence.

Derek Turner – Villain or Victim?

Derek 'Rocky' Turner was appointed as Leeds coach in the summer of 1969, following the departure of Roy Francis the previous autumn. The former Great Britain, Oldham and Wakefield Trinity player had cut his coaching teeth instilling the 'hard man' style of play that he had previously demonstrated out on the pitch, turning Castleford into one of the toughest sides around. At the time of his dismissal in 1973, Turner was criticised for developing a team that played an 'uninteresting' style of rugby, yet the number of points scored and the silverware in the Headingley trophy cabinet did not seem to bear this out, so what are the opinions of the players who served under him?

Graham Eccles:
'Derek Turner didn't care what he called people. He used to say, "You're only as good as your last game." The thing is, he wasn't a bloke who just said it, he meant it. If you didn't do what Derek Turner told you, you were out, international or not. And if you did what he told you, you were back in the team.

'I think I was Derek Turner's type of player. I don't think he liked players who didn't get involved a lot, who tended to just come in when they wanted to. He wanted 100 per cent triers, he'd say, "He tried, so why didn't everybody else?" That's fair enough, really.
'You could ask Derek Turner, "Why am I not in the first team?" and he'd say, "Because you're not doing what I told you to do." He was straightforward and I respected that. Others took it to heart and didn't like him for it.
'His tactical approach was simple. He wanted the forwards to get on top in the first 20 minutes. He said, "Do that and the backs will get you winning money." And he expected his players to be hard. I took a bad knock against St Helens once and our physio Eric Lewis said, "Graham will have to come off, he's seeing double." Turner said, "Just get him back on and tell him to tackle both of them!"'

John Atkinson:
'I scored a lot of tries under Derek Turner, including in his last season, and they said he was a bad coach.
'Derek wanted me to run like Barry Parker, a powerful straight runner in the Jack Austin mould. It was a bit of a shock at that training session. I said, "You want me to play like Barry?" There were a few players standing around, they all turned round and walked off thinking, "Fancy saying that."
'Derek was different to what we'd been used to. He used to say to Smithy, "He's an arrogant bastard is that Atky, but I always pick him first!" That was the quality of the man. I liked him and got on with him and how could I argue when I was still scoring tries?'

Derek Turner covers as Norman Herbert tackles Gilbert Benausse in England's 18-6 victory over France at Leeds in November 1962. Before the decade was out Turner would be in charge at Headingley.

Mick Clark:

'I left Leeds for Keighley because of Derek Turner. He'd just arrived and we'd won our last match by around 50 points. Derek pulled me out of the next training session, I thought "He's going to say something right intelligent here." What he said was, "The Chairman has asked me to have a word with you about your tackling." The Chairman, I knew, never interfered with anything. I said, "We won 50-nil didn't we?"

'I didn't feel as if I should be doing another 20 tackles when we were 50-nil up, and there hadn't been a lot of tackling to do because Mick Shoebottom had been running around madly all the time tackling them before they could get to us. I'd had to say, "Come on he's showing us up here", but we couldn't stop him.

'Anyway, that's what did it, I thought I might as well move on. When I look back I was stupid really, I should have given Derek a chance and taken time to see what he did. But I asked for a transfer; I'd seen this little job at Keighley, as player/coach, so I went to Lawkholme Lane.'

Steve Pitchford:

'Derek Turner was one of the most successful coaches because he won cups. But he was an ignorant man. He had his way, it was his way, and he wasn't bothered. He wasn't a favourite of mine and I wasn't a favourite of his. He didn't like my style, probably because I didn't try to knock everybody out.

'He brought a lot of forwards in; some were good, some were shite. He brought Bobby Haigh from Wakefield, a great forward and a nice man who scored a lot of tries off Ray Batten. And he brought Keith Hepworth and Alan Hardisty. But he had a fixed thing about what a forward should be. A forward, in his opinion, should smack everybody else out.

'He also had a thing about shifting teams around to suit his squad. He played players who weren't fit because he wanted the big nobs in. When I did actually get a game, we had six prop forwards in the pack and a prop forward in the centre. Derek Turner wanted you to break jaws. Fortunately I never had to get into that, there were players there who did the job so I didn't have to.

'The Leeds public had been brought up on the three-quarters scoring tries, with your Atkinsons cutting through. Previously it had been emphasised to the forwards that after two or three tackles we had to get out of the way; John Holmes is coming. Turner changed the whole situation, he brought forwards in, such as Geoff Clarkson who had a great game against us in the Leigh final but who wasn't the Leeds style of player.'

Alan Smith:

'Derek Turner would always say that John Atkinson had a chip on his shoulder and John was always critical of Derek's training techniques. There was no love lost at any time. But Derek was not that daft, he knew he had to have the best winger of the decade on his left wing whether he liked him or he didn't.

'When Barry Parker came it gave Derek great delight – and John used to get so very, very offended – when Derek used to say, "I want you to run like this Parker lad." John's face would be "Am I hearing this?" Derek's reputation preceded him. His tough antics at Castleford followed him to Leeds. He had no training techniques and it was such a contrast to what we'd been used to with Roy Francis, where everything was organised and timed, with programmed training methods. With Derek it was just touch and pass and old style training, as maybe Derek used to train. But we'd all train hard because we all knew we had to sustain it. We still did our sprinting, but we didn't have the same intense training which Roy instilled into us. If that helped sustain Derek Turner's era then Derek must have been delighted because he had some great players with him. And he could spot good footballers. He loved the lads who could mix it and he loved Mick Shoebottom who was maybe Derek Turner's ultimate player.

'He was very upset by Shoey's injury. Barry Seabourne moved on and what did Derek do? He put another lease of life into the side with the Hepworth/Hardisty combination, with Alan Hardisty as a contrast to Shoey. What an artist! Keith Hepworth and Hardisty were almost like Shoey and Seabourne and we backs and the forwards had the benefit of being amongst international players again.'

Les Dyl:

'Derek Turner said that if you weren't fit on Thursday he couldn't pick you on Saturday. Other coaches would be happy to give you a fitness test on the morning of the game but he saw it differently. He frightened me to death. My little old Mini broke down one night in Castleford on my way to training. It meant getting two buses so I phoned up to say that I wouldn't be able to make it. Our kitman Arthur Crowther usually answered the phone but, on this occasion, Derek picked it up. I said, "It's Les Dyl, I've got problems with the car, it's broken down." Derek said, "Les, get a train, get a plane, come by helicopter. Just get here." I said, "Yes, Derek." So I got two buses and I got there at ten to nine, just before the finish, but at least I'd made it.'

Tension shows in the dugout.

Bill Ramsey:

'Derek's idea was to avoid mistakes and don't move the ball about too much, which seemed silly. We were capable of scoring points from any part of any field at any time and why Derek wanted it that way I've no idea.

'He didn't want me playing for him, he said I was no good, but then we go back a long way. I put nine stitches in his ear when he played for Wakefield against Hunslet; he threatened to do all sorts of things to me in retaliation.

'When he took his first session at Headingley I was working for a cooker manufacturer. I'd been in Scotland, drove back and got to Headingley about 5.30 pm, which is early. Of course I had my working suit on. Derek was under the impression that that's how I arrived for training every time. He took a ride out of me and made fun of me in front of all the other players but I got on with it, I played for Leeds.

'The public saw Turner off, they'd had enough of him after being used to a different type of football. A lot of the players had moved and at that time there were quite a few young players who were good enough but needed time to develop; they seemed to get extended runs when they weren't really doing it right.'

Phil Cookson:

'I liked Derek Turner. He gave me my chance, he had faith in me and I repaid him. He was a hard man to work for, he probably wasn't the greatest of coaches, and he wasn't scientific; it was just plain hard work.

'But the fact that the leading try scorers in the season he was sacked were all backs doesn't back up the complaints, does it? He had a different style to Roy Francis. I remember at Cas they used to laugh at the Leeds pack, yet Leeds were getting results despite people saying we were soft. Turner joined Leeds from Castleford, of course, and what did he do? He put some hard men in the pack – and they still got open rugby.

'I liked Derek Turner and I liked Eric Ashton, who followed, him. Eric was a gentleman and I couldn't find a problem. Derek ruled with an iron fist. Whatever was in his mind would come straight out and some didn't like it. A spade was a spade and that was it. He wasn't liked by quite a few players but you can't please everybody, it's impossible. I think it got to Derek, obviously, because he never really got involved again. It's a shame really but that's how it goes, it's a funny game.'

11. A SEASON IN THE DARK

The 1973-74 season was one of readjustment following the departure of Derek Turner.

Leeds, handed a much tougher fixture list with the reintroduction of two divisions, finished third, as in the previous year.

After summer success on their own patch in the Wills Sevens, won for the first time with victories over Halifax (21-18), Dewsbury (17-6) and, in the final, St Helens by 21-18, one major trophy – the Yorkshire Cup – was won under new coach Eric Ashton who was presented with real logistical problems when a power strike was launched in the autumn.

Ashton, who worked in Wales, faced a testing journey to training and his difficulties increased when industrial action forced Leeds to chase around for training facilities.

The season opened with one major change. Hunslet, old rivals in the Lazenby Cup, had folded, to be reborn as New Hunslet. Bramley, who were to gain glory later in the season by winning the BBC2 Floodlit Trophy, stepped forward in their place and were unable to deny Leeds as stand off Alan Hardisty, reappointed as captain, scored a hat trick in the 35-10 win.

Leeds, meanwhile, had offered to field their A team in Division Two should New Hunslet fail to get off the ground. Said Leeds chairman Jack Myerscough: 'If a New Hunslet club comes into being we will be delighted. But if not, we would like to have the chance to run another team in Division Two.

'We have a strong second team and feel they would hold their own. Our two teams could play

A Loiner Looks Back

Ray Batten

Ray Batten, relatively slight of build for a loose forward, began Rugby League life as a scrum-half or stand-off but, lacking pace, was moved to loose forward by his Under 17s coach at Heworth. With a strong pedigree which included his uncle Eric and grandfather Billy, it was perhaps not surprising that Ray Batten was such a success. His qualities, however, were in a different category to those of his family seniors. Quite simply, he was the architect rather than the builder or the decorator; even if the portcullis or the gilded ceiling would have been of the highest quality.

'Some people thought I might be like Don Fox at number seven. My main thing, I suppose, was that I carried the ball in two hands. I can't really explain my ball handling; I suppose it was a gift and maybe the fact that I wasn't fast enough helped me to develop the rest of my game. I played from four years old, so that could also have been a factor. And I watched clever players when I was younger, such as Jeff Stevenson and Tommy Smales, and Brian McTigue.'

A long way from being a half back. Batten, one of the most creative loose forwards in the history of the game, wears the 13 on his shorts almost as a badge of honour.

at Headingley on alternate Saturdays and I am certain there would be no shortage of support.'

Mr Myerscough perhaps revealed, in that statement, the Loiners' preference for Saturday rugby over Sunday, which was by now the favoured day for football by most clubs. Oldham, though, appeared to be a day late for the first Division One game of the season, when Syd Hynes scored four of his side's 10 tries in a 46-2 win.

In a busy opening spell, Leeds overcame Hull in a two-leg Floodlit Trophy Preliminary Round tie, former Hunslet full-back and captain David Marshall landing seven goals from seven attempts on his debut. Marshall was handed the kicking duties following the transfer to Oldham of prop Terry Clawson, who had asked for a move as he was working in Burnley. Scrum-half Keith Hepworth showed the same kind of form, in the first leg against the Airlie Birds, that had helped Great Britain retrieve the Ashes three years earlier.

The Loiners slipped at Warrington, 10-4, between those games before having the chance of exacting early revenge over Dewsbury for the Championship Final defeat.

The champions travelled to Headingley for the first round Yorkshire Cup clash without hooker Mick Stephenson, bound for Penrith. Leeds, no strangers to being the side the rest want to knock off the perch, observed in their programme notes: 'A welcome for the champions. The last match between Dewsbury and Leeds – at Odsal Stadium last May – was

Loiners Big Match

20 October 1973, Yorkshire Cup Final, Leeds 7 Wakefield Trinity 2, Headingley

Alan Hardisty parades the Yorkshire Cup.

Wakefield Trinity coach Neil Fox had no complaints after his side lost a pulsating clash. The Trinity legend, however, did gently make the point that the pressure put on the Yorkshire County committee by sponsors Esso to stage the final at Headingley gave Leeds an advantage.

Fox, interviewed by the Yorkshire Post, said: 'Ground advantage is supposed to be worth five points start in a cup-tie, and that was about it.'

Wakefield's coach, however, was equally adamant that his side had had the chances to win the match and, in the final analysis, resolute defence by the Loiners ultimately won the day.

Trinity were denied on several occasions, including in the early stages when strong cover defence persuaded winger David Smith – a future Loiner – to turn inside when there appeared to be some space out wide.

John Holmes also performed well at full-back, pulling off a try-saving tackle on Wakefield centre Terry Crook late in the first half.

Holmes was switched to centre at half time following

Continued...

an injury to winger John Langley, David Marshall taking over at the back and putting in his customary strong tackling stint.

Leeds' key figure, however, was scrum-half Keith Hepworth who was an incontestable man of the match and picked up each of the 15 votes from journalists present at the match.

Hepworth created the only try of the game, after 14 minutes, when he broke on a typical diagonal run before freeing centre Syd Hynes who, in turn, sent Langley in at the corner.

That score, which Holmes – who had sliced an earlier penalty attempt wide – was unable to convert, put the Loiners ahead after Wakefield had opened with a Crook penalty, awarded after prop Geoff Clarkson had been deemed guilty of a foul. Stand off Alan Hardisty went close a couple of minutes later and from that position Hynes landed a drop goal from 35 yards.

Hooker Mick Morgan responded for Trinity with a darting raid which petered out when he miscued his kick, and Leeds were tested when centre Les Dyl had to pull off a try-saving tackle on second row David Knowles.

But, in heavy rain, Leeds finished the half the stronger, Trinity full-back Geoff Wraith having to withdraw after cutting his head in denying Hepworth.

Marshall made an immediate impact on his introduction for the second half, slamming over a 42-yard penalty within three minutes of the resumption. And despite a 5-2 pull in the scrums in Wakefield's favour, that was the final score of the game. Trinity's Barry Parker was brought back, when clear, for a forward pass and Hynes was hauled down short by Les Sheard, who had replaced Wraith. But neither side could breach the opposing defence.

Leeds duly collected their winning pay packets, containing £65 per man, thanks largely to Hepworth.

Said Fox: 'We could have won if our finishing had been a bit sharper once or twice in the first half, but Leeds did not give much away. Tactically, our plan to keep the ball away from the Leeds wings worked well except for that one flash by Hepworth. I don't think anyone could have held him, the way he played today.'

Leeds: Holmes; Langley, Hynes, Dyl, Atkinson; Hardisty, Hepworth; Jeanes, Ward, Clarkson, Eccles, Cookson, Batten. Subs: Marshall, Ramsey.

Wakefield: Wraith; Smith, Crook, Hegarty, Parker; Topliss, Bonnar; Valentine, Morgan, Bratt, Knowles, Endersby, Holmes. Subs: Sheard, Ballantyne.

Referee: Mr MJ Naughton (Widnes)

Leeds: T: Langley. G: Marshall. DG: Hynes.

Wakefield: G: Crook.

Attendance: 7,621

Leeds RLFC 1973-74.

No way through for Leeds in the Challenge Cup quarter-final defeat at Crown Flatt, Dewsbury

one they will talk about for years at Dewsbury's Crown Flatt home, for it ended with their team becoming Rugby League champions for the first time in the club's history. Dewsbury had made only one other appearance in the Championship Final, and that was back in 1947, when they were beaten by Wigan, but in the Final of 1973 they started and finished the game in the manner worthy of League Champions, and as they pay their first visit to Headingley today, since that game, it gives the Leeds Club and supporters the chance to congratulate the present Dewsbury side upon gaining their well-earned victory by a display which was as entertaining as it was convincing.

'Dewsbury may now find, as Leeds have done previously, that some teams whom they disposed of comfortably in the past will be coming at them just that bit harder this season. Most teams pull out a greater effort when meeting the Champions, for a win over the reigning titleholders brings an added spice to be derived from any other victory. Judging by Dewsbury's excellent team spirit last season, this will be a challenge their players will meet cheerfully, and despite the loss of that fine forward Mick Stephenson if the Crown Flatt side can build upon the good football which coach Tommy Smales helped to establish last season, they may be hard to remove from their lofty position at the top.'

Dewsbury actually improved on their league record of the previous season, rising to sixth compared to eighth in 1972-73; but with the side finishing top of Division One being declared champions, in preference to the old play-off system, the Crown Flatt men were some way shy of retaining the title.

Leeds, meanwhile, were convincing winners

A Loiner Looks Back

Steve Pitchford

'It was a great team to play in during the 1970s and you could have a laugh at the same time, even on the pitch really. The business day was the 80 minutes out there but there were no rules and regulations to stop you having a bit of fun and we made a lot of landlords rich. There was a rule that we used to get paid on a Thursday night and everybody, the secretary included, had to go for a drink, even if it was for only one or two. There might be 20 or 30 of us would go out. The Old Sheepscar was one, then the Smiths Arms. Or we'd go to the Town Hall Tavern and there would be other teams in there as well. The place was full of Rugby League players. It was great.'

at the first stage of the bid to retain the Yorkshire Cup, despite falling behind to a fine early try by Dewsbury centre Nigel Stephenson. The Loiners went on to post eight unanswered tries in a victory as emphatic as had been the previous season's final, centre Les Dyl scorching over for a brace and the remaining touchdowns going to wingers Alan Smith and John Atkinson, second row Bob Haigh, stand off Derek Edwards, prop David Jeanes and second row Phil Cookson.

Centre Syd Hynes, while unable to get on the score-sheet, was in inspired early season form and Brian Batty of the Daily Mail enthused: 'The most encouraging start to the season is the obvious sign that Syd Hynes has recaptured the form that earned him a regular Great Britain place.

'The talented Leeds centre has had a rough time with referees and injuries in recent seasons but he believes he is a different player today. He has shed half a stone, regained his speed and is anxious to prove his ability again. This must be welcome news for the Great Britain selectors, particularly with a vacancy in the centre following the apparent retirement of World Cup star John Walsh.

'The information will be received with far less enthusiasm in Australia where I remember Hynes playing some great rugby in helping Britain regain the Ashes. He touched top form and proved he was fearless when he retaliated against big Artie Beetson to be sent off in the Second Test when Britain had the game won. He tangled with Australia again in the World Cup a few months later and was dismissed in the final after a clash with Billy Smith.

'But the most upsetting incident was when he got his marching orders at Wembley when Leeds lost to Leigh in 1971. I asked Syd if he felt he could live down this murky side of his chequered past. 'As you get older you learn to think twice before getting involved and while I still play it hard I won't be looking for any trouble,' the 29-year-old Hynes replied. 'I feel a different person now and just as sharp as when we toured Australia. It's certainly my aim to try and win a place against Australia and make a second tour. I just hope the selectors have not forgotten me and will give me a chance.'

'If the selectors need any convincing after

Sunday Rugby

A huge crowd packed Headingley for the first Sunday fixture. A trio of defenders deny Wakefield in the 11-5 Challenge Cup quarter final win on 5 March 1972.

Leeds were both the slowest and the fastest of the 30 professional clubs in membership of the Rugby Football League to embrace Sunday football.
Illegal until the mid-sixties, Sunday play was opposed by many players and supporters, all of whom had the support of the Lord's Day Observance Society.
They also had the backing, initially, of the Rugby

Continued...

Football League, which had from the days of the Northern Union contained as one of its byelaws the ruling: 'Professional Football shall not be played on Sundays in Great Britain.'
However, the RFL had been happy to allow Great Britain to play in France on Sundays for several years and, once taken on board as a possibility, Sunday rugby quickly became the accepted norm throughout the north.
Except at Leeds. Despite – or perhaps because of – having played a 'trial match' in November 1966, the Headingley board resisted playing home games on the Sabbath for several years, insisting that Saturday football was what the fans desired.
The rest of the sport went ahead with the revolutionary change during the 1967-68 campaign, although how many clubs abided by a ruling that a 'free' gate be kept open, to remain within the law of the land, remains murky.
Leeds continued to stage their home games on Saturday afternoon until 5 March 1972 when the board finally bowed to the inevitable and staged the third round Challenge Cup tie with Wakefield Trinity on Sunday. The Loiners were rewarded with a gate of 20,855; 5,000 higher than the previous best for the campaign, over 15,000 having been attracted to the Boxing Day clash against the same opposition.
Leeds, however, continued to rail against the trend and it wasn't until the mid-seventies that Sunday football became the norm at Headingley.

Hynes' four-try start to the season they might care to consider his club skipper's views. 'I rate Syd the world's No. 1 centre on this form,' says Hardisty. 'He really looks his old self and he's got the skill and the speed to trouble the Aussies. 'I can't see how the selectors can ignore him.'

'And neither can I for only a surprising slump in form or injury should affect his chances. For we need his skill and strength in the middle for what could be a perfectly balanced partnership with Salford's powerful Chris Hesketh.'

Nigel Stephenson and Brian Murrell show concern, and Allan Agar and John Langley appear to adopt a more philosophical stance, as John Holmes is stretchered off with knee ligament damage at Dewsbury.

Hynes wasn't the only Loiners threequarter in fine form and the qualities in the Leeds backline were recognised by the Yorkshire selectors, who opted for all four – Hynes, Smith, Atkinson and John Holmes – for the game against Lancashire.

Leeds had more Heavy Woollen opposition, in the shape of Batley, in the second round of the Yorkshire Cup, and again there was a 25-point margin between the sides, the Loiners having much the better of the second half to secure a 27-2 win at Mount Pleasant after having been held to 5-2 at the break. Loose forward Ray Batten, so often the creator rather than the finisher, latched onto a pass to score Leeds' only first half try after a five-man move, Bill Ramsey extended the lead early in the second half and three tries in six minutes, by Phil Cookson, Atkinson and Hynes, sealed a win much harder-earned than the final scoreline would indicate; Holmes landed six goals.

That success brought tougher opposition to Headingley for the semi-final, Bradford Northern arriving as a team determined to put behind them the memory of the previous season's heavy Wembley defeat at the hands of

Headingley Hero

John Holmes

Born not much more than a stone's throw from Headingley, John Holmes was the epitome of the local boy made good.

A cultured stand-off half who also featured impressively at full-back and centre for much of his career, Holmes was the master of the incisive pass and the pivot around which the various Leeds sides of the late 1960s and 1970s flourished.

After joining Leeds from Kirkstall Boys, at the age of 16, on 23 March 1968, Holmes quickly became a fixture in the first team, initially at full-back, where he had excelled with Kirkstall.

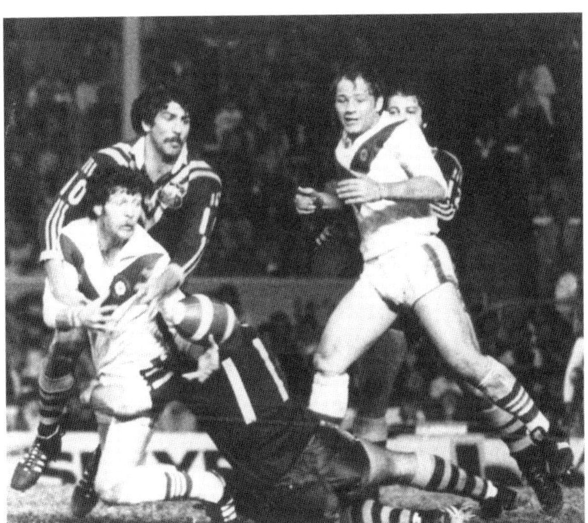

John Holmes fires out a textbook pass against Australia, while David Ward looks on, on the 1979 tour.

His impact was immediate. The youngster netted 23 points, with a try and 10 goals, on his debut in the Lazenby Cup game at Hunslet on 12 August 1968, and in a glittering 20-season career, Holmes amassed 1,554 points with 153 tries and 553 goals from 626 appearances.

There was, however, much, much more to Holmes' game than the scoring of points.

A quick-fire intelligence more than made up for a perceived lack of pace, and the ability to carve open the tightest defence with an astute Rugby League brain – plus the facility to float out the necessary

Continued...

Featherstone Rovers. The Loiners had, nine days earlier, won 34-12 at Odsal in the first round of the Players No 6 Competition but the opposition was in entirely different fettle at Headingley and it took a strong defensive effort to procure a place in the final. Leeds won 10-5, thanking their lucky stars that Northern full-back Eddie Tees landed only one goal from five attempts and that winger Mike Lamb, a former Loiner, knocked on with the tryline begging.

Tries for second row Bob Haigh – with a blistering turn of pace – and Holmes scored the Leeds tries with Marshall landing a goal and Hynes adding a drop goal.

In a season packed with knock-out competitions, Leeds travelled to Odsal a little over a month later for the first round of the ill-fated Captain Morgan Trophy, which lasted for only one season and was a straight knockout competition involving first round survivors in the Lancashire and Yorkshire Cups. Hardisty scored two tries and a drop goal in the 34-12 romp, Marshall notched a try and six goals, Hynes kicked a drop goal and David Ward, Haigh and Dyl grabbed the remaining touchdowns to leave Northern way adrift.

The in-form Hardisty followed up his success at Bradford with a hat trick in the second round 32-21 win over Swinton but Warrington, the eventual, and one-and-only Captain Morgan Trophy winners, beat Leeds at Headingley in an abrasive semi-final in which Alex Murphy was carried off after finding himself on the wrong end of an altercation with Tony Fisher.

finely-weighted pass – made Holmes one of the leading half-backs in a generation in which Great Britain selectors were generally spoilt for choice.
John Holmes earned 20 caps, including six as substitute, between 1971 and 1982.
He made a huge impact in Great Britain's successful assault on the 1972 World Cup, scoring 26 points with two tries and 10 goals against New Zealand.
It is, however, as a Leeds player that he is best remembered, and many good judges will insist that he is the finest player to have worn the blue and amber.
Holmes featured prominently in the Leeds sides of the 1971, 1972, 1977 and 1978 Challenge Cup Finals. The first two finished in disappointing defeat against Leigh and St Helens respectively, but Holmes had a huge impact in the 1977 success over Widnes, confirming his under-rated defensive prowess with a try-saving tackle, in the early stages, on Widnes winger Dennis O'Neill which helped pave the way for the 16-7 victory. And his late drop goal, achieved despite a two-man tackle, helped set up the 14-12 verdict, 12 months later, against St Helens.
The maestro also collected Championship medals in 1968-69 and 1971-72, League Leaders trophy medals in 1968-69, 1969-70 and 1971-72, and an array of other medals in the Yorkshire Cup, Yorkshire League, Regal (formerly John Player) Trophy, the Floodlit Trophy and the Premiership. And his very late try at Central Park in the summer of 1975 helped Leeds break a duck with a first-ever victory in the Wigan Sevens.
His team-mates were not slow to recognise his talents and Graham Eccles rates him as Leeds' best player: 'If only for the number of games he played, and swapping from full-back to centre to stand-off to second row even. I think people often overlook the tremendous amount of tackling he did. And when he gave a ball he gave it flat on the line, as they were tackling him, so he put the player through the gap. He didn't stand two yards back and throw a 30 yard pass, he was prepared to go in where he could get hurt – which did happen – he never shirked.'
It's a view shared by David Ward, who took over from Holmes as Leeds captain in the mid-seventies. He says: 'John Holmes was an all-time great, his playing ability second to none. Holmesy wouldn't take his coat off until 25 minutes before kick-off time, he was very much a calming influence. If I wanted to strangle one of our team mates during a match he would say, 'leave him, I'll have a word.' That might have been the right approach for that young junior. Mind you, I'd also say, 'and make sure you tell him, Holmesy!' He and I worked closely together. And when he said he wanted the ball, he got it. An all time great.'
Adds Neil Hague: 'John was a tremendous reader of a game. He'd spot something which no one else could see and he'd tell you to go with him. You went because he'd always be proved right, he would create a gap and you'd be put through.'

The nature of the defeat, which followed a disappointing exit in the BBC2 Floodlit Trophy at Hull KR, where the Robins gained retribution for a 35-2 league defeat less than three weeks earlier, led to calls for Ashton to strengthen the side – despite the fact that only two league matches had been lost, at Wakefield and at Warrington.

Other than in the Yorkshire Cup, Leeds were unable to quite reproduce their impressive league form in knockout competitions. The Loiners had to work hard before beating Batley away 18-7 in the first round of the Challenge Cup, courtesy of two Phil Cookson tries, a John Langley touchdown and a try by Geoff Clarkson, with Marshall landing three conversions. Eventual champions Salford were accounted for 10-6 at Headingley in the second round, Dyl and Alan Smith netting the tries and Marshall and Hynes (with a drop goal) adding goals, but Dewsbury proved to be a step too far in the Crown Flatt quarter-final, limiting Leeds to a

Syd and Norma Hynes share the joy of broken legs.

win 23-10 and bring the curtain down on a season that, apart from the Yorkshire Cup success, never quite got going.

Highlights in the league, however, included a 10-match unbeaten run from October to March but the bread and butter fare ended limply with three defeats in four days, the opposition scoring 17 points on each occasion. Bramley won 17-13 at Headingley on 12 April, Castleford 17-11, also at Headingley, the following day, and there was a 17-10 victory for Whitehaven at the Recreation Grounds on 15 April.

Marshall penalty in the 9-2 defeat.

The Loiners also fell slightly short in the Championship play-offs. Keighley put up a strong challenge in the first round and should have been ahead at the break before conceding four tries to Langley, two to Atkinson and one to Batten as Leeds prevailed 31-12. Widnes had the better of much of the second round clash and were 7-3 ahead before Leeds, inspired by Hepworth, at last took a grip with 17 points in the last 17 minutes. Hepworth, bested by Reggie Bowden in the first half, scored the try that brought Leeds back into the game, and Jeanes, Cookson and Dyl also nipped over with Marshall kicking two goals.

Leeds experienced the other side of the coin in the Headingley semi-final against St Helens. Tries by Cookson and Langley, both converted by Marshall, put the Loiners 10-3 up at the interval but the Saints, inspired by full-back Geoff Pimblett, dominated the second half to

A Loiner Looks Back

Les Dyl

'Graham Eccles used to hate the big money Rugby Union signings. We all did but Graham really had it in for them. He really used to get among the lads in the Salford pack.'

Salford's backs seem to be doing most of the defensive work as Leeds mount an attack through David Ward and Phil Cookson. Graham Eccles didn't like ex-Rugby Union forwards – perhaps the Red Devils' packmen were keeping out of the way.

12. FRANCIS RETURNS

After the relative disappointment of the 1973-74 campaign, Leeds sought a return to the glory days of the late 1960s with the reappointment of Roy Francis as coach.

Francis returned to the hot seat as Eric Ashton, worn down by travel difficulties from his work in north Wales for training and for matches, parted company with the Loiners.

A storm broke out when Headingley folk hero Lewis Jones was overlooked for the role of A team coach, Castleford's John Sheridan being handed the task of nurturing the young talent at Headingley. And, also off the field, 74-years-young Arthur Crowther retired after a 55-year stint as a jack-of-all-trades which included the job of kit man in his later years.

There was some rebuilding to do on the field. Alan Hardisty headed Down Under, accepting a three-year contract with Australian country club Rockhampton as player/coach. And Hardisty's former Cas colleague Derek Edwards, who had never quite settled at Headingley, moved to Keighley on a free transfer.

Leeds picked up what had been an elusive trophy during the summer, winning the Wigan Sevens. A try by John Holmes in the last 30 seconds snatched a 16-11 victory over the hosts in the final. Holmes had scored two tries, and Syd Hynes kicked a goal, in establishing an 8-0 lead, with Hynes crossing as Wigan fought back. The success, in which Leeds also beat Wigan B 17-10 and Salford 16-11, was notable for the performance of 18-year-old Peter Judson, a surprise call-up from the Colts and A teams.

Apart from the Lazenby Cup, retained with the 42-4 win over Bramley, Leeds picked up one major trophy; and they left it late, collecting the last available piece of silverware available.

Mick Harrison makes the hard yards in the Challenge Cup semi-final defeat by Warrington.

That was the Premiership Trophy, contested by the sides finishing in the top eight in the First Division.

There was an instant exit from the BBC2 Floodlit Trophy, St Helens easing to a 30-6 win at Knowsley Road, and massive disappointment at the semi-final stage of the Challenge Cup.

Leeds qualified for the Premiership by finishing third, for the third successive season, albeit with a declining record, winning 19 and drawing one of their 30 games.

The Loiners effected a major capture in prop Mick Harrison, a real players' player who cost £10,000 from a Hull outfit that stuck firm after an initial bid of £7,500. Harrison, signed as a replacement for David Jeanes who was intent on pursuing his accountancy studies, was to have a

A Loiner Looks Back

John Atkinson

'Roy Francis was into the big philosophy of the right decision. The right decision was when you'd only got 18 inches to get by down the touchline; if you had the ability and the pace, that was the way to go. The safe decision was to come off your left foot, beat two men and get tackled and the people would still be satisfied. They'd think "oh, he's beaten two men, he's been tackled, well that's alright." They'd still clap you. The wrong option obviously, whatever you do that's totally wrong but the right decision is, "I can see 18 inches down there and if I accelerate I can get through and once I'm through I'm in." Good players should be making the right decisions more than the safe decisions.

'Roy and Syd would always back us, even if it went wrong, because more often than not the right decision would pay off.

'The forwards still take the Mickey out of me, "we'd just come up from a scrum and Atky's kicked on the first tackle," but when they get serious about it they say, "but he's won us an awful lot of matches with that, hasn't he?" You wouldn't get Syd, when he was coach, stopping me because he knew I was doing it for a reason. I thought I'd at least a 50-50 chance of getting the ball back and hopefully causing trouble for the opposition.

'The supporters understood that as well. I think the South Stand knew that we were trying very hard to be entertainers. People spent their money to come and see us and we had a duty to try and entertain them. Although there were times when we didn't and when that happened they let us know, which they had a right to do.

'I think they enjoyed watching Les Dyl and me. I stood all my early career on the left wing watching Smithy and Hynesy thinking, "how do they do that?" and Les and I worked our own partnership out. Les's game was based on pace and power and I used to say, "you go as far as you can Les and I'll shout when I

Continued...

huge impact and be a galvanising effect on his colleagues, over several seasons. Leeds, meanwhile, were in pursuit of stand off Bruce Burton from Halifax as the man seen as the ideal replacement for Hardisty.

Harrison's old club were to deny Leeds in the Yorkshire Cup, winning 12-8 in the second round clash at the Boulevard despite having Brian Hancock and Len Casey sent off late in the first half, with Keith Hepworth also departing in the second period.

Promising half-back Chris Sanderson had scored a try in the 16-5 first round win over Keighley, replacing a Welsh trialist who had had two first team outings and facing a former colleague in Edwards.

Leeds suggested a stronger impact in the Players No 6 competition and were in scintillating form in their first meeting with New Hunslet. Left winger John Atkinson scored four tries and Alan Smith had a hat trick on the right flank in the 49-10 romp, while full-back Dave Marshall kicked eight goals against the club he had served with such distinction.

Keighley were seen off 39-4 in the second round with Syd Hynes nipping over and centre Les Dyl, who had crossed twice against Hunslet, again bagging a brace as he continued his fine form on Great Britain's Australian tour. Dyl had been in hot water when he returned home with a pair of 'tomato-red' boots which didn't sit too well with a club that 'prides itself on its style.' Despite tempting offers from Down Under, Dyl made it clear that he was happy at Leeds.

want the ball." And he'd do that, you'd see two or three men pushing him in and the ball would come out, overhand into my arms.

'We scored a try at Hull when I was on the dead ball line when we started out, Neil Hague and John Holmes opened it up from under our posts, gave Les an edge and he broke away. I got knocked over by somebody, got back up and Les was still running, pushing people away. By the time I'd made it back up to him again he'd got three of them hanging on; the ball came out to me and I ended up scoring under the posts. That proved how powerful and strong he was.

'It was service like that which enabled me to become the first Englishman since St Helens' Alf Ellaby to top the tryscoring list in successive seasons. That was wonderful but you can't do it unless the side are doing it for you. I think it epitomised the style of rugby that we played at Leeds.'

Prop Steve Pitchford, in whom Francis was showing huge faith which would be amply repaid, crashed over for a try in the same game but Pitchford's touchdown in the quarter-final at Odsal was the Loiners' only score, other than two Marshall goals, in a 17-7 defeat at the hands of Bradford Northern.

Coach Roy Francis, reported to have £30,000 to spend, was said to have nine players on his shopping list, including Scottish RU full-back Andy Irvine who opted to spurn any overtures. The Loiners, however, had high hopes of success in the Challenge Cup and boosted their prospects with the capture, prior to the registration deadline, of 21-year-old stand off Mel Mason from Featherstone Rovers. Mason made his debut against St Helens, just seven days after the Loiners had slumped to a 12-11 defeat at the hands of York at Clarence Street in a game dominated by home winger David Barends.

Headingley Hero

Graham Eccles

It takes players of widely differing skills and attitudes to forge a successful side. A top team must also possess 'heart'; an attribute which the Leeds teams of the era had in abundance.

No player, however, boasted that quality more than Graham Eccles. At around five feet seven inches tall and with a playing weight of just over 13 stones he should, in theory, have been easy meat for the many giants who lined up, week in, week out, against him.

The reality was quite the opposite. Long-serving Leeds kitman Billy Watts recalls standing alongside John Mantle in the Knowsley Road tearoom after the Loiners had ground out a hard-earned win at St Helens. Mantle had been kept on a tight rein that afternoon and chuntered to anyone who would listen: 'If it wasn't for that Graham Eccles we'd have got winning pay today.'

Praise enough from someone whose opinion should matter most to the Market District product who joined Leeds in 1968 and, after Derek 'Rocky' Turner arrived as coach for the 1969-70 season, became a fixture in the first team for 14 years.

A try scorer on his debut at Bradford Northern in the final league fixture of the 1968-69 campaign, he had at one stage been unable to break into the second team and there was even talk of converting him into a scrum-half. With Turner in charge at Headingley he was given his chance. And it wasn't one he would allow to slip.

A Yorkshire County Championship medal: an honour bizarrely denied the redoubtable Graham Eccles.

Eccles recalls: 'I was a fit 13 stones, I could get about the field and play a full 80 minutes. A lot of the bigger players couldn't play the full game out, so by the end of the match I was still going strong and they were slowing down. That made a big difference.'

That input helped Leeds win a

Continued...

trophy in each of the following 12 seasons, with Eccles an important component in the Loiners machine.

He picked up a Championship medal in 1972, when his trademark tackling was vital in the 9-5 success over St Helens in the final at Station Road, Swinton, and a runners-up medal in the defeat at the hands of Dewsbury 12 months later.

Five Yorkshire Cup winners' medals before the end of the 1970s were placed in the Eccles trophy cabinet, together with two Premiership winners' gongs.

Eccles was also prominent in the 1977 and 1978 Challenge Cup Finals and was unlucky not to collect the Lance Todd Trophy for his epic display in the second of those games when his huge tackling stint, especially in the early stages when the Loiners were on the ropes, was a major factor in his side eventually lifting the trophy.

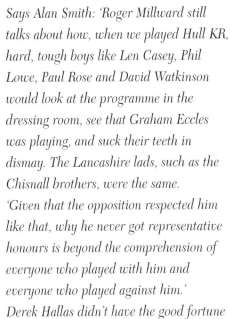

Graham Eccles was renowned as arguably the finest tackler in the game. Here he shows his ball-handling skills with David Ward ready to benefit.

The award, however, went to St Helens' George Nicholls in what many still regard as a travesty of justice that almost equals his lack of representative honours.

It is a scandal that Eccles, rated so very highly by his peers, was not even recognised by Yorkshire, let alone Great Britain, and it remains a sore point among Loiners fans, his team mates and, indeed, many of his opponents.

The explanation – that he was too lightweight for the international arena – was feeble, a dereliction of duty, and never carried any credence with anyone outside the smoke-filled rooms of the county and international selection committees.

Says Alan Smith: 'Roger Millward still talks about how, when we played Hull KR, hard, tough boys like Len Casey, Phil Lowe, Paul Rose and David Watkinson would look at the programme in the dressing room, see that Graham Eccles was playing, and suck their teeth in dismay. The Lancashire lads, such as the Chisnall brothers, were the same.

'Given that the opposition respected him like that, why he never got representative honours is beyond the comprehension of everyone who played with him and everyone who played against him.'

Derek Hallas didn't have the good fortune to play alongside a man who is often rated as fine a defender as the game has seen but he saw enough to add the accolade: 'I'd endorse that. He not only tackled hard but he hurt them, that's the thing I liked. When you play against somebody like that you've got one eye looking for where he is. He was the most under-rated second row without a doubt.'

There was only one point in it against the Saints, this time in Leeds' favour as Mason displayed plenty of courage in a physical clash in which Hepworth was forced to retire 10 minutes from time. The victory, despite a subsequent 22-16 defeat at Castleford, put the Loiners in fine fettle for the Challenge Cup opener at Whitehaven – the second Sunday game in succession, reported to be 'something of a shock' for Leeds fans – where a try after only three minutes put the side on the way to a 16-7 win in which Atkinson notched two tries, Holmes and David Ward nipped over, and Marshall and Holmes scored a goal each.

There could hardly have been a tougher task, in the second round, than a visit to reigning champions Salford but the knowledge that they had won 12 of the previous 14 games against the men from the Willows in a sequence stretching back to 1971 served the Loiners well. The late withdrawals of Tony Fisher and Ray Batten, as the coach travelled on the M62 to Lancashire, could have scuppered Leeds' prospects but the hoodoo was maintained with a superb performance. Second row Graham Eccles, who had played only one A team game since

A Loiner Looks Back

Neil Hague

'Roy Francis, he was a fantastic coach and he was years before his time. I used to drink in the True Briton in Meanwood and I dropped in one Friday night. I was playing for the A team the next day. I was at the bar and ordered a pint and the man in front of me turned round and said, "that will be a shandy, will it?" It was Roy. From that day on he called me Tetley.'

Christmas – and that a mere 24 hours before the Salford clash – stepped into Batten's boots and produced a trademark display while Bob Haigh, best known for his try-scoring exploits, confirmed his defensive prowess with a cracking tackle on rampant Salford prop Mike Coulman.

Marshall kicked four goals, including one from the touchline which transformed a 12-11 deficit into a 13-12 lead, and Pitchford was running into the type of form which would make him the scourge of opposing packs for several seasons. Sanderson, Hynes and (thanks to an audacious dummy by Sanderson), Alan Smith scored Leeds' tries against the out-gunned Red Devils to set up a big third round tie, at Headingley, with Bradford Northern.

Leeds' best crowd since March 1972, 12,979, witnessed another impressive show as the Loiners swept to a 22-6 victory, spurred by a reported bonus of £100 a man. Sanderson had another big game, outshining former Headingley favourite Barry Seabourne in a marked contrast of styles, the Yorkshire Post's Raymond Fletcher highlighting that Seabourne rarely ran with the ball, passed on over 70 occasions and was only twice tackled in possession while Sanderson was always ready to run, passed fewer than 20 times, was tackled in possession 17 times and scored the Loiners' final try.

A Loiner Looks Back

John Holmes

'I never used to get changed early. I'd walk in and David Ward would be there, stripped, with the Vaseline on. He'd ask if I was playing or not and at twenty to three, or maybe quarter to, I'd get changed and away I went. That's just how I was; I couldn't sit there for an hour building myself up. I'd have left my energy in the dressing room. Later in my career, when we started doing warm-ups on the cricket pitch, I used to sneak off to the toilet.

'I was captain of Leeds and they took it off me. I wasn't playing well. They made Wardy captain, and we went to Wembley two years later. People said that it could have been me up there lifting the cup but it didn't bother me. You knew damn well that when you went on the pitch with him he'd do the business. You just had to calm him down, get him back to where he should be. I think we were good for one another. Some people reckon we have a fan club for one another. "They're off again," they'll say, when we start singing each other's praises. But I did have a huge amount of respect for him. He was a really great player, a great leader, and a tough man. Very under-rated, because he had it up there as well. He could see things immediately. I'd just have to give him a nod or a shout about something I'd seen off the cuff and he'd know damn well what was happening.'

Contrasts in temperament. John Holmes was coolness personified in the changing room, declining to change until 15 minutes before kick off. Graham Eccles was the dressing room joker, while David Ward preferred to psyche himself up for at least an hour prior to the start.

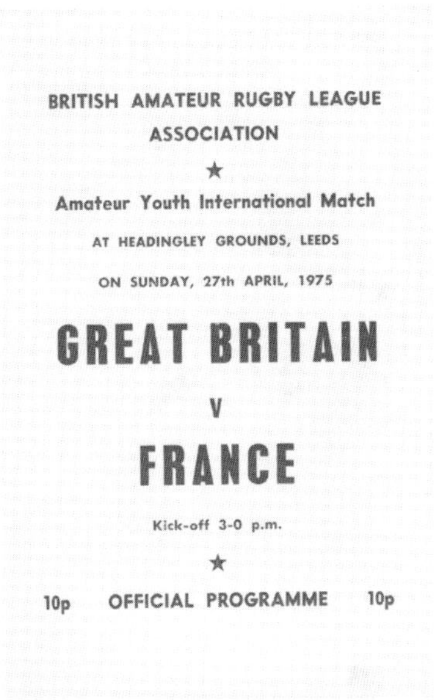
BRITISH AMATEUR RUGBY LEAGUE ASSOCIATION

★

Amateur Youth International Match

AT HEADINGLEY GROUNDS, LEEDS

ON SUNDAY, 27th APRIL, 1975

GREAT BRITAIN

V

FRANCE

Kick-off 3-0 p.m.

★

10p OFFICIAL PROGRAMME 10p

Headingley has been used regularly as a major venue by all sections of Rugby League.

Fisher, Dyl and Marshall scored Leeds' other tries, with Marshall kicking five goals from a platform laid by the likes of Pitchford, as Leeds edged closer to a return to Wembley.

It wasn't to be, however. Warrington won the semi-final at Wigan 11-4, winger John Bevan scoring three tries including one very late in the first half when referee Fred Lindop and his officials were unable to hear the half-time hooter, and another in injury time when Lindop had taken control of the time-keeping.

The defeat left the Loiners with only one trophy available – the Premiership Trophy – and football chairman Jack Myerscough declared 'an assault' on the new competition which had been launched to replace the old Championship play-offs.

Three defeats in the last six league games prevented the Loiners from overhauling second-placed Wigan. St Helens were clear champions, 11 points better than the Pie Eaters and 14 ahead of Leeds – an unbeaten Headingley record being undermined by poor away form which led to defeats at Wigan, St Helens, Rochdale Hornets, Wakefield Trinity, Warrington, York, Castleford, Featherstone Rovers, Salford and Widnes – but final league placings did not appear to be too important to

Loiners Big Match

17 May 1975, Premiership Final, Leeds 26 St Helens 11, Central Park, Wigan

It was a rarity, during the 1974-75 season, for Leeds players to be given standing ovations in Lancashire. A dismal record of six defeats in as many league games across the Pennines, added to the 30-6 thumping at St Helens in the BBC2 Floodlit Trophy, suggested severe travel sickness on the part of Roy Francis' men and the only respite came with the notable win at Salford, preceded by the victory in Cumbria at Whitehaven, in the Challenge Cup.

John Holmes and David Marshall are thoughtful at half time in the Premiership Final against St Helens. Marshall, introduced at full-back because of a Holmes injury, produced a superb defensive display in the second half to help seal the Loiners' 26-11 win.

The portents, therefore, were none too promising as Leeds prepared to take on St Helens at Central Park, Wigan, in the final of the Premiership Trophy. However, youth knows no fear, and the selection of a frighteningly (some would say just frightened) young front row of Steve Pitchford, David Ward and Roy Dickinson for the last game of the campaign – and one that had to be won to preserve the Loiners' record of lifting a trophy in each season since 1966-67 – was a typical Francis masterstroke.

Francis, under pressure for his job as the Leeds board had not responded to his call for clarification over his future, opted for the youngsters ahead of veteran Mick Harrison, while hooker Tony Fisher was suspended.

Continued...

Dickinson, at just 18, had impressed after having been snapped up from junior rugby and Francis had no qualms about pitching him, Ward and Pitchford in against a highly experienced Saints front row which, in John Mantle, Tony Karalius and John Warlow, had an average age of 32 compared to Leeds' 21. He told the Yorkshire Evening Post: 'I have no worries about our lads. I'm just wondering how long St Helens can last the pace against them. In the last 10 matches, Roy and Steve have propped against some of the best forwards in the League; they've learned the hard way and they've done it well. David Ward has played in all the Premiership matches and he has plenty of big match experience.'

The agony and the ecstasy. Syd Hynes races over for his second try and pulls a hamstring.

The trio fully repaid Francis' faith, setting a wonderful platform for their side, and the men behind were not in the mood to waste it. Mel Mason, the stand off half captured from Featherstone Rovers earlier in the campaign, had possibly his finest game for Leeds and, after full-back John Holmes had opened the scoring with a penalty, netted a superb try, latching onto loose forward Ray Batten's intelligent pass before leaving St Helens scrum-half Jeff Heaton sprawling whilst racing in an arc for a morale-boosting score which Holmes improved. Mason's touchdown followed some important work up front, Warlow having to withdraw after eight minutes with damaged ribs, and the loss of Mantle after half an hour with a gashed head was another blow for St Helens. Those injuries dictated that substitute Ken Gwilliam moved to stand off, with John Walsh switching to his usual position of centre, taking the place of David Hull, who moved into the pack, second row pair George Nicholls and Eric Chisnall moving up to prop. Saints coach Eric Ashton may have pondered, at that point, on the wisdom of having selected second row-cum-centre Eddie Cunningham as substitute ahead of Welsh prop Mel James.

Leeds, with Mason revelling in his forwards' dominance, couldn't have cared less. The loss of Holmes, replaced by David Marshall, did nothing to limit the side. A raid by scrum-half Keith Hepworth established the position for Syd Hynes to drop a goal, and another attack inspired by Hepworth, with a delayed pass, brought Mason into yet more incisive action, Hynes popping up to tear through for a score in which not a single defender was anywhere close.

Continued...

the Rugby Football League which operated a random draw of 16 teams comprising the leading 12 in Division One and the top four in Division Two.

The Loiners had to travel to fourth-placed Featherstone in the first round on 27 April 1975 where there were no question marks regarding Leeds' superiority. An ineffective Featherstone side could do little to deny Leeds and, in particular, Dyl who scorched over for a hat trick in the 27-8 win. Haigh netted two tries, Alan Smith scored a 60-yard thriller in which Ken Kellett was left sprawling, and Hynes raced over with Holmes kicking three goals as Leeds belied their previously mediocre travelling form.

Castleford, drawn at Headingley at the next stage, fared no better against a Leeds side installed as competition favourites. Cas were, in fact, a point worse than their pitland neighbours, going down 28-8 as the Loiners set up their win with a 15-point blitz shortly before half time. Pitchford, disappointed by his form in the Challenge Cup defeat by Warrington, was back in top fettle and powered his way over for Leeds' first try. That block-buster was followed by a touchdown for Alan Smith after Haigh and

Hynes had linked, Haigh was next to cross and Holmes' three conversions helped Leeds to a 15-0 lead which Cas were never going to retrieve. Smith, Atkinson and Hynes all raced over in the second half, Holmes adding two more goals, for a victory which took the Loiners a step nearer preserving their record of having won at least one major trophy in each season since 1966-67.

Hull KR, who had finished as runners-up in Division Two, travelled to Headingley for the semi-final and put up a better show than either Featherstone or Castleford before losing 18-8. The young front row of Roy Dickinson, Ward and Pitchford was now establishing itself as one of the best around and helped pave the way for an 8-3 interval lead through tries by Dyl and Alan Smith, Leeds going on to victory with

Hynes, however, touched down in a mix of joy and agony as his hamstring went, Graham Eccles stepping off the bench as Marshall improved.

As the Loiners considered how they would rearrange their side, the avalanche of points continued, centre Les Dyl scorching through and timing his pass to Atkinson to perfection, the winger ending full-back Geoff Pimblett's hopes with a perfectly-executed hand off.

The ovation as the players trooped off at the interval was heart-warming and important. Leeds recognised that following their own spate of injuries they, too, could be under the cosh. Alan Smith moved in from the wing to the centre to cover for Hynes, and Bob Haigh switched from the second row to the wing, for a second half in which the defensive talents of Marshall were important. The full-back pulled off one superb tackle on Hull which came to nothing, the next move resulting in right winger Les Jones squeezing in at the corner, loose forward Kel Coslett converting.

Cunningham, who had set up the Jones try, was again the catalyst, with centre Frank Wilson, for left winger Roy Mathias to sprint down the touchline where Marshall, used to plenty of tackling practice during his days with bottom-of-the-table Hunslet, again earned his spurs with a copybook stop.

Mason, who collected the Harry Sunderland Trophy as man of the match for his top-notch performance, went a long way towards that accolade when he raced back to deny Cunningham what looked like a certain try, and Marshall was called upon once more to halt Matthias in his tracks.

Despite the draining nature of their defensive task, Leeds still had plenty in reserve in attack, however, and a move involving several players resulted in Alan Smith forcing his way past Pimblett.

Although St Helens did manage to register tries by Matthias and Heaton, the Loiners had done enough and stayed in the comfort zone, in their first-ever Premiership Final, with Atkinson's second try – courtesy of an intelligent switching of play by Pitchford – and two more goals by David Marshall as Saints went down to their biggest defeat in six years.

Leeds: Holmes; A Smith, Hynes, Dyl, Atkinson; Mason, Hepworth; Dickinson, Ward, Pitchford, Cookson, Batten, Haigh. Subs: Marshall, Eccles.

St Helens: Pimblett; Jones, Wilson, Hull, Mathias; Walsh, Heaton; Warlow, Karalius, Mantle, Chisnall, Nicholls, Coslett. Subs: Gwilliam, Cunningham.

Referee: Mr WH Thompson (Huddersfield).

Leeds: T: Atkinson 2, Mason, Hynes, Smith. G: Marshall 3, Holmes 2. DG: Hynes.

St Helens: T: Jones, Mathias, Heaton. G: Coslett.

Attendance: 14,531

second half touchdowns from Mason and Batten, Holmes landing three goals. Leeds, though, were grateful that the legendary Neil Fox had an off day with his kicking. Fox, who broke Cyril Kellett's club record of 145 goals in a season in the game, only managed one success and his three first half failures were costly, as was a mistake by Ian Madeley who appeared to have broken through for a try but instead looked for his support, his pass to Roy Holdstock going to ground.

The victory set up a Premiership Final against St Helens at Wigan, won in style.

Leeds parted company with Roy Francis at the end of the season. The man who had moulded one of the most attractive sides in the history of the game in the late 1960s had not quite been able to repeat the feat and, against a background of poor away form, particularly in Lancashire, had sought clarification – which was not forthcoming – over his future.

In a letter to the board, sent in mid-April, he stated: 'My contract ends on May 31st and knowing the board's preference for forward planning I would assume my services are not required for the coming season. I can assure you that every effort will be made towards winning the Premiership.'

It was a sad end to Francis' links with the club and he told the Evening Post: 'This was in no way a letter of resignation. I was trying to clarify things so I could arrange my holidays and make plans for the club's summer school for youngsters.'

Atkinson Halts Jewel Thief;

Yorkshire Evening Post

'Leeds Rugby League star John Atkinson made the tackle of his life in the crowded city centre today and brought down a man after a diamond ring disappeared from a jeweller's shop.

'John (27) answered cries of "stop him" as the man was chased through the streets by staff of the jewellers.

'As passers-by watched the chase in Albion Street, the star winger appeared on the scene and pulled off a text-book tackle, for which he is so famous at Headingley.

'Later, John explained from his Cookridge home: "A man shouted 'stop thief' and I saw a man running towards us. My wife just nudged me and said, 'Go get him' and before I really knew what was happening I was tackling him."

'A passer-by said: "I saw this tackle and thought, this man knows what he is about. Then they told me that he is a Leeds RL man, and I am not surprised."'

Atkinson, though, wasn't quite the man of the moment later in the season when he was an hour late reporting for training with England at Castleford after having missed a previous session. His explanation – that he had pranged his car a week or two earlier and had been let down over a lift, having to travel to Castleford by car – didn't go down well with the England management and Manager Bill Oxley said: 'I intended giving Atkinson only a few more minutes when he turned up. If he had not reported than he would have been out of the side against France.'

The Loiners acted swiftly, appointing Syd Hynes, then 30, as Francis' replacement on a one-year deal. Hynes was Leeds' first player/coach.

13. MORE SILVER AMASSED

The success story of the 1960s and 1970s continued in 1975-76 and, unlike in the previous campaign, the Loiners didn't have to wait until the very last match to make certain of serious silverware.

For the fourth successive season, player/coach Syd Hynes and his men finished third in the First Division, albeit with a slightly improved record on the previous two campaigns.

Hynes and his captain, scrum-half Keith Hepworth, led the Loiners to 21 victories in their 30 league games, although the side scored fewer points (571 to 581) and conceded more (395 to 359) than in 1974-75.

Sport, however, is primary about winning rather than its manner, even if style-conscious Leeds have often abjured that philosophy.

In the event the Loiners were only three points adrift of champions Salford at the close of the campaign. And while Championship issues invariably come down to ifs and buts, the 7-5 defeat at the Willows on 20 February, important enough at the time, turned out to the most crucial result of the league campaign.

A Loiner Looks Back

John Holmes

'Neil Hague and I would practice crazy passes and kicking drop goals backwards before training. We used to go out 10 or 15 minutes early and mess about, taking goal kicks, and I used to practice taking them off my left foot. Not for any reason, we were just doing silly things for a laugh.

'Billy Francis came at me that day at Wembley, in 1978. I knew where the posts were and I just let go. I didn't see the ball go over, I was on my back, but it went between the sticks and the rest is history.

'The second one, which David Ward got, I was going to have a peg at myself. But I got blocked off so I gave it to Wardy and he landed it. They came back and nearly scored in the corner; if we'd thought about that we would probably have played it out down at their end. Whether Derek Noonan would have scored I don't know. We had four or five coming across. Hopefully he would have been put in the stand but at the end of the day it didn't really matter. It was nice to win after being beaten in 1971 and 1972.

Headingley heroes line up in 1975-76

The Red Devils had been beaten easily enough at Headingley a month earlier, the Loiners easing to a 28-14 victory with a try and five goals by full-back David Marshall and touchdowns by right winger Alan Smith, centre Les Dyl, left centre John Atkinson, second row Butch Adams and Hepworth.

But it was to prove a different story in the return.

Leeds, despite lacking seven regulars including Hepworth, loose forward Ray Batten,

Loiners Big Match

15 November 1975, Yorkshire Cup Final, Leeds 15 Hull KR 11, Headingley

If any one game epitomised the never-say-die spirit of the Leeds side of the 1970s it was the Yorkshire Cup Final win over Hull Kingston Rovers that brought the Loiners their thirteenth success in the competition, going back to the 1921-22 season.

The victory edged Leeds ahead of Huddersfield (12) in the hierarchy of Yorkshire Cup winners, with Wakefield Trinity just in the frame on nine.

Yet Leeds, taking part in their seventeenth decider, looked down and out with five minutes remaining and facing an 11-9 deficit.

Despite being forced to play the game at Headingley, at the behest of the sponsors, the Robins had had the better of the match, helped by a lion's share of possession earned by hooker Clive Dickinson, who out-heeled an Ian Payne standing in for the injured David Ward.

They were also helped by the fact that Leeds had played the Robins' neighbours and bitter rivals Hull less than 48 hours earlier at Headingley in the replayed second round John Player Cup clash.

The Loiners, given that testing run-up to the final, had no right to be in contention as the hooter beckoned but, with time running out, ever-alert centre Les Dyl saw an opportunity from a play-the-ball on the Robins' line and using skipper Syd Hynes – at scrum-half for the injured Keith Hepworth – as a decoy, scampered over from dummy half with veteran Neil Fox buying an outrageous dummy from the young speedster.

That score, recorded under the posts, was converted by stand off John Holmes and with seconds remaining Holmes landed a drop goal to make certain of the Yorkshire Cup and leave Hull KR reeling at the injustice of it all.

Second row Graham Eccles could also ponder on the

Continued...

Smith and Atkinson, took an early lead when Phil Cookson, at loose forward, linked with Hynes to send John Holmes over the whitewash.

But the Red Devils hit back to go ahead 5-3 at the interval through two goals and a drop goal by stand off David Watkins, who extended the lead with a penalty midway through the second half.

Leeds rallied with a goal by Marshall when Salford scrum-half Steve Nash was penalised for feeding. But the home side held on for a win that turned out to be seminal.

The Red Devils were castigated locally for an indifferent performance, and it was reported that half-back Ken Gill, the lynchpin of his side's attacks, was kept under wraps by Neil Hague who 'harassed him to the point of being perilously offside.'

Hague was partnering young Kevin Dick, a scrum-half who six days earlier had featured for Leeds Colts against Bradford and had then played for the A team at Hull before ending a hectic week with his first team appearance at the Willows.

The Loiners, in fact, could take a lot of satisfaction from their performance with Pitchford and Adams particularly outstanding and it was noted that referee Fred Lindop penalised them six times for offside, and Salford not at all. But the points went to the Red Devils, who scraped another important win seven days later against St Helens in another stuttering display.

When the end-of-season run-in arrived Leeds, Salford and Featherstone had each *iniquities of this world, having played a huge part in his side's win with a superlative defensive performance only to see the White Rose Trophy, sponsored by the Yorkshire Federation of Supporters Clubs for the man of the match, go to Fox who had helped Rovers assume a stranglehold with a try and two goals.*

Dyl, too, was an obvious contender and if Hynes had had his way would probably have collected the individual memento if only for following his coach's instructions, after his quiet performance against Hull, to go looking for the ball.

There was a feeling that Rovers perhaps deserved a replay, particularly as Great Britain winger Clive Sullivan had had a 'try' controversially ruled out for stepping into touch as he raced over the Leeds line for what would have been his second try of the game.

In a match in which the lead changed hands on five occasions Phil Cookson, switched to loose forward with Ray Batten operating in the second row, scored the Loiners' first try after Holmes and prop Mick Harrison had linked, Holmes scoring a conversion and a penalty in the first half.

Leeds: Marshall; A Smith, Hague, Dyl, Atkinson; Holmes, Hynes; Harrison, Payne, Pitchford, Eccles, Batten, Cookson. Subs: Dickinson.
Hull KR: Wallace; Dunn, A Burwell, Watson, Sullivan; Turner, Millward; Millington, Dickinson, Lyons, Rose, Fox, Hughes. Subs: Holdstock.
Referee: Mr JV Moss (Manchester).
Leeds: T: Cookson, Dyl. G: Holmes 4. DG: Holmes.
Hull KR: T: Sullivan, Fox. G: Fox 2. DG: Millward.
Attendance: 5,743

Champagne celebrations after the Yorkshire Cup Final victory.

played 29 games and had accumulated 43, 42 and 42 points respectively. Those statistics made it imperative that the Loiners won their last game, at Wigan, to have any chance of denying the men from the Willows, who had to travel to Keighley. In the event, Hynes' men went down 27-15 at Central Park and Salford won at Lawkholme Lane after having scored three tries in the first 15 minutes.

There was consolation, however, in the Yorkshire Cup, always the first trophy on offer.

Leeds were in devastating form on the way to the final, overwhelming Halifax in the first round with a 32-5 stroll in which Holmes excelled at Headingley in the late-August sunshine.

The game was in the bag by the break, when a 23-0 lead had been established, and the Loiners understandably eased off in the last 40 minutes.

Holmes, at stand off, finished with 20 points from three tries and four goals, with other tries going to Cookson, second row Bob Haigh, Atkinson, stand off Mel Mason and Marshall.

An emphatic 22-2 verdict against Bradford Northern, at Odsal, followed. Holmes, again, was an important figure, landing five goals, while Cookson, Haigh, Dyl and Hepworth grabbed the tries.

The Loiners were required to head west, once more, for the semi-final, this time grinding out an 11-2 win over Keighley. Leeds laid strong foundations in the first half, carving out an 8-2 interval lead, before holding out for victory in

A Loiner Looks Back
David Ward

'Leeds sides of the 60s and 70s always used to win a trophy; when it got down to the important game and the important point, the quality player loved it, "it's big time rugby now, it's game on now, boys, we ain't gonna lose this one." That's where big players come into it. You win the big point, the semis, the third round, the final. I put my hand up in those games and the other lads didn't crack either. Certain players are your best players when you're 20 points up but not so much when it's nil-nil with only about 10 minutes to go and you're looking for somebody who is going to crack. That's the weakness in the chain. Most times, the players who played for Leeds in that era had the ability to win the important games.

'The big point.' David Ward, a player ready to rise to the occasion, seeks a crucial drop goal at Warrington.

'Workington away, in 1977 in the third round of the Challenge Cup, was a great example. That was a draw and a half that nobody ever wanted, when Workington were flying high; you just didn't go up there and win. Alan Smith scored a try in the corner and Brian Murrell had to kick the goal to seal the game. We slugged that out, in wintry conditions, and that is a win that stands out very much in my mind.

Continued...

the second half. Holmes, again, was a mainstay with a try and a goal, and there was a brace for Mason.

While the path to the final had been relatively straightforward, the decider itself against Hull KR was another matter entirely. With home advantage – Headingley having become a permanent venue for the competition at the behest of sponsors Esso – the Loiners admittedly should have had the upper hand. But it didn't look that way as the Robins went into the last five minutes 11-9 in front before Dyl saved the day with a late try.

Leeds also made good progress in the BBC2 Floodlit Trophy, battling through to the semi-finals before going down 7-0 at Dewsbury. The Loiners opened with a Preliminary Round 21-10 win over Castleford at Headingley when Hague raced over from the centre for two tries in a match dominated by prop Steve Pitchford, described by the Evening Post's Arthur Haddock as having 'emerged as an unusual type of personality at Headingley.'

The victory set up a first 'derby' clash with New Hunslet at the fledgling club's Greyhound Stadium, where the pitch was notoriously narrow and Hunslet had installed their famous (or infamous) 'TV aerial' goal-posts, mounted on a single upright standing on the dead ball line.

That feature had become notorious earlier in the campaign when an opposing winger crossed without a defender in sight and, glancing up, raced out of play in the belief that the upright was on the try-line.

'The semi-final was a huge game as well. The week before, I'd made my debut for England against France in Carcassonne in the European Championship. I came off in the second half because I'd copped for one and my eye had closed. They had to do a bit of surgery to open it up and get me to play in that semi-final, and I won the man of the match. That gives me a lot of satisfaction.'

The goalposts were again a focal point in a match won 10-9 by Leeds, who struggled to adapt to the cramped pitch and posted just one try, by Howard, and three goals and a drop goal by Holmes. Hunslet supporters insisted that one of Holmes' three goals had drifted wide of an upright. The south Leeds outfit, however, could have won the game if Bob Gaitley, who had landed four goals, had opted to kick for goal with a last-minute penalty rather than kick to the corner.

An abrasive Wigan outfit were beaten 17-10 at Headingley in the semi-final, Holmes not lasting the course after being flattened off the ball by Pie Eaters hooker Terry Hollingsworth in an incident missed by the referee and his touchjudges but certainly spotted by Hynes, who made his views clear to the officials in addition to netting two tries in the win.

But the semi-final at Dewsbury, who had been beaten 25-16 in a league game at Crown Flatt a couple of weeks earlier through Leeds' expansive approach, ended in a 7-0 defeat as the Loiners made the mistake of playing it 'up the middle.'

Leeds' interest in the John Player competition ended in the second round. Swinton were disposed of easily enough at the first hurdle, Alan Smith and Atkinson scoring two tries each, Hague crossing and Marshall kicking four goals

Headingley Hero

Alan Smith

The contrast between Alan Smith, on Leeds' right wing, and John Atkinson on the opposite flank could not have been more marked.

Where Atky was the flamboyant flyer, capable of netting tries from anywhere on the pitch, Smithie was the battering ram whose tries mostly came from relatively short range and often from seemingly impossible situations.

The bludgeon to Atkinson's rapier, Smith's scoring feats owed much to an indomitable spirit, an unquenchable hunger for tries, and to sheer unadulterated courage.

The former amateur from Brookhouse, Wakefield, may also have been spurred on by a mixed beginning to his professional career.

Having put pen to paper with the Loiners in 1962 Smith, then playing on the left wing, netting four tries on his debut in the August of that year in the Eastern Division win at Headingley over Dewsbury.

That bright start, though, turned to despair when Smith suffered a broken leg in an A team game.

The injury put his career on sharp hold – not that he was anything but delighted just to be part of the Headingley scene. But, as with several other Headingley Heroes, it is interesting to speculate on how Alan Smith's subsequent career owes something to fate.

When Football Chairman Jack Myerscough suggested a loan spell at Bramley in 1965, Smith was happy enough to oblige but was also delighted to return to Headingley after a four-week spell. Noting the big-money signing at that time of Roundhay Rugby Union man John Atkinson, also a left winger, Smith made a conscious decision to switch flanks, asking – and getting – a run on the right wing in the A team.

The metamorphosis was astonishing. An improvement in form and fortunes led to a return to first team action in December 1966. This time it would be permanent, sparked by an impressive two-try display

Continued...

in the Boxing Day win over Wakefield Trinity.
No touchdown ever went begging for Alan Smith for want of passion or commitment, with three, four or more defenders often left sprawling and reflecting on having conceded a try that few if any other players would have been capable of scoring. Smith had one particular trick of leaning into opponents, a ploy which somehow threw

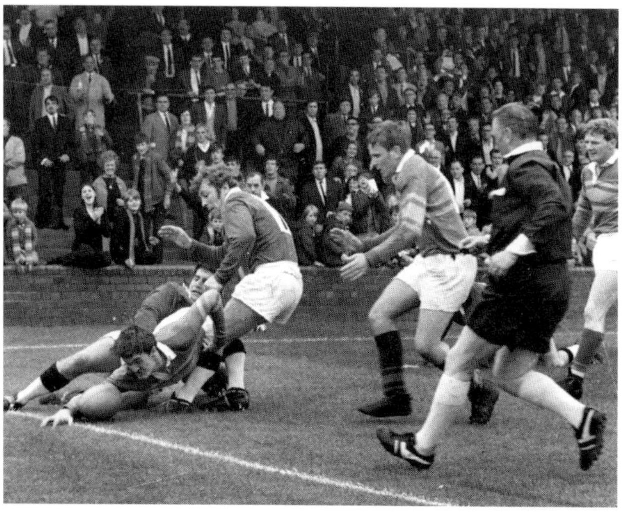

Alan Smith shows typical determination in battling his way to the tryline despite a posse of Bramley tacklers including former Great Britain full back Arthur Keegan.

them off guard before a forceful hand off sent them sprawling. Atkinson, the man who indirectly led to Smith's rebirth as a Rugby League player, soon forged a lasting friendship with his opposite number and remembers: 'We discussed it and he said, "I just lean into them and they automatically start to lean backwards, then I push 'em." I played against him just once, for Great Britain against Leeds at Headingley. And he did it to me! He came towards me, leaned in, and the next thing I was flat on my backside. And I'd known what he was going to do. He used that trick time and time again, and nobody told him how to do it. Nobody told him, either, how to come in off the wing and take the outside centre. Again, it was just a natural thing.'
Smith forged an almost telepathic right-wing partnership with Syd Hynes, a magician with the ball. The duo bamboozled opposing defences with a variety of tricks, Hynes either using Smith as a decoy or just as often feeding his winger, harassed would-be tacklers invariably not knowing exactly which of the pair actually had the ball until it was too late.
Alan Smith went on to play for Leeds until his retirement in 1983. Along the way, after brushing aside retirement pangs in 1976, he played at Wembley in 1968, 1972 and 1977, missing out in 1971 because of injury.
The winger also featured in the Championship Finals of 1970 (when he scored in each of the four rounds) 1972 and 1973, a shoulder injury ruling him out in 1969. Added to that list is a host of Yorkshire Cup, Premiership, John Player Trophy and BBC2 Floodlit Trophy medals, not to mention three Tests against the Australians in the Ashes series success of 1970. Not a bad record for a player who, once, was grateful simply to be on the Headingley scene.

in the 23-7 success, and the Loiners were only denied a fine win in the second round against Hull at the Boulevard when Airlie Birds substitute Chris Davidson landed a late drop goal for a 9-9 draw.

The Loiners lost the replay – played the day after the game between England and Australia at Headingley and two days before the Yorkshire Cup Final against Hull KR – 23-11, Alan Smith providing a highlight with a trademark try in which he simply battered his way through four defenders, but the prize of a lucrative home semi-final with St Helens went to Hull.

Hopes were high, though, of progress in the Challenge Cup to ease the disappointment of the previous season's semi-final defeat at the hands of Warrington. A first round tie at Huddersfield posed few problems, Leeds accounting for the Fartowners 34-10 after Hynes and Smith had crossed in the early stages. Touchdowns for Atkinson, Mick Harrison, Hepworth and, with a brace, Cookson completed a comfortable win.

Bradford, too, were unable to cope with the

TV Gantry

Leeds became a popular venue for the BBC TV cameras in the 1960s and 1970s.
Almost certain that a game at Headingley would go ahead regardless of the weather, TV bosses were quick to plump for the Loiners' home games. And the cameras became such a regular fixture at the ground that a gantry was built over the South Stand.
It wasn't easy, however, reaching the gantry in the years before the famous spiral staircase was erected. In an interview in 1974 legendary commentator Eddie Waring reflected: 'In an effort to find a "Twickers" position for cameras, TV producers go higher and higher over the top of stands. It's like climbing the steep steps to heaven (to quote the hymn 'midst toil, peril and pain'). There are certainly some risky ascents to be made. I've known colleagues refuse to climb up to some positions, and only two years ago a well-known player and a well-known manager refused to climb the Leeds ladder. This has been altered a little now, particularly since I suggested the club chairman should try it for himself.'

Loiners, despite trailing by only a point early in the second half in the second round tie at Headingley. Northern, who lacked former Leeds prop Terry Clawson, unwell after inoculations for a forthcoming trip to Australia, conceded two quick penalties close to their own posts, followed by a sensational try in which Eccles sent Dyl away, the speedy centre finding Atkinson with a smart inside pass to present Hynes, who had taken over the goal kicking duties from Holmes, with his fourth goal.

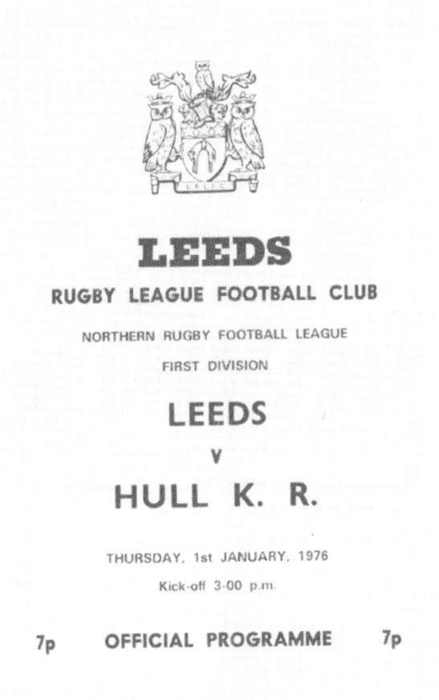

Leeds v Hull KR, 1 January 1976. The first year in which New Year's Day was a Bank Holiday. Fans gave a resounding thumbs up to Rugby League games on a cold winter's day as a more enjoyable way of clearing a hangover than having to go to work.

Cookson ended Northern's challenge, charging over from short range, and tries for Atkinson and Hague wrapped up a notable win.

Post Office Road, Featherstone, however, had long been a graveyard of Challenge Cup dreams for leading sides throughout the league and it was Leeds' turn to slip to the Rovers in the quarter-finals. The Loiners headed to the pit village full of confidence, boosted by the knowledge that they had won nine of 11 games at Post Office Road in the previous 11 seasons.

Not this time, though. Hepworth was absent, reported as having a cold but said, in subsequent years, to have been delayed returning from a greyhound meeting in Ireland. His absence, not announced on the tannoy, didn't become apparent until the first scrum, which was fed by Chris Sanderson. Sanderson played well but Hepworth's abilities as a 'seventh forward' were missed and Leeds crashed to a 33-7 defeat, the heaviest Challenge Cup reverse in the Loiners' history up to that point but put in better perspective when Featherstone gave champions Salford a similar hiding a few weeks later.

The defeat left Leeds focusing on the Championship and on retaining the Premiership. Aware of the pressures involved on an injury-hit squad, with Atkinson another addition after dislocating his left ankle in the 17-12 win over Wigan on 24 March, the Loiners called off their proposed trip Down Under where a fixture had been arranged for June with champions Eastern Suburbs.

Hynes, like many coaches before him, found himself the butt of pressure from the fans, despite the crippling injury list which included long-term absentee Haigh. But a comfortable 12-2 win over Widnes in the first round of the Premiership, with Eccles and Dickinson crossing and Marshall kicking three goals, suggested that the trophy could remain on the Headingley sideboard.

It wasn't to be. The two-leg semi-final against St Helens involved a 12-5 defeat at Headingley, Eccles scoring the Loiners' only try and Marshall kicking a goal, followed by a 21-6 defeat at a Knowsley Road arena celebrating a Challenge Cup Final victory over Widnes – the side's sixth successive setback on Saints' soil – which owed much to the harsh dismissal of Ward for an alleged trip on home full-back Geoff Pimblett. It was Ward's first dismissal in five years as a professional.

A Loiner Looks Back

Billy Watts

'Jack Myerscough was a gentleman. He didn't suffer fools gladly, but you could always speak to him. I wasn't in a position to go to him and moan about anything but if ever you wanted to say anything he would listen. He also had a good sense of humour, he used to come out with some little sayings but people used to look and see the funny side of what he'd said and laugh away. And he could keep a straight face.'

Football Chairman Jack Myerscough revelled in presentations for players and former players.

14. RISING TO THE OCCASION

> **A Loiner Looks Back**
>
> **Graham Eccles**
>
> *'When we played on Saturdays we all went out together after the match. When they first switched to Sunday, sometimes you'd had so many knocks that if you worked on a building site or down the pit you didn't feel like going to work. The lads had to have somewhere to meet so that's how the Monday Club started!*
>
> *'We all went out together and we were all friends together so if you didn't play well you not only let your team down, you let your friends down. You put that little bit of extra effort in.*
>
> *'I always put 100 per cent into whatever I did and I never missed training, although I didn't enjoy it. How people can complain about playing two games a week I don't know; I'd rather play twice and not train. But you're training to play the game you love. There were some players who played Rugby League for money, the players who moved around many clubs, but most players were in the game because they loved to play.*
>
> *'We all worked a full working day and we played 80 minutes rugby, and of course we were scrumming down.'*

David Ward was left with a fulsome shiner after making acquaintance with a French fist in the France v England game in 1977.

Leeds embarked on the 1976-77 season as Yorkshire Cup holders and aware that the 1975-76 Championship had only been denied them by the 7-5 defeat mid-February by eventual table-toppers Salford.

Despite a strong opening to the campaign the serious challenge was not to be repeated, the Loiners slumping to ninth – their lowest position since 1964-65 – a ranking which failed to qualify them for the Premiership play-offs.

There was, though, to be ample solace in the retention of the Yorkshire Cup and, perhaps more importantly, in the retrieval of the Challenge Cup after a gap of nine years.

Leeds fans, in addition, had another wing hero to celebrate. David Smith, a former teammate of skipper David Ward at Shaw Cross, was snapped up from Wakefield Trinity as veteran pacemen John Atkinson and Alan Smith continued to suffer from injuries.

David Smith went on to top the try-scoring table with 25 – Atkinson was second with 16 – in a season which was to end in joy on the pitch but, off it, would be blighted by tragedy with the death of Chris Sanderson.

The scrum-half, who had been battling to be first choice since making his debut in the 1971-72 season, was in line for a first appearance at Wembley as the Loiners travelled to the Willows on 24 April 1977 in pursuit of a win which would have hoisted them into the top eight, above Bradford Northern. The final league game of the season wasn't completed as the half-back went into a tackle and never got up again.

Ward remembers the occasion with typical and understandable emotion. 'That was the lowest point of my career. It was very, very sad.

Loiners Big Match

16 October 1976, Yorkshire Cup Final, Leeds 16 Featherstone Rovers 12, Headingley

Games against Featherstone Rovers, who boasted one of the best packs in the league in the 1970s, often turned into an arm-wrestle, a war of attrition. But the 1976 Yorkshire Cup Final fell into the opposite category.

A crowd of 7,615 witnessed a classic as the Loiners and Featherstone served up one of the best finals in the history of the competition.

Leeds, the holders after the previous season's last-gasp win over Hull KR, were again pushed all the way and Great Britain centre Les Dyl, who had snatched victory 12 months earlier against the Rovers of the east coast, was once again a central figure, troubling the inland Rovers throughout.

So did the young Leeds pack, which had been expected to struggle against the vaunted Featherstone six. Rovers, who lacked the injured Jimmy Thompson, came off second best. Loiners hooker David Ward, who a few years earlier had struggled to secure enough possession for his side and had been told that Rovers' Keith Bridges was on the Headingley shopping list, had the satisfaction of out-raking the Featherstone man – and that factor was crucial to Leeds' success.

Ward, flanked by Roy Dickinson and Steve Pitchford, with Graham Eccles, Chris Burton and Phil Cookson providing plenty of push at the rear, won six of the first eight scrums to give the Loiners the platform of early possession from which the game was won.

Dyl's second try came from a quick heel, the centre racing over from 40 yards after cleverly using his winger David Smith as a foil.

That score, in the 25th minute, was the fourth occasion on which the lead had changed hands but Leeds were never to trail again.

Continued...

The Leeds squad that fought for the Yorkshire Cup and the Challenge Cup in the 1976-77 season.

Chris and I went on the first ever English Schoolboys' trip to France; he came from York and we both signed on in the same summer. The game was abandoned, of course.

'Rugby League is like life; you're in the trenches, in the front line, you've got to get up, you've got to shake your feathers and you've got to kick on. You have your period of mourning but as a young man born to play Rugby League you have to get on with your career. You have to go forward and, as captain, it was my role to lead them out again, whether it's a week later or a fortnight later. 'Are we going out there or are we not? Because I am. And let's go. Because you just have to keep playing. You've done your mourning – you never ever forget, mind you – but the game goes on.

'Death transcends everything. You can go right through 400 or 500 games and say, 'it's a tragedy that we lost this game, and it's a tragedy that we lost that game.' But just hold on – it's only a game. The tragedy was that somebody lost a life there. If it had happened to me I wouldn't have wanted people to be moping about. You play the game of Rugby League, you know the consequences, you give one or two out and invariably you might have to take one or two shots. If it had been my turn to go on the rugby

Player-coach Syd Hynes, operating at right centre, made certain that his side were in a comfort zone at the break, slipping a neat pass to loose forward Phil Cookson who ploughed over unstoppably against his hometown team. Full-back David Marshall landed his first goal of the afternoon to help send the Loiners in at the interval 11-5 ahead. Featherstone responded early in the second half with centre Steve Quinn's second long range goal and a series of Rovers' raids came to nothing in the face of resolute defence, winger Ken Kellett and second row Peter Smith both being held short.

Having ridden the storm, Leeds extended their lead when the huge-hearted Eccles, latching onto Ward's smart reverse pass, powered through a posse of defenders, with Marshall improving.

Featherstone, aided by possession from four successive scrums as Bridges found his heeling powers, gave the Loiners a late scare when second row Peter Smith forced his way over a minute from time. Quinn landed the goal, reducing the deficit to four points, and Rovers came close to snatching a win which they themselves conceded would not have been deserved, a last-second attack petering out when possession was spilled near the Leeds line.

Phil Cookson raises arms aloft after another victory over Featherstone Rovers at Odsal.

That inability to retain the ball had also proved costly for Featherstone in the early stages, Dyl having fly-kicked a loose ball on the Rovers 25 and winning the race to the touchdown for a score that wiped out Quinn's fourth-minute penalty. Winger Graham Bray retrieved Rovers' lead with a try created by scrum-half Dale Fennell, Bridges and stand off John Newlove.

But Dyl, with his long range score, soon got Leeds back into gear and those two touchdowns went a long way to earning the centre the White Rose Trophy, as the man of the match; an honour which many felt should have been his 12 months earlier for his performance against Hull KR.

Featherstone, meanwhile, drew comfort from the fact that they had played so well in a final staged at the home of their opponents. Rovers' undoubted abilities were confirmed later in the season when they won the Championship for the first time in their history. And for Leeds? The little matter of Wembley glory!

Leeds: Marshall; Hague, Hynes, Dyl, D Smith; Holmes, Banner; Dickinson, Ward, Pitchford, Eccles, Burton, Cookson.

Featherstone: Box; Bray, Coventry, Quinn, Kellett; Newlove, Fennell; Gibbins, Bridges, Farrar, Stone, Smith, Bell.

Referee: Mr MJ Naughton (Widnes).

Leeds: T: Dyl 2, Eccles, Cookson. G: Marshall 2.

Featherstone: T: Bray, Smith. G: Quinn 3.

Attendance: 7,615

field I'd have wanted everybody still to have played.'

The Loiners very next game was at Wembley, against favourites Widnes, when Syd Hynes' men were given little chance of adding the Challenge Cup to the Yorkshire Cup, which had been won in a second successive Headingley final.

The controversial decision to stage the White Rose decider at Leeds, made to please sponsors Esso who favoured the palatial backdrop – and the certainty that the game would go ahead – undoubtedly favoured Leeds, who for the second season enjoyed a narrow success, this time against Featherstone Rovers. It was still necessary, however, to win three games to get

Headingley Hero

Steve Pitchford

If any one player of the 1970s epitomised the popular image of the Rugby League prop, it was Steve Pitchford.

The barrel-chested powerhouse forward, packing 16 stones into his five feet nine inches frame, possessed an awesomely low centre of gravity which made him a tremendously difficult man to stop.

Never was this more evident than in the match which was possibly his finest hour – the 1977 Challenge Cup Final against Widnes.

Pitchford collected the Lance Todd Trophy that afternoon for a blockbusting display, over the full 80 minutes, which left the much-vaunted Widnes six floundering.

That performance led directly and deservedly to a call-up to Great Britain for the World Cup in Australia where more epic displays caused the Kangaroos – not Pitchford's favourite people – huge problems.

All four of the local product's caps were earned in that tournament, with the highlight his try in the World Cup Final against Australia at Sydney.

To his consternation Wigan full-back George Fairbairn inexplicably missed the conversion which would have turned a 13-12 deficit into a 14-12 success, leaving Pitchford with a rare loser's medal in a collection otherwise consisting entirely of gold.

Steve Pitchford signed for Leeds in 1968 and was obliged to learn the virtue of patience before finally consolidating his first team spot with a big match against Warrington in September 1974.

A sensational tackle on Wire flyer John Bevan which denied the winger a score and sustained the Loiners' 23-18 victory capped a display in which he outshone highly-rated opposite number Brian Brady.

The match marked the end of a period in the wilderness for Pitchford, who had suffered from a personality clash with Derek Turner, Leeds' coach from 1969 until 1973. Turner had a penchant for

Continued...

Steve Pitchford shows the kind of bullocking charge that brought him this try at Keighley in 1974 and the Lance Todd Trophy at Wembley three years later. Referee Stan Wall struggles to keep up.

there and the Loiners were handed a tough draw in each round.

The defence of the trophy began at Odsal, a little over a week after the Lazenby Cup had been retained with a 25-18 win over Bramley at McLaren Field in which David Smith scored a hat trick and Sanderson netted a brace. Peter Banner, a capture from Featherstone Rovers, grabbed one of Leeds' three tries in the 11-9 win. Graham Eccles and Alan Smith completed the scoring, with a John Holmes goal – the only one of the game – ultimately seeing Leeds through.

Leeds had to tough it out at the second round stage with another daunting away trip, this time to Wheldon Road. Castleford, typically, were not ready to lie down and the Loiners did well to force a 12-12 draw, Holmes scoring a try and two goals, David Smith nipping over and David Marshall landing a goal.

It was almost as close, four nights later, in the replay when a Holmes drop goal separated the sides in a 21-20 win. Centre Les Dyl raced over *forwards of a highly physical bent, a trait which was not in Pitchford's nature. And, for whatever reason, he failed to make a mark during Eric Ashton's single term of office. The waiting, now, was over. After having made a mere handful of first team appearances since his promising debut at Featherstone in April 1970, followed by an equally daunting game at Castleford in the following season's Yorkshire Cup (when he arrived at Wheldon Road with a full set of teeth and left with rather fewer, courtesy of the front row academy that was Dennis Hartley), Steve Pitchford retained the number 10 shirt for the next 27 games and was first choice blind side prop at Headingley for the remainder of his career. Coach Roy Francis, also impressed by hooker David Ward and open side prop Roy Dickinson, kept faith with the trio in preference to the more experienced Mick Harrison, Tony Fisher and Mervyn Hicks and his confidence in the youngsters was repaid with victory in that season's Premiership Final, when Pitchford picked up the first of his 20-odd medals in the 26-11 victory over St Helens.*

Steve Pitchford's display in the Challenge Cup final helped secure a place in Great Britain's 1977 World Cup squad. RFL secretary David Oxley presents the prop, and hooker David Ward, with their caps while Football Chairman Jack Myerscough beams with pride.

A prop forward with a notable turn of pace, Pitchford was also valued by his colleagues for his intelligent approach to Rugby League, one such moment when he moved the ball wide near his own line in the Challenge Cup semi-final of 1977 sparking a move which led to John Atkinson scoring the match-winning try. Pitchford followed up his big performance in that season's final with an impressive display, 12 months later, in the win over St Helens. He also pocketed winners' medals in the Yorkshire Cup in 1975-76, 1976-77, 1979-80 and 1980-81, and a second Premiership medal in 1978-79.

Those scant statistics, however, hardly illustrate his importance to the side. Rugby League has changed continually since the birth of the Northern Union in 1895. There has, though, been one eternal verity. If your front row is not going forward, or at the very least holding its own, no team will achieve much, regardless of the quality of its backs. Steve Pitchford was one of the men who laid the platform without which none of Leeds' glorious successes would have been possible.

in typical style for two tries, Holmes sidestepped over for his second try of the series and second row Phil Cookson contributed an important touchdown, with Marshall's four goals also being crucial.

The semi-final, at home to Dewsbury, proved to be the most straightforward of Leeds' games in the Yorkshire Cup that year. The Loiners were in unstoppable mien and booked a place in the final with seven tries to three in the 31-15 success. Alan Smith, Neil Hague, Cookson, Chris Burton, Paul Fletcher, Holmes and Steve Pitchford all forced their way over the whitewash, and Marshall kicked two goals, to set up a final against a strong Featherstone Rovers side which was to secure its first Championship a few months later.

The bid to win the BBC2 Floodlit Trophy for the first time in six years foundered at home to eventual winners Castleford after Hynes' men had overcome New Hunslet at Headingley in the first round. Hunslet, who were to gain promotion from Division Two at the end of the campaign, performed creditably enough but

A Loiner Looks Back

Harry Jepson

'We signed Chris Sanderson from a team in York, opposite where the York ground was, I remember going to watch him. He was a very good player. That was a dreadful day at Salford. 24 April 1977. Awful. I think I could take you to the blade of grass where he was injured. We had to take him to hospital and I had to identify him. They had to have a formal identification. Then I had to go and tell his parents. I'd known them, because I was involved in his signing for Leeds. I think he swallowed his vomit; awful thing. Chris had been in line to play in the 1977 Challenge Cup Final. There was a lad called Steve Dickens who was dreadfully upset, because they were both the same age. Over £20,000 was raised for his widow.'

were unable to deny a Leeds outfit which posted tries by Holmes, Roy Dickinson, Ward and Eccles, with former Hunslet skipper Marshall kicking four goals against his old club.

Castleford, though, wounded by their Yorkshire Cup exit, travelled to Headingley on 9 November, only three days after Leeds had edged Salford by a single point in a tough John Player tie, and were in rip-roaring form in attack and defence, limiting the Loiners to a Marshall goal and scoring four tries in the 17-2 victory.

It was Cas, again, who ended Leeds' hopes in the John Player competition. Leeds romped through their first round tie with Rochdale Hornets, treating the Headingley crowd to eight tries, including two for Dyl and one each by David Smith, Cookson, young scrum-half Kevin Dick, Dickinson, Pitchford and Marshall, who kicked four goals with Holmes landing the other. Salford were the next victims in a much tougher clash, the Loiners winning 18-17 through tries for Hague, Dyl, David Smith and Hynes,

Loiners Big Match

7 May 1977, Challenge Cup Final, Leeds 16 Widnes 7, Wembley

Six years previously, Leeds had prepared for the Challenge Cup Final with Leigh in the knowledge that stand off Mick Shoebottom was seriously injured after an incident in a Championship play-off fixture a couple of weeks earlier against Salford.

The cruel ironies of history took another twist in 1977. Chris Sanderson, Leeds' young scrum-half from the York area, was building up to the match of his career when he stepped onto the turf at the Willows, Salford, in the last league game of the season.

Sanderson was to lose his life that day in a moment that puts sport in its proper perspective. The half-back made a perfectly normal tackle, stayed on the ground, and never recovered.

The game was abandoned and with the Loiners' other scrum-half Peter Banner on his way to Australia for personal reasons Leeds, forced to get on with the business of running a Rugby League club and with a Challenge Cup Final to circumvent, had to look elsewhere within the camp for a man capable of

Leeds players are focussed and determined as they return to the pitch at half time.

taking on not only the redoubtable Widnes scrum-half Reggie Bowden but also with the capacity to face up to the fearsome Chemics pack.

Coach Syd Hynes settled, readily, on 19-year-old Kevin Dick. The youngster, signed three years earlier,

Continued...

had captained Great Britain Colts to victory over France the previous season and, in a performance which echoed that of David Barham against St Helens in the 1972 Championship Final, not only held his own against opposition of the highest standard but proved to be a major figure.

Dick quashed fears that he would be affected by nerves in his first Challenge Cup tie by landing a penalty after only three minutes, brushing aside the effects of a robust challenge by Widnes prop Bill Ramsey, the former Leeds player.

The half-back could, perhaps, have been fazed by his failure to land conversions by tries for winger John Atkinson and centre Les Dyl – the second was from a kickable position but left the Loiners trailing by the odd point in 15 – but Dick's irrepressible spirit shone through with the decisive try of the match.

Neil Hague carries skipper David Ward shoulder high, and Roy Dickinson parades Kevin Dick, as Leeds retrieve the Challenge Cup after nine years.

It came after a thundering run by prop Steve Pitchford, an unforgettable Lance Todd Trophy winner. The task of Dick, stand off John Holmes and the rest of the pedigree Leeds backs had been made much easier by the impact of the men up front with Pitchford producing a powerhouse performance which made him an unavoidable choice as man of the match. Yet another of Pitchford's rampaging runs left the Widnes defence wilting and, from the prop's play-the-ball on the Chemics' line, Dick sold the most audacious of dummies to scamper over for a try which, with his conversion, extended Leeds' lead to six points with 19 minutes left.

The tiring Widnes side had little left in the tank and the rest of the scoring fell to Dick with, in the last three minutes, a drop goal and a penalty.

Centre Les Dyl and his team-mates made sure that Chris Sanderson's young widow was invited into the changing rooms to take part in the celebrations, skipper David Ward saying: 'We tried that much harder for Chris today.' 'It was the greatest tribute they could have paid to him,' was her reply.

The Loiners had fully deserved their win against a side, acknowledged as the cup kings, which had appeared at Wembley for the third successive season – equalling Bradford Northern's record of the late 1940s – and which would return in 1979, 1981, 1982 and 1984.

Despite having finished ninth in the league, albeit a place above a Widnes outfit notorious for focusing on the Challenge Cup, the Leeds board had given coach Hynes a vote of confidence prior to the game which was repaid handsomely.

After Dick had established that early lead, Holmes showed his defensive abilities with a try-saving tackle on Widnes winger Dennis O'Neill, before Atkinson had a 'try' vetoed by referee Vince Moss, of Manchester, for a forward pass.

The Chemics drew level when full-back Ray Dutton landed a penalty and took the lead when Bowden switched play, centre Mal Aspey ghosting past several defenders and Dutton again improving.

Continued...

Marshall again proving influential with three goals.

The assault came to a close, however, with Castleford's second visit to Headingley in 11 days. The Wheldon Road outfit gained further revenge for the Yorkshire Cup exit with a 20-14 win in which Leeds matched the visitors' four tries with touchdowns for Alan Smith, Cookson, David Smith and Hynes. But a solitary goal, by Kevin Dick, wasn't enough to prevent defeat. If there was any consolation, however, it came with the fact that, as in the Floodlit Cup, Leeds had gone out to the eventual winners. Castleford went on to beat Blackpool Borough in one of the most romantic of finals, adding the John Player Trophy to the Floodlit Trophy.

With league form indifferent – Lancashire and Cumberland, in particular, were less then fertile hunting grounds, with defeats at Workington Town, Widnes, Wigan, Leigh, St Helens, Warrington and Rochdale Hornets – Hynes' attention focused on the Challenge Cup.

Batley, struggling in the lower reaches of Division Two, were no match for their hosts in the first round. Leeds amassed 10 tries in the 40-6 victory, including a hat trick for Alan Smith, two for Eccles, and touchdowns by Fletcher, David Smith, Banner, Cookson and Holmes, with Holmes (3) and Cookson (2) kicking the goals.

But a well-placed Holmes kick bamboozled Widnes' Great Britain winger Stuart Wright, Atkinson winning the race to the ball, to bring Leeds back into the game at half time at just 7-5 adrift. And a touchdown for centre Les Dyl in the second half, allowed after a pass on his own 25 yard line by Bowden had hit the referee – Ward winning the resultant scrum – helped Leeds retrieve the lead. Dick, from the scrum, flung out a reverse pass to Holmes who switched play for Dyl to blast through the defence for a stunning score. And although Dick missed the goals, the scrum-half's eight subsequent points were enough to win the Cup.

Leeds: Murrell; A Smith, Hague, Dyl, Atkinson; Holmes, Dick; Harrison, Ward, Pitchford, Eccles, Cookson, Fearnley. Subs: David Smith, Dickinson.
Widnes: Dutton; Wright, Aspey, Eckersley, O'Neill; Hughes, Bowden; Ramsey, Elwell; Mills, Dearden, Adams, Laughton. Subs: George, Foran.
Referee: Mr V Moss (Manchester)
Leeds: T: Atkinson, Dyl, Dick. G: Dick 3. DG: Dick.
Widnes: T: Aspey. G: Dutton 2.
Attendance: 80,871

Headingley Hero
Kevin Dick

Kevin Dick was perhaps the ultimate big match player. His performance in his first-ever Challenge Cup tie – the 1977 Final against Widnes, at the age of just 19 – is testimony to that and for any doubters there were many other epic displays by the stocky scrum-half to savour.
Dick always had an edge to his game, an aggressive arrogance which both charmed and infuriated the likes of his skipper David Ward.
The local lad made good went very close to picking up the Lance Todd Trophy for his display at Wembley against Widnes and collected two other Man of the Match awards during his glittering career with Leeds. And, each time, the opposition arguably had only themselves to blame.
The last trophy garnered by Leeds in a 15-season run of success stretching from 1966-67 to 1980-81 was the Yorkshire Cup. Dick was the scourge of Hull KR that day, and his inspiration was Rovers chairman Colin Hutton.
Hutton was also the Great Britain Manager and had been instrumental in dropping Dick for the Third Test against New Zealand.
Dick took great pleasure in being Leeds' match-winner with a late drop goal and a couple of touchline goals to have a major say in the 9-8 result.
It had been a similar story 18 months earlier. The Great Britain side to tour Australia and New Zealand had been announced on the eve of the Premiership Final and Dick was given an ideal opportunity to prove a point.
Bradford's Alan Redfearn had been selected ahead of Dick and, from the Leeds scrum-half's point of view, the timing could not have been better scripted.

Continued...

With Dick bossing the show, Leeds swept to a 24-2 victory over Northern. His eight goals were a record for the final and, added to his contribution in the loose, earned him the Harry Sunderland Trophy.

His finest hour was, perhaps, his Wembley debut in 1977 when he was called up following the death of Chris Sanderson and grabbed an astonishing try, direct from acting half-back, when several experienced Widnes players were somehow persuaded to buy his outrageous dummy.

A wonderful score by a player, totally unfazed by the occasion, who now reflects: 'I was so young, so exuberant. But your feet are kept on the ground in this game and that had certainly been the case when I missed the easy conversion of Les Dyl's earlier score. But we knew we had it won with 15 minutes to go; we were laughing and giggling, we had it all in hand and we had the chance to actually enjoy the occasion.'

A magical memory for a player of true star quality who achieved something of a record the following season when he stepped onto the Wembley turf as a substitute to become perhaps the only man to play in two Challenge Cup Finals without having featured in any of the previous rounds.

Typically, Dick reflects of the St Helens game: 'Much is still made of Noonan's knock on. He wouldn't have scored. If he'd caught the ball, he'd have come inside and I'd have taken his head off. As it happens we finished with the longest scrum of all time. It went on forever, I messed around not putting the ball in right, and we didn't bind properly.'

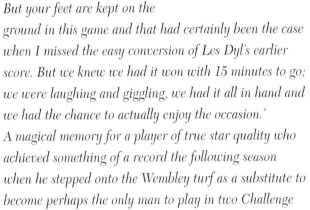

Hugs for Kevin Dick from John Holmes, John Atkinson and Les Dyl as the young half back scores an outrageous try in the 1977 Challenge Cup Final. Ex-Leeds man Bill Ramsey can hardly believe it.

Dick's ability, at such a young age, to retain his composure in those closing moments when as the feeding scrum-half he held the key to the match, says much for his maturity. As his skipper David Ward says: 'You have to have whatever Kevin had to be a great player. He had 'bounce'. How other people view that is another matter. Your Shaun Edwards and Ellery Hanleys, they have to have something that the average guy has not got. It's not just talent; it's having arrogance without the sharpness, having the confidence and the panache and knowing deep down, 'I'm the man today, I'm in control of this position."

Barrow belied indifferent league form which would cost them a place in the top flight with a battling performance in the next round. Leeds, while never in serous trouble, could never quite cut loose but were happy enough to settle for a 21-11 win which involved a brace by John Atkinson, with Hague, Dickinson and Pitchford also crossing and young full-back Brian Murrell landing three goals.

Challenge Cup quarter-final ties didn't come any tougher than trips to Cumberland and Workington Town, who had won the Lancashire Cup at around the same time as Leeds were lifting the Yorkshire Cup, presented a more than daunting hurdle.

That testing prospect became reality in a game in which just one try was scored. The youngster who had made the full-back role his own in preference to the veteran Marshall was the hero in what is remembered as Murrell's match. His touchline conversion – his second goal of the game – of a late Alan Smith try, combined with a Holmes drop goal, put Leeds 8-2 ahead in a truly hard-fought contest. The

A Loiner Looks Back

John Atkinson

'We set our stall out to win the Challenge Cup in 1977, and we did it. It wasn't an easy passage, we had to go to Workington in the third round, they were a good side, and we gritted our teeth and won 8-2. And we beat Widnes, who were a magnificent side, in the final. We played well and we deserved to win with some great performances. Stevie Pitchford, Graham Eccles and Kevin Dick, for example, were superb.'

Loiners' reward? A semi-final tie at Wigan against St Helens, who had been beaten 23-13 at Headingley in a league game in October but had won the December return 17-6.

The day dawned and the big-match mentality now prevalent under Hynes was apparent in the 7-2 victory. As in the third round, Leeds' opponents were denied a try (only Barrow, with two touchdowns in the second round, could breach the Loiners' goal-line) and a long range try by John Atkinson, with a goal by Murrell and two Holmes drop goals, sealed a return to Wembley.

That victory atoned for the indifferent league form which was epitomised by a poor December in which all three league games were lost, 17-4 at St Helens, 14-10 at Warrington and 18-8, on Boxing Day, at home to Wakefield Trinity.

There were, however, commendable successes along the way. Barrow were bested 16-8 at Craven Park in a game in which Stuart Johnston and Holmes crossed and Willie Oulton, a £600 signing from Batley, kicked five goals. Hapless Oldham, who finished bottom of Division One after a 'devil' of a season in which 666 points were conceded, shipped 56 of those at Headingley in mid-March when Atkinson raced over for four super tries. And a young loose forward by the name of David Heron, a major signing from Hunslet Parkside, scored a try on his debut in the 13-12 win at Castleford played between the Challenge Cup games with Batley and Barrow.

A Loiner Looks Back

David Ward

'Being given the captaincy was a real high spot. Dear me, look at the history of the place. Captain of Leeds Rugby League Club? Jesus Christ, I'll take this! We were on the big stage, we won every trophy, and I felt as though I was the King of the World. When you are captain of Leeds you are captain of the greatest Rugby League club in the world; even if they are bottom of the league.

'I'd started as a kid, in awe of the senior players in the dressing room, to being a senior player encouraging the youngsters, to being captain.

'1977 was the Queen's Silver Jubilee. Her Majesty cannot have had a better year than David Ward, it was a golden year for me. Everything I touched went right. I got the captaincy, I went to Wembley, I made my Great Britain debut, I get picked for the World Cup, I get the Young Player of the Year award and I get the Man of Steel Award. You can't touch that year. But to be a good 'un, it's easy getting to the top, it's harder stopping there.'

Loose forward Stan Fearnley aims to breach the defence with David Ward in support.

15. WONDER WEMBLEY WIN

Leeds' ability to rise to the occasion was again in evidence in the 1977-78 season in which the Challenge Cup was retained despite continued indifferent league form.

St Helens were beaten at Wembley in a classic final, the victory ensuring that the Loiners' record of having won a major trophy in each season since 1966-67 was maintained.

The Yorkshire Cup, however, fell by the wayside after two pulsating second round ties against Hull. And the Lazenby Cup was also lost as the Loiners went down to an 18-16 defeat at Bramley on 12 August in a game in which scrum half Kevin Dick scored a try and two goals, Roy Dickinson crashed over and Steve Dickens touched down.

Leeds were out of the Yorkshire Cup before September arrived. The competition, almost a

Big match mentality – the Leeds squad which rose to the occasion in 1977-78.

preseason tourney, got underway on 20th August, the holders overcoming Batley at Mount Pleasant 33-6 with two tries each for John Holmes and half-back David Treasure. Prop Mick Harrison and winger John Atkinson also touched down, with Dick chipping in with a try and six goals.

Hull FC, however, came to Headingley seven days later and fought a classic 18-18 draw, Dick keeping Leeds in the contest with a try and three goals to supplement two Treasure tries and an Atkinson touchdown. But the Airlie Birds had the better of matters in the Boulevard return, winning 19-11 as the Loiners could only muster tries by Alan Smith, David Smith and Neil Hague, plus a Willie Oulton goal.

The League programme began brightly and Leeds were unbeaten in September. Only three days after the Yorkshire Cup defeat at the Boulevard, there was quick revenge against Hull with a 25-13 Division One win at Headingley in which pacemen Les Dyl and David Smith bagged a brace apiece, Atkinson crossed and prop Steve Pitchford forced his way over, Oulton adding three goals and Holmes landing a timely

> A Loiner Looks Back
>
> **Billy Watts**
>
> *'Syd Hynes never lost a final as coach. I don't know the secret. We didn't always do that well in the league but somehow, when it came to cup football, Syd seemed to have that magical touch. He got all the players performing when it really mattered including twice at Wembley, when we were behind both times and fought our way back.*
>
> *'It was maybe a stroke of luck that he had Kevin Dick on hand to take over from Chris Sanderson in 1977. Dick had a wonderful temperament but Hynes must take much credit for handling him right. Syd was awesome, somehow with finals he used to stamp his authority.'*

A Loiner Looks Back

John Atkinson

John Atkinson scored 340 tries in a career with Leeds spanning 16 years and 518 matches, from his debut on 25 March 1966 against York to his final game, at Widnes, on 5 May 1982.

His abiding memory, however, is not of any of those touchdowns, many of which are firmly lodged in the collective consciousness of his legion of fans, but of one that got away.

It was during a match against Hull KR at Headingley when Atkinson looked a certain scorer after having been given a glimmer of space when scrum-half Sammy Sanderson worked the blind side at a scrum. Try no 341 was, however, denied him by the rare talent that was Rovers half-back Roger Millward, who halted the winger with a wonderful cover tackle.

Reflects Atkinson: 'Roger talked to me a while ago about how I patted him on the head and said, "what a wonderful tackle." But it was. I was playing against a great player and he'd read it. Despite my pace and everything, he'd read the situation and he tackled me. He said it was one of the best moments of his career when I congratulated him and my response was, "Roger I was home and dry, then out of the corner of my eye I saw you and the next thing you had me round the ankles. I'd ended up in touch but I hadn't done anything wrong." It was a fabulous piece of rugby, a great decision from our scrum-half, I'd taken the right decision to take this very short gap, and out of the blue came Roger.

'It's like a piece of great fielding in cricket. You don't have to score a run for great cricket and it's the same in rugby. I just thought, "where the hell did he come from?"'

John Atkinson and John Holmes are among the Great Britain players being put through their paces at Headingley by Jim Challinor in preparation for the 1974 tour to Australia.

Steve Evans had the better of John Atkinson, Willie Oulton and Sammy Sanderson on this occasion. But the April Fools Day joke was on Featherstone, Leeds winning the Odsal Challenge Cup semi-final 14-9 to book a Wembley date with St Helens.

drop goal.

Bramley were denied the chance to add to their Lazenby Cup success, Leeds going back to McLaren Field and securing a hard-earned 22-20 win with tries by Hague, Atkinson, Treasure and David Smith, Oulton's five goals garnering a derby win.

The next game, at Workington, suggested that the Loiners could make an impact at league level. Town, hard-bitten members of the top flight, were not accustomed to losing many games at Derwent Park and were still mindful of the previous season's Challenge Cup quarter-final defeat. Leeds were unable to come away with both points and were obliged to settle for a 15-15 draw but their tenacity was illustrated by the fact that they earned winning pay – for an away draw – having scored only two tries to Town's three, Paul Fletcher and David Smith crossing and the accurate Oulton kicking four goals, Treasure's drop goal ensuring parity.

Dewsbury were hammered 40-11 at home in the last game of the month, Brian Murrell and Sammy Sanderson (no relation to the unfortunate Chris) scoring two tries each with

A Loiner Looks Back

Harry Jepson

'Dave Heron was a fine player. The first time he touched the ball for Leeds he scored a try, he went under the posts at the St Michael's Lane end. He and Tim Wilby both played for Hunslet Parkside and for Great Britain Colts. I always felt that Alan Hardisty spoiled Wilby, when he was coaching Leeds' second team. We'd signed him because he was a bone-crushing tackler. One day at Keighley, I said to Alan Horsfall, "what's the matter with Tim Wilby?" He was standing back and using the ball. After that match he said he'd changed his style. Alan Horsfall said, "forget about that. You're not a creative Rugby League player. You're just an absolute bloody destroyer." I'm sure that Alan Hardisty saw something in him that he felt he could develop, and who am I to question? But Wilby's basic ability was as a ruthless destroyer, and he never really recovered.

'One of Dave Heron's great assets was that he was a wonderful tackler. His tackling was intense, players who had been tackled by him knew about it, and yet he had this wonderful ability with the ball as well.'

Tim Wilby looks on as Frank Myler congratulates Syd Hynes on the 1977 Challenge Cup win.

Headingley Hero

David Ward

A feature of Leeds' success in the sixties and the seventies was the obviously strong team spirit.

That priceless commodity, which has so often eluded big money sides at Headingley and elsewhere, owed much to the fact that many of the players came through the Colts ranks and were more than ready to give that vital little bit extra, for the club and for each other.

None typified that approach more than David Ward, a captain who wore his blue and amber heart on his sleeve.

Ward, a Shaw Cross lad and a man of indomitable spirit, joined Leeds in 1971, rose to become captain and memorably led Leeds to successive Challenge Cup victories in 1977 and 1978.

The 1977 success over Widnes was achieved against a background of turmoil and grief following the death of half-back Chris Sanderson in a game at Salford.

And the 1978 verdict, against St Helens, was mounted despite a dreadful opening quarter in which the Saints established a 10-point lead.

Both triumphs owed much to Ward's powers of leadership. The hooker, who had captained junior

Continued...

David Smith, Dickinson, Graham Eccles and Atkinson completing the rout, goals going to Chris Gibson (5) and Oulton (3). Nothing, however, illustrated Leeds' inconsistent league form more than the fact that the Loiners would lose the return, at Crown Flatt in mid-December, 18-12, when Pitchford and David Smith grabbed the Loiners' only two tries and Oulton kicked three goals.

Hopes of making an impact on the Championship were ended by seven defeats in the 10 games before Christmas, Wigan, St Helens (twice), Castleford, Bradford Northern and Widnes joining Dewsbury in getting the better of Leeds. A hard-earned win at Warrington, 16-10, when Alan Smith and David Smith notched tries and Holmes kicked two goals and two drop goals, Dick also landing two goals, served evidence of the Loiners' true abilities and New Hunslet, on their way to relegation – albeit just three points shy of safety – were beaten 27-15 courtesy of two David Smith tries and touchdowns from Sanderson, Pitchford and Cookson, with Oulton kicking six goals.

sides from an early age, led by persuasion and by example and it was that noteworthy resilience that so often inspired those around him.

Not that Ward wasn't without many of the finer touches expected of a Leeds player. A tireless defender and an astute tactician, Ward relished controlling the momentum of a match.

Possibly his finest moment in that regard came at Wembley in 1978 when he landed a drop goal a minute into the second half which crucially maintained Leeds' impetus.

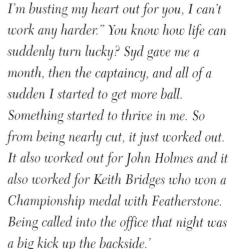

Tears of joy and relief for David Ward in 1978 as Leeds hold out against St Helens to win the Challenge Cup.

And his worst moment probably came towards the end of the same game when he kicked a second drop goal. That effort stretched Leeds' lead to two points but also gave St Helens the chance to gain possession deep in Loiners' territory.

The Loiners survived and Ward, who still crucifies himself over his tactical gaffe, was in a highly emotional state at the end of the game.

His reaction typified a captain who led his unit with a heady mix of sheer physical example and cunning savvy.

Ward shares with several former colleagues the knowledge that it could all have been so very different. The dividing line between success and failure in sport is frighteningly narrow and there was a time when the hooker could have found himself on the way out of Headingley but for a masterstroke by coach Syd Hynes.

Ward reflects: 'John Holmes was captain but it didn't suit his character and I was struggling because I wasn't getting enough ball. Syd said, "there's pressure from them above. They've put an offer in for Keith Bridges at Featherstone and I don't want to buy him." I said, "Syd, I'm busting my heart out for you, I can't work any harder." You know how life can suddenly turn lucky? Syd gave me a month, then the captaincy, and all of a sudden I started to get more ball. Something started to thrive in me. So from being nearly cut, it just worked out. It also worked out for John Holmes and it also worked for Keith Bridges who won a Championship medal with Featherstone. Being called into the office that night was a big kick up the backside.'

'He epitomised the local lad wanting to make good,' recalls Harry Jepson. 'We once lost at Widnes and David kicked John Carroll out of his car at Tingley crossroads. David was still very upset by the defeat and Carroll had said "it's only a game!" He did go back for him though, he found him walking down the roadside.

'I've seen David so strapped up after a game they couldn't get him into the bath. Once in, he couldn't get out, he'd put himself through so much. He had a massive, wonderful heart and he led by example.'

Ward himself admits: 'Being captain of Leeds was a great honour and I still feel a bit humble talking about it. I never asked anybody to do anything I wouldn't do and I think it was something I was destined to do; I captained every team I played for, from school onwards.'

Those wins, however, were undermined by a 25-22 home defeat by Wigan in the first round of the John Player competition in which two tries for Sanderson, touchdowns for Eccles and Dyl and five Dick goals weren't enough to ensure progress. The game has entered the annals of folklore, particularly in Wigan, as 'Green Vigo's match,' the winger producing a once-in-a-lifetime display which netted a hat trick. The experience left Atkinson, the perfectionist, so shattered that he immediately announced his retirement – a decision which was, happily, quickly rescinded.

Between times, Leeds made an impact on the BBC2 Floodlit Trophy, beating Widnes 16-13 in the Preliminary Round with tries from Brendan White, Cookson and Sanderson, Ward's drop goal nicely complementing Dick's three goals.

Rochdale Hornets, rare visitors to Headingley, were beaten 19-5 in the second

John Holmes moves in to help Roy Dickinson in the Challenge Cup semi-final. Sammy Sanderson is also on hand if need be.

round, Gibson scoring a try and two goals and David Smith, Atkinson, Dyl and Stan Fearnley, a loose forward snapped up from Bradford, forcing their way over the whitewash.

Leeds got themselves back into the winning mood needed for an assault on Wembley with a 22-6 Boxing Day win over Wakefield Trinity, and comfortable victories in January over Hull KR, Workington Town and, in the Belle Vue return, Wakefield. Featherstone Rovers and Salford put a brake on the winning run but the 15-5 and

A Loiner Looks Back

Steve Pitchford

The meat in the sandwich. St Helens Tony Karalius, about to be compressed by Steve Pitchford and Mick Harrison.

'Syd Hynes was one of the boys. He didn't mess about too much as coach although I do remember him bringing the tackle count in. It was half time in one game and although we were winning, we weren't playing very well. Syd says to Mick Harrison, "Mick, I need you to do more tackles, you've only done three tackles in the first half." Big Mick says "well would you run at me?" Everybody looked and went, "Oh no!" That just brightened the whole dressing room and we played a lot better in the second half. That was Syd and his first attempt at tackle counts.'

Loiners Big Match

13 May 1978, Challenge Cup Final, Leeds 14 St Helens 12, Wembley

David Ward, the Leeds captain in the Challenge Cup successes of 1977 and 1978, was a leader who wore his heart on his sleeve. The former Shaw Cross junior unashamedly wept at the final whistle when the Loiners retained the game's most glittering domestic prize. And his tears were undoubtedly the result of a mix of both joy and relief.

Joy at the retention of the game's major trophy. And relief that his late tactical gaffe had not led to defeat. As honest as they come, Ward has long held up his own error as a lesson to young players as an example of the fact that scoring is not necessarily the be-all and end-all.

A strange assertion, on the face of it? Ward takes up the tale at the point where, after stand off John Holmes had put Leeds ahead for the first time five minutes from the close with a sensational drop goal with his 'wrong' left foot, he himself added his second one-pointer with just two minutes left on the clock.

'We were in control, we were winning the game. Looking back on it, as a coach I tell the story to kids now. Why did I kick my second drop goal? I should never ever have kicked it. I knew there were only a couple of minutes left and I should have closed the game down. We should have camped on the Saints line and stayed there. That drop goal was only worth a point, and we're two points in the clear now, but what does that matter? Because look where we are. Our arses are on our own tryline now. They kick off to us, and we're under our own posts, and we all start dithering. And lo and behold, we drop the ball. St Helens have it. There's now about 30 seconds on the clock and they run it at us. And they get an opportunity. I'm not saying they would have scored, but there was a chance, but Derek Noonan dropped the ball. He didn't drop it over the line, he was 10

Continued...

yards away from the line, but there was plenty of movement. There was plenty of forward movement among the Saints, but there was also plenty of sideways movement with the seventh cavalry coming across.

'There was now about 15 seconds to go, it was a scrum down, and we just messed around. We were slow getting in, we collapsed it, we got up, we didn't get in, the scrum-half wouldn't come round. Then the hooter went while we were still scrummaging down. And me, did I heave a sigh of relief! Because after I'd dropped that goal and done a little bit of celebrating I thought, 'what have I done here now? Did we really need that one?"

Steve Pitchford, 1977 Lance Todd Trophy winner, congratulates 1978 recipient George Nicholls.

Ward's leadership skills, illustrated by his willingness to criticise himself, were in evidence throughout the game which in the early stages went as predicted by the pundits, who reckoned that full-back Willie Oulton would be given a torrid time under the bomb.

The prophesies came true after only four minutes, St Helens loose forward Harry Pinner hoisting a high kick which Oulton was unable to smother, the ball bouncing out his arms towards winger John Atkinson who was also unable to defuse the situation. Saints hooker Graham Liptrot pounced for one of the easiest touchdowns of his career and full-back Geoff Pimblett added the extras. The Lancastrians, coached by former Leeds boss Eric Ashton, were five points up and Leeds were in trouble.

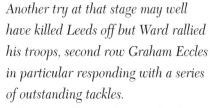

Willie Oulton and Mick Harrison reflect on a job well done.

The lead was doubled after 13 minutes, and the Loiners' woes increased, when St Helens half-back Ken Gwilliam fed stand off Bill Francis from the base of a scrum and the Yorkshireman scythed through his fellow county-men for another devastating score, Pimblett adding salt to the wound with his second conversion.

Another try at that stage may well have killed Leeds off but Ward rallied his troops, second row Graham Eccles in particular responding with a series of outstanding tackles.

Atkinson, in his 400th game for the club and in his fifth Challenge Cup Final, clawed his side back into contention with a glittering score, racing onto a well-timed pass by his centre Les Dyl and rounding Pinner and Pimblett to cross in the corner.

Oulton – with Atkinson, at fault for the first Saints score – joined his team-mate in making amends for the error by landing the touchline conversion but St Helens kept their noses in front with a Pimblett penalty six minutes before the break. Ward, however, knew that St Helens were busted. 'We were behind at half time, but not in terms of the flow of the game. When that half time whistle went we were the side on top. You have to smell that. Don't worry about the score-line, because there's another 40 minutes to be played. 'We're on top now, boys,' and we ran in. We didn't walk in; the whole Leeds team ran in, over the back and the dog track. We passed the St Helens guys, who were walking, and that hit them psychologically.

'Even though they were winning 12-5, we were in control of the game; but we had to keep our impetus going. The first time we got down to their end we had to come back

Continued...

21-3 reverses did nothing to deter Leeds as they prepared for a home tie with Halifax intent on the defence of the Challenge Cup.

Halifax, at that time, were at rock bottom. The Thrum Hall men had lost to amateurs Cawoods in the John Player Cup a couple of months earlier and would finish the season at the foot of Division Two with only two victories. Against that background the Pennine side, who that month appointed Maurice Bamford as coach – the future Great Britain and Leeds boss taking over from Harry Fox – were stoical in the 25-5 defeat. Leeds' qualities could not be dimmed, though, and the Loiners went into the last 16

with a score. So, straight after half time, we get down there, I made the decision, and I popped one. That was my first drop goal of the game, and it kept the momentum going, and we now have a roll on.'
Centre Neil Hague helped bring Leeds closer, sending winger David Smith over, and after Pimblett had seen a drop goal attempt drift wide with 14 minutes remaining, the Loiners drew level nine minutes from the close with a try for second row Phil Cookson. And, for Ward, the tale of the late drop goals is that Holmes' won it and his own almost lost it.

Leeds: Oulton; D Smith, Hague, Dyl, Atkinson; Holmes, J Sanderson; Harrison, Ward, Pitchford, Cookson, Eccles, Crane. Subs: Dick, Dickinson.
St Helens: Pimblett; Jones, Noonan, Glynn, Mathias; Francis, Gwilliam; D Chisnall, Liptrot, James, Nicholls, Cunningham, Pinner.
Referee: Mr WH Thompson (Huddersfield)
Leeds: T: Atkinson, D Smith, Cookson. G: Oulton. DG: Ward 2, Holmes.
St Helens: T: Liptrot, Francis. G: Pimblett 3.
Attendance: 96,000

with two tries each for David Smith and Atkinson, together with tries for Fletcher, Eccles and former Hull loose forward Mick Crane.

The second round draw handed Leeds a trip to Belle Vue for a meeting with a Wakefield Trinity side that, 12 months later, would be featuring at Wembley themselves. Not in 1978, however, as Leeds beat them by a slightly higher margin than they had Halifax. The Loiners eased to the quarter-finals with a 28-6 victory in which Cookson crashed over for two tries, supported by touchdowns from Dyl, Hague, Crane and Sanderson, with in-form Oulton kicking five goals.

A crowd of 18,637 turned up for the third round clash with Bradford Northern. Northern would finish as Championship runners-up but the Odsal outfit were unable to contain Leeds on that day. Atkinson, in particular, was in big match mood and gave Northern winger David Barends a torrid time, racing over for two tries with Hague scoring Leeds' other touchdown. Oulton's three goals and a drop goal from Holmes ensured a 16-8 win and a semi-final against a Featherstone Rovers side which had ended Leeds' hopes at the third round stage two years earlier with the Loiners' biggest ever

The Greatest Drop Goal?

John Holmes making an impossible point.

The drop goal has been a vital part of a team's armoury for as long as rugby football, of either code, has been played.
Its ranking has always been higher in Rugby Union, which has traditionally valued kicking as of more value than handling, but Rugby League has also long recognised its importance.
Intriguingly, a mode of scoring which had slipped out of vogue somewhat became fashionable again when its value was reduced from two points to one in the 1974-75 season.
The Loiners, though, had long benefited from what can be one of the most dramatic means of winning a match, notably in the 1957 Challenge Cup semi-final against Whitehaven at Odsal when scrum half Jeff Stevenson landed a long-range effort which transformed what seemed a certain one-point defeat into a 10-9 victory. The Challenge Cup, famed for producing moments of

Continued...

unrivalled drama, came up with the goods again in 1978, when Leeds met St Helens in a pulsating Wembley final.
There had been much debate, pre-match, regarding full back Willie Oulton's capabilities under the high kick and, sure enough, the Saints set out to test Oulton in the early stages.
One effort produced a demoralising try, and the Loiners were quickly 10 points down when the Saints scythed through a hesitant defence for another converted score.
Leeds, though, bounced back in glorious fashion to equalise. And, with the match in the balance, John Holmes produced a moment of magic with a drop goal that many rate as the greatest-ever – in any form of rugby.
The stand-off was under intense pressure as he took the ball on the last tackle and with a one-pointer clearly on. Impressive spoiling play by the Saints appeared to have averted the danger for the Lancastrians as a couple of defenders closed in on the moustachioed wonder.
But, despite going down in a two-man tackle, Holmes somehow managed to retain his balance and, with his left and 'wrong' foot, coolly kicked a magnificent drop goal, from an almost prone position and from almost 25 yards out, which put his side ahead for the first time.
That score was followed by a second drop goal of the game for skipper David Ward – and a let-off for Leeds when Saints bombed a last-second try scoring opportunity.
The laurels, though, went to Holmes. There have been, in the history of rugby, a multitude of drop goals which players, in truth, should have scored as the recognised experts in their respective positions. And there have been drop goals which players of any quality had no right to kick.
Holmes' effort belongs firmly in the latter category, an amazing goal which, like the bumble bee, defies the laws of physics. A true and possibly unassailable contender for the accolade of the Greatest Drop Goal ever.

Willie Oulton's goalkicking was an important factor in Leeds making an immediate return to Wembley in 1978.

Challenge Cup defeat. As Rovers had also thwarted hot favourites Leeds in the 1967 semi-final, recent history suggested that the gods would not favour Headingley hopes.

The match was played on April Fool's Day, at Odsal, but the jokes were, this time, on Featherstone. Hague and Holmes, two of the jesters in the lively Leeds dressing room, scored the tries in the 14-9 win, with Oulton again a major figure with four goals.

With a return to Wembley guaranteed, Leeds made certain of a place in the Premiership play-offs with victories at New Hunslet and at home to Widnes, followed by home wins over Salford and Warrington.

In a busy close to the season, the Loiners slipped at Hull and Castleford and at home to Bradford Northern, who hosted Leeds in the first round of the Premiership play-offs on 30 April. Leeds, clearly and understandably committed to the Wembley dream, were outgunned by a Northern outfit which went on to win the Premiership with a 17-8 win over Widnes at Swinton. Dyl scored two tries and Gibson added two goals in the 18-10 defeat but glory in the competition which transcended all others was to belong to Leeds.

16. LEAVING IT LATE

Leeds rose, in 1978-79, to fourth in the table from the disappointing ranking of eighth the previous year and ninth in 1976-77. The improvement came despite (or maybe because of) the Loiners' exit from the Challenge Cup at the first round stage as just one game was subsequently lost – at home to Workington Town – after what was undoubtedly a demoralising defeat.

As David Ward, as proud a captain as it's possible to find, explains: 'The two Challenge Cup Finals, and the run-ups to them, were out of this world. In the third season, in 1979, after we'd won the Challenge Cup in 1977 and 1978, we got drawn at Hull in the first round. And we got beat. We'd just had two years of having the Challenge Cup in the cabinet at Leeds; what you have to do when you have a trophy like that is you just close your eyes, soak the atmosphere in and embrace all the prestige that it gives you as a player. It gives you status as a player; it gives the whole club so much kudos in the world of rugby. To lose it in your first match … well, dear me, I really cried then. It wasn't just the one game we'd lost, we'd lost the trophy in our first game, we hadn't even got through to the semis.

'Of course it was a tough call and somebody had to go. That, I suppose, is the magic of the Challenge Cup.'

The magic of the Leeds sides of the 1960s and 1970s was their capacity to bounce back from shattering disappointments, such as the 17-6 defeat at the Boulevard on 10 February 1979, in the best possible fashion; by collecting the next

A Loiner Looks Back

Graham Eccles

'The Stevie Pitchfords and the Mick Harrisons would be on for the full game and they would still be playing at the end of that time. Pitchford was very deceiving, he was very quick over the first 30 yards. And although he looked fat, he was so solid. It was like running into a barrel. He was a tremendous runner with the ball. Mick Harrison was a fantastic player. Some people used to ask me, "what does he do?" And I'd say, "you want to hear people moan when he hits them." Mick used to hit them across the chest, and you could hear the breath come out of them when he hit them. Mick Harrison is, certainly, the strongest bloke that I played with.

'Leeds made some tremendous signings. Mick travelled from Hull for I don't know how many years, and he never used to miss training. The other Mick Crane used to miss a few times but he was a different type of footballer, more the Ray Batten type perhaps. Ray would slide into a tackle and players didn't know the ball had gone. And there was David Ward, a captain who led by example. You'd want him in your team every week, you certainly wouldn't want him against you. He played with all his heart, with that Leeds shirt on, and I don't think it would have mattered to him what money he was on, he just went on that field and played his heart out.'

Pure theatre. Mick Harrison and Steve Pitchford pack down, together with hooker David Ward. Scrum-half Keith Hepworth prepares to feed and stand-off half John Holmes awaits the outcome with interest.

Headingley Hero
Neil Hague

There is a story of how the eccentric England cricketer Derek Randall once ducked as a slogged ball skied downward towards him on the boundary. The six cost his county, Nottinghamshire, the game, and his team-mates were not best pleased; until, that is, Randall, with a broad smile, produced the ball as confirmation that his team had won.

*'What the f*** did you think you were doing?' the Notts lads blasted. 'I just wondered if I could catch it behind my back,' was Randall's response.*

Neil Hague would recognise a kindred spirit. The hugely talented utility player liked nothing more than trying something different and, to their credit, a succession of coaches including Roy Francis and Syd Hynes were happy to indulge him.

Hague would often catch a rugby ball behind his back in training sessions and jokes: 'I was better at catching it that way than in front! As a team we did like to try things and we had a very relaxed approach to the game, although that doesn't mean that we weren't taking it seriously.

'I remember Brian Murrell running down the wing, he had the ball in his right hand as if he was going to pass, but instead transferred it behind his back to his left hand and off he went.

'We had a lot of players with that touch of class. They would try things on the spur of the moment; Syd Hynes was a great example. Things don't always work out but if you don't try them you regret it.'

Hague had a penchant for the unorthodox, including passing the ball between his legs. 'I used to get so many rollickings off Syd Hynes if I'd tried to slip a pass out of a tackle, but he never dropped me for it.'

Neil Hague, who signed in 1973, played in every position in the backs for Leeds. A creative player, he felt wasted on the wing and admits that stand-off was his preferred role. He also impressed at scrum-half, centre and full-back, but the problem with being a utility player is that the specialists tend to take the

Continued...

major trophy on offer.

At the time of the Hull defeat, Leeds had played 20 Division One games. Of those, 10 had been won, one drawn, and nine had ended in defeat, leaving the Loiners in mid-table and uncertain of a top eight place that would secure a position in the Premiership play-offs.

Rehabilitation began immediately with an emphatic 21-7 victory over a Warrington outfit that, at the close of the season, could look back on that defeat as the one that prevented them from finishing level with Hull KR at the top of the table.

That win, which involved two John Atkinson tries and touchdowns by Neil Hague, Butch Adams and Alan Smith, with the irrepressible Kevin Dick landing three goals, was due revenge for the 24-13 defeat at Wilderspool in November, when youngster Tim Wilby and Roy Dickinson had crossed for the Loiners.

Leigh were the next to pay for embarrassment in Lancashire, the 18-2 early October reverse being eclipsed by a 49-6 stroll at Headingley in

'Singin' in the Rain.' Nothing fazes Leeds wingers of the class of the two Smiths – Alan and David and John Atkinson.

which there were two tries each for Alan Smith, Les Dyl, Graham Joyce and Dick, who also kicked eight goals; David Smith, Atkinson and Dickinson grabbed the remaining touchdowns for the Loiners.

Salford, who had been accounted for 30-16 back in September at Headingley with the help of two Hague tries, a try and six goals by Gibson and touchdowns from Paul Fletcher, Atkinson and Mick Crane, found themselves conceding the 'double' when Leeds carved out a 3-0 success at the Willows in which Dyl scored the only points of the game with a try. And that achievement was followed by another, equally impressive 'double', St Helens being beaten 20-15 at Knowsley Road to back up the 26-11 success at Headingley in January. Atkinson notched two tries in the second game to add to his touchdown at Headingley, with Hague and Crane also nipping over and Dick landing four goals.

Workington Town, who had been held to a 9-9 draw at Derwent Park on the opening day of the season, recorded a notable win at

available spots if all players are fit for a major match. 'That can happen, but I was lucky in my career, and I played a lot of games. We all drank together, we built up a tremendous team spirit from that and we took it out onto the pitch. And we treated the game seriously; we trained very hard during the week, and pre-season training was gruelling. There were mornings when I could hardly get down the steps.'

Hague scored his first try for Leeds on 14 March 1974 in the 17-16 win over Dewsbury at Crown Flatt. A memorable occasion and an important touchdown but he derived just as much pleasure from the creative aspect as from scoring.

Neil Hague (left) looks on as his switching of play creates space for David Ward and Phil Cookson.

There were, however, two tries which linger in the memory. One was the vital touchdown from stand-off in the Challenge Cup semi-final against Featherstone Rovers in 1978, when he scampered over straight from a scrum for a converted try which helped Leeds to a 14-9 win. And the other was in a match against St Helens, again from stand-off, when he went the length of the field. 'They asked me how I did it. I said, 'if it hadn't have been for that bloke standing near the flag with a pint I wouldn't have got there!"

John Atkinson, another free spirit, remains a fan. He says: 'In some ways he'd got a screw loose. He'd do something and you'd think what's he done that for? The next thing we'd be away. He had that little bit of something extra, something different.

'He'd get the ball in his dead ball area and he'd flick it backwards, 30 yards, to you. You'd end up getting tackled on the halfway line so we'd come from under the posts simply because he had decided to do something. That's what made him special, he was unpredictable. You never knew what he was going to do from one minute to the next and I don't think he knew either.'

Loiners Big Match
27 May 1979, Premiership Final, Leeds 24 Bradford Northern 2, Fartown, Huddersfield

A glorious record of having won a major trophy over a period spanning 13 seasons came under severe scrutiny when Leeds squared up with Peter Fox's Bradford Northern before a 19,489 crowd.

With the memory of first round exits in the Yorkshire Cup (at Odsal, by the odd point in 47, after a nine-point lead, with only 12 minutes remaining, had been lost), the BBC2 Floodlit Trophy and the Challenge Cup still haunting Syd Hynes and his men, Leeds now had just one last chance to maintain their run.

Holders Northern had forced their way into the final, despite having finished eighth in the league, with wins at Hull KR and at Warrington. On each occasion, as in the game against Leeds in the Yorkshire Cup, Fox's men had battled back from the dead, overturning a 13-0 deficit to prevail 18-17 at Craven Park and brushing aside an 11-2 disadvantage at Wilderspool to eventually win 14-11.

Leeds, then, were aware that Bradford could not be discounted at any stage but Northern's strong opening assault, with heavyweight packmen Jimmy Thompson, Jeff Grayshon and Len Casey prominent, suggested that Fox, perhaps having had enough of late recoveries, had instructed his men to mount an early lead.

That was, in fact, gained as stand off Steve Ferres landed a quick penalty, and Northern's prospects were improved when Leeds centre Les Dyl was taken off injured after eight minutes, Paul Fletcher entering the torrid fray. But that was as far as Bradford, who lacked injured David Redfearn and David Barends in the three-quarters and fielded inexperienced Les Gant and Eddie Okulicz, got.

Okulicz and Gant in particular, and Northern in general, were tormented throughout by incisive, probing kicks from the Leeds half-back pairing of

Continued...

Headingley, prevailing 31-11 in a match in which Leeds were limited to a try and goal by Dick and touchdowns for Hague and Atkinson.

From that point the five remaining league fixtures, and three Premiership Trophy ties, were all won. And in style.

Leeds visited Castleford on the last day of March and swept to a stunning 34-10 victory in

John Holmes races over against Hunslet.

which Dick scored a try and eight goals, finding grand support from Holmes, Atkinson, Ward, Sammy Sanderson and Graham Eccles who all crossed the Wheldon Road whitewash to confirm another memorable 'double' after the 19-12 win at home involving tries by Alan Smith, Hague, Holmes and Adams.

A couple of days later, on April Fool's Day, the Loiners embarked on a schedule of three away games in 14 days with a 20-8 win at Huddersfield, Dick leading the way with two

Sammy Sanderson and Kevin Dick, with Dick operating, unusually, at stand off despite wearing the number seven shirt.

Time after time, Bradford's pack was driven back by the pair's intelligent punts and chips and Leeds, who lacked the injured John Holmes and Tim Wilby, prospered, despite massive defensive efforts by the likes of Northern full-back Keith Mumby and hooker Keith Bridges.

Play-anywhere Neil Hague, slotting in at full-back, was a huge presence and was involved in the only try of the first half, collecting a memorable long ball from prop Mick Harrison to send centre David Smith over eight minutes before the break.

A 50-yard burst by Hague, minutes earlier, had come to nothing when winger Alan Smith had been hauled down short. On this occasion, though, Bradford had no answer, and further damage was added when Dick hoisted a touchline conversion, followed by a penalty, to give his side a 7-2 interval lead.

With second row pair Graham Joyce and Graham Eccles blocking up the middle, Northern could find no way through when the second half got under way. Dick, meanwhile, kept the scoreboard clicking for Leeds, landing two penalties and a drop goal to stretch the Loiners' lead to 10 points. And it was Dick, the Harry Sunderland Man of the Match winner, who put the game beyond Northern with a timely interception, feeding David Smith who was hauled down spectacularly by Gant, Alan Smith racing over from dummy half.

Put the game beyond Northern? Given Bradford's habit of staging impossible fight-backs that season, few in the large contingent of Leeds fans in the Fartown crowd felt too sure about that. But Leeds, this time, were not going to be denied. Two more Dick goals represented a couple more nails in Northern's coffin and victory was assured when skipper and hooker David Ward strolled over, Dick adding the conversion to total 15 of his side's 24 points in a record margin for the final.

Second row Graham Joyce impressed, with a strong defensive performance, in the Premiership Final victory over Bradford Northern. Joyce is pictured, earlier in the year, on the offensive against Widnes. Sammy Sanderson, David Smith and Graham Eccles are in attendance.

The victory was also a success for coach Syd Hynes who once again confirmed his tactical acumen, instructing winger John Atkinson to switch occasionally to the centre, to devastating effect.

Leeds: Hague; A Smith, D Smith, Dyl, Atkinson; Dick, Sanderson; Harrison, Ward, Pitchford, Joyce, Eccles, Cookson. Subs: Fletcher, Adams.

Bradford: Mumby; Parker, Okulicz, Gant, Spencer; Ferres, A Redfearn; Thompson, Bridges, Forsyth, Trotter, Grayshon, Casey. Subs: Van Bellen, Mordue.

Referee: Mr WH Thompson (Huddersfield).

Leeds: T: D Smith, A Smith, Ward. G: Dick 7. DG: Dick.

Bradford: G: Ferres.

Attendance: 19,489

tries and four goals and Atkinson and Crane also crossing. Bradford Northern, who had pulled off a surprise at Headingley at the turn of the year with a 10-5 win, when Leeds mustered a Dickinson try and a Dick goal, came off second best in an equally tight game at Odsal, Leeds winning 13-10 with a try and a goal by Holmes, a Crane touchdown and three Gibson goals.

Wakefield, who had been beaten 22-6 at Headingley on Boxing Day when Gary Hetherington, who had recorded 16 goals in his previous three outings, landed his last goal for the club, could do little to prevent a 16-7 victory at Belle Vue when Dyl bagged his second brace of the season against Trinity, Atkinson, and Adams also touching down. Already certain of fourth spot, the Loiners finished on a high with the 23-11 home win over relegated Rochdale Hornets, courtesy of two tries for Sanderson, touchdowns by Dyl, Cookson and Atkinson and four Gibson goals.

Leeds hosted fifth-placed St Helens in the Premiership first round and deservedly

A Loiner Looks Back

Phil Cookson

Phil Cookson enjoyed a glittering career with Leeds. Noted for his powerhouse charges, he turns his hand here to defence in the 1973 John Player Final victory over Salford.

'Probably the hardest decision I ever made was when I finished. I didn't fall out with the club. I'd just had enough, my body was telling me that and I'd lost the heart to train and play. It took a while, I was hoping I'd get by it and get through it and find a new lease of life but it never came and I wasn't enjoying my rugby. It's time to go then, it's no good lingering.

'I was working 40 to 50 hours every week, and I was at night school on Fridays, in between training and playing, so that didn't help.'

Loiners Big Match

27 October 1979 Yorkshire Cup Final, Leeds 15 Halifax 6, Headingley

The Smiths were to the fore as the Loiners maintained their record of lifting a trophy in each season since 1966-67 with a hard-fought success over Maurice Bamford's Second Division Halifax.

The Yorkshire Cup Final was, for the last time, played at Headingley regardless of whether Leeds were in the decider or not. Few, however, contested the right of Syd Hynes to continue his remarkable record of not having lost a final since stepping into the coaching hot seat in the summer of 1975.

Leeds denied Halifax a single try, the underdogs having to be content with three goals by full-back Jimmy Birts.

By contrast, the Loiners posted three touchdowns, shared by the unrelated Alan and David Smith who were teamed on the right flank for the game.

David, who had been signed several years earlier to cover for his senior namesake, who had been struggling for many years with knee trouble, grabbed one touchdown from the centre position. Alan, meanwhile, crashed over for a trademark brace in a display which confirmed that the hunger which had sustained him for almost two decades was as rapacious as ever.

Alan Smith's performance earned him the Yorkshire Federation of Rugby League Supporters' clubs sponsored White Rose Trophy, as the man of the match.

A crowd of 9,134 turned up for the game, in which Leeds scrum-half Kevin Dick landed three goals.

Leeds had reached the final the hard way, opening with a tough home clash in the first round with Castleford, who were usurped 26-14 in another game in which the Smiths dominated, David leading the way on this occasion with a brace and Alan netting the one. Brian 'Butch' Adams, David Heron and Steve

Continued...

progressed, having scored five tries to two. Dyl, handed the kicking duties, scored a try and three goals, Sanderson crossed twice and David Smith and Holmes touched down.

Wigan, who had collected the 'double' over Leeds in the league campaign – Hetherington scoring his only try, with Eccles, in the 23-14 defeat at Headingley – traversed the Pennines for the semi-final and became the next club to wilt as Leeds' big match temperament took a hold. Sanderson, in fine form, scored two tries for the third game in succession, and Atkinson and Hague raced over with Dick (3) and Dyl adding goals to set up the final with Bradford who, coincidentally, had ended Leeds' hopes in the first round of the Yorkshire Cup with a 24-23

Pitchford forced their way over among the forwards and Dick kicked four goals while Cas could only muster two tries by Bruce Burton, touchdowns for Bob Spurr and Terry Richardson and a Steve Norton goal.

A trip to Batley in the second round posed few problems, the Loiners prevailing 29-6 in a game in which Gary Hetherington starred with two tries and four goals for a personal haul of 14 points. There were two touchdowns each, also, for Adams and Phil Cookson, and Alan Smith had yet another try.

The semi-final at Belle Vue attracted 7,494 fans who saw a tough Wakefield Trinity side which had featured in the previous season's Challenge Cup Final, outwitted 12-7. Leeds, despite the early loss of David Smith – carted off after a robust challenge by former Trinity team-mate Trevor Skerrett – were generally on top and edged matters with tries by John Holmes and Cookson, with Hetherington adding three goals. McDermott netted Wakefield's only touchdown and Bill Ashurst added two goals.

Leeds went on to extend their trophy-winning sequence to 15 seasons with the 8-7 victory over Hull KR in the 1980-81 Yorkshire Cup Final. The event's seven-year sojourn at Headingley was brought to an end with the decision to stage the decider at Fartown, Huddersfield, where 9,751 paid to see Leeds edge the issue with the help of an Alan Smith try and two goals and a drop goal by Dick, who collected the White Rose Trophy man of the match award as a result.

In the following season, 1981-82, the Loiners, for the first time since 1965-66, failed to lift a trophy.

Leeds: Hague; A Smith, D Smith, Dyl, Atkinson; Holmes, Dick; Dickinson, Ward, Pitchford, Eccles, Heron, Cookson. Subs: Sanderson, Adams.
Halifax: Birts; Howard, Garrod, Cholmondley, Waites; Blacker, Langton; Jarvis, Raistrick, Ward, Scott, Sharp, Busfield. Subs: Snee, Callon.
Referee: Mr M Naughton (Widnes).
Leeds: T: A Smith 2, D Smith. G: Dick 3.
Halifax: G: Birts 3.
Attendance: 9,134

The decision to drop Kevin Dick from the Great Britain side had immediate repercussions for Hull KR chairman Colin Hutton, who was also the Great Britain manager. Suitably riled, Dick inspired Leeds to an 8-7 win.

A Loiner Looks Back

Gary Hetherington

'My early memories of Jack Myerscough are of how he would come into the dressing rooms, before a game or at half time, with an offer of an extra winning bonus. The players looked forward to his appearances! Jack and Alf Rutherford had a certain style, we'd have champagne on the bus after an away victory, with Jack and Alf Rutherford sitting at the front. I also got to know Harry Jepson at that time, especially on long trips to places like Workington, which were a bit of a finishing school of my Rugby League education. People like those three and Bill Carter and Joe Warham had a wealth of experience in Rugby League management.'

defeat in a thriller at Odsal in which the Loiners scored five tries (through Hague, Alan Smith, Sanderson, Cookson and Crane) slipping when Gibson's four goals were topped by Northern's six.

The Loiners had also gone out of the John Player competition at the first round stage, missing out 16-11 at St Helens despite tries for David Smith, Crane and Sanderson. A Preliminary Round victory over Bramley in the Floodlit Trophy (Leeds winning 47-11 with an Alan Smith hat trick, two tries each for Sanderson, David Smith, Brendan White, a try and three goals for Gibson and a Cookson touchdown), all supplemented by four Hetherington goals, was followed by first round defeat against Hull, who won 14-8 in a game in which Dick scored the Loiners' only try, Willie Oulton kicking two goals and Ward landing a drop goal.

However, the far-seeing decision of the Leeds board of the early 1960s to install the famous electric blanket once again paid dividends as the Loiners' mediocre league form was ended with the help of a sequence of seven out of eight league matches between mid-December and early March being played at home. Aided by that advantage a number of victories were recorded which helped improve confidence, in addition to preventing a fixture backlog.

LEAGUE TABLES

TABLES FROM THE SEASONS 1959/60 TO 1979/80

League 1959/60

	P	W	D	L	F	A	Ps
St Helens	38	34	1	3	947	343	69
Wakefield T	38	32	0	6	831	348	64
Hull	38	28	1	9	758	474	57
Wigan	38	27	2	9	828	390	56
Featherstone R	38	27	0	11	730	437	54
Whitehaven	38	22	3	13	594	533	47
Warrington	38	22	2	14	650	482	46
Swinton	38	22	2	14	654	503	46
Oldham	38	22	1	15	744	461	45
Hunslet	38	21	3	14	595	488	45
Leigh	38	20	4	14	600	502	44
Huddersfield	38	21	1	16	603	510	43
Hull KR	38	20	1	17	517	575	41
Leeds	38	20	0	18	641	573	40
Salford	38	19	2	17	629	583	40
Batley	38	18	3	17	476	506	39
Widnes	38	18	1	19	598	519	37
Castleford	38	18	0	20	561	630	36
Workington T	38	18	0	20	448	530	36
Keighley	38	17	1	20	575	659	35
York	38	17	0	21	579	698	34
Halifax	38	15	2	21	627	561	32
Rochdale H	38	15	0	23	435	519	30
Barrow	38	13	1	24	422	562	27
Bramley	38	10	2	26	393	673	22
Bradford N	38	9	3	26	450	645	21
Liverpool C	38	9	3	26	383	720	21
Blackpool B	38	9	1	28	400	819	19
Dewsbury	38	4	1	33	337	982	9
Doncaster	38	2	1	35	284	1084	5

League 1960/61

	P	W	D	L	F	A	Ps
Leeds	36	30	0	6	620	258	60
Warrington	36	27	1	8	701	269	55
Swinton	36	27	1	8	647	271	55
St Helens	36	27	0	9	773	304	54
Wigan	36	26	0	10	689	334	52
Leigh	36	26	0	10	588	299	52
Wakefield T	36	26	0	10	576	326	52
Oldham	36	25	1	10	667	359	51
Featherstone R	36	23	1	12	520	403	47
Workington T	36	21	0	15	515	468	42
Hull	36	20	1	15	606	448	41
Hull KR	36	19	2	15	472	462	40
Halifax	36	19	1	16	500	436	39
Huddersfield	36	18	2	16	449	429	38
Hunslet	36	18	0	18	442	415	36
Whitehaven	36	17	2	17	448	478	36
Castleford	36	16	2	18	465	502	34
York	36	16	2	18	502	547	34
Batley	36	16	1	19	343	415	33
Widnes	36	16	0	20	396	514	32
Blackpool B	36	14	3	19	405	443	31
Bramley	36	12	1	23	333	517	25
Salford	36	11	2	23	341	689	24
Bradford N	36	10	2	24	312	580	22
Keighley	36	10	1	25	349	553	21
Barrow	36	9	2	25	305	578	20
Dewsbury	36	8	3	25	296	573	19
Rochdale H	36	9	0	27	296	733	18
Liverpool C	36	5	1	30	296	768	11
Doncaster	36	3	0	33	287	768	6

League 1961/62

	P	W	D	L	F	A	Ps
Wigan	36	32	1	3	885	283	65
Wakefield T	36	32	1	3	822	288	65
Featherstone R	36	28	1	7	621	370	57
Huddersfield	36	25	2	9	494	351	52
Workington T	36	25	0	11	658	362	50
Widnes	36	25	0	11	508	309	50
Leeds	36	25	0	11	593	390	50
Hull KR	36	24	0	12	513	451	48
St Helens	36	23	0	13	606	302	46
Oldham	36	22	1	13	643	344	45
Swinton	36	21	1	14	527	326	43
Castleford	36	21	0	15	501	369	42
Bramley	36	19	4	13	450	393	42
Warrington	36	19	2	15	576	435	40
Halifax	36	18	3	15	400	334	39
Hull	36	18	1	17	573	415	37
Leigh	36	17	0	19	388	497	34
Barrow	36	14	1	21	423	558	29
Keighley	36	13	2	21	365	467	28
York	36	12	1	23	462	531	25
Salford	36	12	1	23	385	740	25
Whitehaven	36	11	2	23	383	539	24
Blackpool B	36	11	1	24	335	600	23
Rochdale H	36	9	4	23	317	595	22
Hunslet	36	10	1	25	350	582	21
Batley	36	9	2	25	255	538	20
Dewsbury	36	8	2	26	260	543	18
Doncaster	36	8	1	27	294	668	17
Liverpool C	36	6	0	30	224	753	12
Bradford N	36	5	1	30	288	766	11

First Division 1962/63

	P	W	D	L	F	A	Ps
Swinton	30	22	1	7	372	231	45
St Helens	30	19	1	10	525	260	39
Widnes	30	19	1	10	325	301	39
Castleford	30	16	3	11	370	321	35
Wakefield T	30	16	1	13	432	359	33
Warrington	30	15	2	13	391	337	32
Leeds	30	16	0	14	333	364	32
Wigan	30	14	2	14	476	393	30
Huddersfield	30	14	0	16	298	278	28
Hull KR	30	13	1	16	389	387	27
Featherstone R	30	12	3	15	389	407	27
Workington T	30	12	3	15	410	441	27
Halifax	30	13	1	16	354	417	27
Hull	30	10	2	18	352	462	22
Oldham	30	9	1	20	288	432	19
Bramley	30	9	0	21	266	580	18

First Division 1963/64

	P	W	D	L	F	A	Ps
Swinton	30	25	0	5	401	202	50
Wigan	30	21	2	7	530	294	44
St Helens	30	20	1	9	418	266	41
Featherstone R	30	18	1	11	485	364	37
Workington T	30	18	1	11	436	332	37
Castleford	30	18	0	12	436	338	36
Wakefield T	30	16	0	14	488	339	32
Halifax	30	15	1	14	368	388	31
Hull KR	30	15	0	15	448	368	30
Warrington	30	15	0	15	374	380	30
Hunslet	30	14	0	16	371	487	28
Widnes	30	13	0	17	338	386	26
Leeds	30	10	0	20	323	493	20
Huddersfield	30	10	0	20	264	413	20
Keighley	30	5	0	25	253	599	10
Hull	30	4	0	26	267	551	8

League 1964/65

	P	W	D	L	F	A	Ps
St Helens	34	28	0	6	621	226	56
Wigan	34	26	0	8	626	260	52
Castleford	34	25	1	8	555	294	51
Wakefield T	34	24	2	8	486	228	50
Warrington	34	24	1	9	416	292	49
Workington T	34	23	1	10	497	326	47
Halifax	34	22	1	11	629	335	45
Hull KR	34	22	0	12	587	377	44
Oldham	34	20	1	13	444	312	41
Leeds	34	20	0	14	469	349	40
Swinton	34	19	1	14	334	250	39
Leigh	34	19	1	14	446	349	39
Hull	34	19	0	15	412	381	38
Hunslet	34	19	0	15	477	466	38
Featherstone R	34	18	0	16	436	463	36
Barrow	34	18	0	16	383	408	36
Bradford N	34	15	1	18	345	347	31
Huddersfield	34	15	0	19	368	419	30
Widnes	34	14	2	18	348	410	30
Whitehaven	34	14	1	19	308	402	29
Dewsbury	34	13	2	19	298	407	28
Salford	34	11	2	21	307	420	24
Liverpool C	34	10	2	22	248	519	22
Bramley	34	10	1	23	309	456	21
York	34	10	0	24	347	535	20
Batley	34	9	1	24	263	613	19
Keighley	34	9	0	25	303	592	18
Doncaster	34	9	0	25	296	616	18
Rochdale H	34	7	1	26	293	493	15
Blackpool B	34	6	2	26	248	554	14

League 1965/66

	P	W	D	L	F	A	Ps
St Helens	34	28	1	5	521	275	57
Swinton	34	27	1	6	510	283	55
Wigan	34	27	0	7	604	302	54
Wakefield T	34	25	2	7	562	239	52
Castleford	34	23	3	8	524	233	49
Leeds	34	24	0	10	493	295	48
Bradford N	34	21	1	12	375	247	43
Workington T	34	21	1	12	423	306	43
Oldham	34	20	3	11	398	347	43
Halifax	34	21	0	13	482	318	42
Huddersfield	34	20	0	14	420	267	40
Hull KR	34	20	0	14	496	321	40
Hull	34	20	0	14	447	346	40
Widnes	34	17	0	17	444	347	34
Featherstone R	34	17	0	17	408	399	34
Warrington	34	16	1	17	287	339	33
Hunslet	34	15	2	17	378	436	32
Salford	34	15	1	18	360	438	31
Keighley	34	15	0	19	266	452	30
Leigh	34	14	1	19	309	418	29
Barrow	34	13	1	20	410	367	27
Bramley	34	12	2	20	331	475	26
York	34	11	0	23	316	507	22
Dewsbury	34	10	1	23	257	424	21
Rochdale H	34	10	0	24	284	387	20
Liverpool C	34	9	2	23	307	494	20
Blackpool B	34	9	1	24	331	549	19
Batley	34	6	2	26	196	576	14
Doncaster	34	6	0	28	228	586	12
Whitehaven	34	4	2	28	191	585	10

League 1966/67

	P	W	D	L	F	A	Ps
Leeds	34	29	0	5	704	373	58
Hull KR	34	26	2	6	691	335	54
Wakefield T	34	27	0	7	631	339	54
St Helens	34	22	3	9	551	344	47
Bradford N	34	22	2	10	506	346	46
Workington T	34	22	1	11	517	345	45
Swinton	34	20	3	11	472	354	43
Castleford	34	21	0	13	560	409	42
Hull	34	18	3	13	492	430	39
Oldham	34	18	2	14	466	362	38
Halifax	34	18	2	14	567	477	38
Warrington	34	18	1	15	423	438	37
Leigh	34	17	3	14	412	433	37
Salford	34	18	1	15	398	424	37
Barrow	34	17	2	15	479	407	36
Widnes	34	15	5	14	366	412	35
Wigan	34	17	0	17	513	456	34
Rochdale H	34	15	4	15	408	395	34
Dewsbury	34	15	1	18	374	390	31
Featherstone R	34	12	3	19	401	477	27
Huddersfield	34	13	0	21	369	379	26
York	34	13	0	21	457	615	26
Bramley	34	12	0	22	371	488	24
Keighley	34	11	1	22	413	615	23
Hunslet	34	9	2	23	402	578	20
Blackpool B	34	9	2	23	333	509	20
Whitehaven	34	10	0	24	313	593	20
Liverpool C	34	9	0	25	332	552	18
Doncaster	34	8	1	25	361	677	17
Batley	34	7	0	27	280	610	14

League 1967/68

	P	W	D	L	F	A	Ps
Leeds	34	28	0	6	720	271	56
Wakefield T	34	24	1	9	600	295	49
Hull KR	34	24	1	9	620	348	49
St Helens	34	24	1	9	472	334	49
Warrington	34	24	0	10	539	290	48
Bradford N	34	24	0	10	560	309	48
Leigh	34	22	1	11	426	254	45
Castleford	34	22	1	11	510	344	45
Salford	34	22	0	12	470	313	44
Workington T	34	21	1	12	522	355	43
Wigan	34	21	0	13	602	350	42
Hull	34	21	0	13	530	432	42
Halifax	34	19	2	13	441	459	40
Swinton	34	18	1	15	485	448	37
Huddersfield	34	17	2	15	343	336	36
Widnes	34	17	1	16	538	420	35
Dewsbury	34	17	0	17	329	426	34
Featherstone R	34	16	0	18	455	437	32
Barrow	34	14	0	20	420	485	28
Bramley	34	14	0	20	380	498	28
Hunslet	34	13	0	21	430	507	26
Oldham	34	13	0	21	433	559	26
Rochdale H	34	13	0	21	335	489	26
Liverpool C	34	11	2	21	363	493	24
Whitehaven	34	10	1	23	300	577	21
York	34	9	1	24	368	687	19
Keighley	34	8	0	26	295	475	16
Blackpool B	34	6	1	27	307	634	13
Doncaster	34	4	2	28	264	768	10
Batley	34	4	1	29	247	711	9

League 1968/69

	P	W	D	L	F	A	Ps
Leeds	34	29	2	3	775	358	60
St Helens	34	27	2	5	669	262	56
Wigan	34	25	2	7	732	368	52
Castleford	34	24	2	8	462	255	50
Swinton	34	23	0	11	503	412	46
Salford	34	19	5	10	573	309	43
Featherstone R	34	21	1	12	523	346	43
Workington T	34	21	0	13	512	379	42
Leigh	34	19	4	11	447	371	42
Hull KR	34	20	0	14	566	445	40
York	34	20	0	14	477	440	40
Wakefield T	34	19	1	14	473	375	39
Hull	34	18	3	13	494	419	39
Widnes	34	19	1	14	506	434	39
Keighley	34	18	1	15	380	407	37
Oldham	34	18	0	16	479	474	36
Warrington	34	17	1	16	561	546	35
Halifax	34	16	2	16	468	485	34
Bradford N	34	16	0	18	525	475	32
Barrow	34	13	1	20	454	559	27
Rochdale H	34	13	0	21	342	485	26
Dewsbury	34	12	1	21	306	430	25
Hunslet	34	11	0	23	439	554	22
Doncaster	34	11	0	23	279	622	22
Huddersfield	34	9	1	24	296	553	19
Batley	34	8	1	25	294	577	17
Huyton	34	8	0	26	273	657	16
Bramley	34	7	0	27	313	575	14
Blackpool B	34	7	0	27	382	752	14
Whitehaven	34	6	1	27	360	539	13

League 1969/70

	P	W	D	L	F	A	Ps
Leeds	34	30	0	4	674	314	60
Castleford	34	25	1	8	493	298	51
St Helens	34	23	1	10	702	292	47
Wigan	34	23	0	11	698	420	46
Hull KR	34	22	2	10	566	395	46
Salford	34	22	1	11	572	332	45
Leigh	34	21	3	10	554	325	45
Featherstone R	34	22	1	11	558	385	45
Swinton	34	20	4	10	550	351	44
Widnes	34	21	2	11	473	355	44
Hull	34	20	2	12	420	357	42
Bradford N	34	19	0	15	511	404	38
Whitehaven	34	18	2	14	404	450	38
Warrington	34	17	2	15	559	421	36
Huddersfield	34	17	1	16	377	395	35
Halifax	34	16	0	18	395	454	32
Batley	34	15	1	18	388	485	31
Bramley	34	14	1	19	374	498	29
Barrow	34	14	1	19	379	511	29
Rochdale H	34	13	3	18	334	524	29
Wakefield T	34	13	2	19	521	452	28
Dewsbury	34	13	1	20	383	451	27
Hunslet	34	13	1	20	391	574	27
Workington T	34	12	2	20	416	483	26
Keighley	34	13	0	21	370	555	26
York	34	11	1	22	378	502	23
Doncaster	34	7	0	27	264	564	14
Huyton	34	5	3	26	177	643	13
Oldham	34	6	0	28	343	590	12
Blackpool B	34	6	0	28	318	762	12

League 1970/71

	P	W	D	L	F	A	Ps
Wigan	34	30	0	4	662	308	60
St Helens	34	29	0	5	748	231	58
Leeds	34	28	0	6	856	352	56
Leigh	34	26	0	8	636	380	52
Wakefield T	34	24	1	9	760	330	49
Keighley	34	21	0	13	448	375	42
Salford	34	20	1	13	641	432	41
Hull	34	20	1	13	610	444	41
Workington T	34	20	1	13	504	467	41
Halifax	34	20	0	14	538	497	40
Dewsbury	34	17	3	14	474	406	37
Castleford	34	18	0	16	467	403	36
Hull KR	34	18	0	16	447	524	36
Batley	34	16	2	16	492	411	34
Huddersfield	34	16	2	16	440	434	34
Oldham	34	12	7	15	487	434	31
Bramley	34	15	1	18	385	528	31
Widnes	34	14	2	18	439	422	30
York	34	14	1	19	428	451	29
Featherstone R	34	14	1	19	572	635	29
Barrow	34	14	0	20	479	483	28
Warrington	34	13	2	19	449	657	28
Swinton	34	13	0	21	404	505	26
Huyton	34	11	2	21	229	508	24
Rochdale H	34	9	3	22	318	533	21
Blackpool B	34	10	1	23	380	647	21
Bradford N	34	8	2	24	339	662	18
Doncaster	34	7	3	24	306	695	17
Whitehaven	34	8	1	25	298	698	17
Hunslet	34	6	1	27	355	739	13

League 1971/72

	P	W	D	L	F	A	Ps
Leeds	34	28	2	4	750	325	58
Bradford N	34	26	2	6	724	357	54
St Helens	34	26	1	7	661	297	53
Wigan	34	25	0	9	702	314	50
Salford	34	25	0	9	720	338	50
Swinton	34	23	2	9	554	368	48
Featherstone R	34	23	1	10	632	372	47
Rochdale H	34	21	1	12	429	306	43
Wakefield T	34	21	0	13	587	414	42
Castleford	34	20	1	13	488	368	41
Widnes	34	19	3	12	476	388	41
Dewsbury	34	18	2	14	431	352	38
Oldham	34	18	1	15	573	480	37
Hull KR	34	18	0	16	432	498	36
Warrington	34	16	3	15	537	397	35
Leigh	34	17	0	17	421	407	34
Huddersfield	34	17	0	17	394	435	34
Barrow	34	16	2	16	375	508	34
Hull	34	16	0	18	488	495	32
York	34	15	2	17	465	498	32
Halifax	34	14	0	20	398	564	28
Bramley	34	13	0	21	333	542	26
Whitehaven	34	12	0	22	394	523	24
Workington	34	11	2	21	303	533	24
Blackpool B	34	11	0	23	351	560	22
Keighley	34	8	0	26	330	740	16
Huyton	34	7	1	26	277	610	15
Batley	34	5	2	27	249	628	12
Doncaster	34	5	0	29	234	729	10
Hunslet	34	2	0	32	300	662	4

League 1972/73

	P	W	D	L	F	A	Ps
Warrington	34	27	2	5	816	400	56
Featherstone R	34	27	0	7	768	436	54
Leeds	34	26	1	7	810	324	53
St Helens	34	24	2	8	623	298	50
Wakefield T	34	25	0	9	814	398	50
Salford	34	25	0	9	723	383	50
Castleford	34	25	0	9	704	404	50
Dewsbury	34	23	0	11	534	354	46
Oldham	34	20	2	12	604	349	42
Hull KR	34	20	1	13	731	522	41
Rochdale H	34	20	1	13	438	426	41
Widnes	34	19	0	15	592	458	38
Leigh	34	18	2	14	479	390	38
Bramley	34	18	1	15	452	453	37
Whitehaven	34	18	1	15	408	512	37
Wigan	34	17	1	16	577	491	35
York	34	17	1	16	586	575	35
Halifax	34	17	0	17	543	562	34
Batley	34	15	0	19	537	600	30
Keighley	34	15	0	19	451	505	30
Swinton	34	14	1	19	441	458	29
Workington T	34	12	1	21	444	464	25
Bradford N	34	12	0	22	582	685	24
Huddersfield	34	10	2	22	465	598	22
Hull	34	11	0	23	494	693	22
Barrow	34	7	0	27	351	775	14
Doncaster	34	6	0	28	298	911	12
Hunslet	34	5	0	29	371	916	10
Blackpool B	34	4	0	30	324	972	8
Huyton	34	3	1	30	243	879	7

League 1973/74

	P	W	D	L	F	A	Ps
Salford	30	23	1	6	632	299	47
St Helens	30	22	2	6	595	263	46
Leeds	30	20	1	9	554	378	41
Widnes	30	18	1	11	431	329	37
Warrington	30	16	1	13	414	368	33
Dewsbury	30	16	1	13	389	474	33
Wakefield T	30	16	0	14	470	411	32
Featherstone R	30	14	2	14	443	397	30
Castleford	30	12	4	14	420	411	28
Rochdale H	30	13	2	15	379	415	28
Wigan	30	12	3	15	427	364	27
Bramley	30	11	3	16	344	457	25
Oldham	30	12	1	17	341	494	25
Hull KR	30	9	2	19	428	552	20
Leigh	30	7	0	23	326	655	14
Whitehaven	30	7	0	23	308	634	14

League 1974/75

	P	W	D	L	F	A	Ps
St Helens	30	26	1	3	561	229	53
Wigan	30	21	0	9	517	341	42
Leeds	30	19	1	10	581	359	39
Featherstone R	30	19	1	10	431	339	39
Widnes	30	18	1	11	382	305	37
Warrington	30	17	1	12	428	356	35
Bradford N	30	16	1	13	393	376	33
Castleford	30	14	3	13	480	427	31
Salford	30	14	1	15	451	351	29
Wakefield T	30	12	5	13	440	419	29
Keighley	30	13	0	17	300	424	26
Dewsbury	30	11	0	19	350	506	22
York	30	10	0	20	359	498	20
Bramley	30	9	0	21	338	493	18
Rochdale H	30	8	0	22	219	400	16
Halifax	30	5	1	24	269	676	11

League 1975/76

	P	W	D	L	F	A	Ps
Salford	30	22	1	7	555	350	45
Featherstone R	30	21	2	7	526	348	44
Leeds	30	21	0	9	571	395	42
St Helens	30	19	1	10	513	315	39
Wigan	30	18	3	9	514	399	39
Widnes	30	18	1	11	448	369	37
Wakefield T	30	17	0	13	496	410	34
Hull KR	30	17	0	13	446	472	34
Castleford	30	16	1	13	589	398	33
Warrington	30	15	2	13	381	456	32
Bradford N	30	13	1	16	454	450	27
Oldham	30	11	1	18	380	490	23
Dewsbury	30	10	1	19	287	484	21
Keighley	30	7	0	23	274	468	14
Huddersfield	30	5	0	25	370	657	10
Swinton	30	3	0	27	238	581	6

League 1976/77

	P	W	D	L	F	A	Ps
Featherstone R	30	21	2	7	568	334	44
St Helens	30	19	1	10	547	345	39
Castleford	30	19	1	10	519	350	39
Hull KR	30	18	1	11	496	415	37
Warrington	30	18	0	12	532	406	36
Salford	29°	17	1	11	560	402	35
Wigan	30	15	2	13	463	416	32
Bradford N	30	15	2	13	488	470	32
Leeds	29°	14	2	13	467	439	30
Widnes	30	15	0	15	403	393	30
Wakefield T	30	13	2	15	487	480	28
Workington T	30	13	1	16	352	403	27
Rochdale H	30	11	0	19	367	449	22
Leigh	30	8	1	21	314	634	17
Barrow	30	8	0	22	345	628	16
Oldham	30	7	0	23	322	666	14

°Match Abandoned.

League 1977/78

	P	W	D	L	F	A	Ps
Widnes	30	24	2	4	613	241	50
Bradford N**	29	21	2	6	500	291	44
St Helens	30	22	1	7	678	384	45
Hull KR	30	16	3	11	495	419	35
Wigan	30	17	1	12	482	435	35
Salford	30	16	0	14	470	446	32
Featherstone R	29	15	2	12	443	452	32
Leeds	30	15	1	14	512	460	31
Warrington	30	15	0	15	561	367	30
Castleford	30	13	2	15	515	583	28
Workington T	30	11	4	15	406	519	26
Wakefield T	30	12	1	17	393	450	25
Hull	30	10	3	17	358	480	23
New Hunslet	30	11	0	19	318	518	22
Bramley	30	5	4	21	281	608	14
Dewsbury	30	2	2	26	207	579	6

** Bradford N second on percentage as last game was cancelled following Featherstone's strike.

League 1978/79

	P	W	D	L	F	A	Ps
Hull KR	30	23	0	7	616	344	46
Warrington	30	22	0	8	521	340	44
Widnes	30	21	2	7	480	322	44
Leeds	30	19	1	10	555	370	39
St Helens	30	16	2	12	485	379	34
Wigan	30	16	1	13	484	411	33
Castleford	30	16	1	13	498	469	33
Bradford N	30	16	0	14	523	416	32
Workington T	30	13	3	14	378	345	29
Wakefield T	30	13	1	16	382	456	27
Leigh	30	13	1	16	406	535	27
Salford	30	11	2	17	389	435	24
Barrow	30	9	2	19	368	536	20
Featherstone R	30	8	1	21	501	549	17
Rochdale H	30	8	0	22	297	565	16
Huddersfield	30	7	1	22	314	725	15

League 1979/80

	P	W	D	L	F	A	Ps
Bradford N	30	23	0	7	448	272	46
Widnes	30	22	1	7	546	293	45
Hull	30	18	3	9	454	326	39
Salford	30	19	1	10	495	374	39
Leeds	30	19	0	11	590	390	38
Leigh	30	16	1	13	451	354	33
Hull KR	30	16	1	13	539	445	33
St Helens	30	15	2	13	505	410	32
Warrington	30	15	2	13	362	357	32
Wakefield T	30	14	2	14	435	466	30
Castleford	30	13	2	15	466	475	28
Workington T	30	12	2	16	348	483	26
Wigan	30	9	3	18	366	523	21
Hunslet	30	7	1	22	346	528	15
York	30	6	1	23	375	647	13
Blackpool B	30	5	0	25	230	613	10

Yorkshire League 1960/61

	P	W	D	L	F	A	Ps
Leeds	28	25	0	3	526	199	50
Wakefield T.	28	21	0	7	479	234	42
Featherstone R.	28	20	1	7	417	235	41
Hull	28	19	1	8	510	293	39
Hull KR	28	18	1	9	399	271	37
Huddersfield	28	15	2	11	387	349	32
Hunslet	28	15	0	13	344	299	30
Batley	28	13	1	14	269	302	27
Castleford	28	12	2	14	347	383	26
York	28	12	2	14	358	415	26
Keighley	28	9	1	18	297	385	19
Bramley	28	9	1	18	254	409	19
Bradford N.	28	7	2	19	234	441	16
Dewsbury	28	5	2	21	225	471	12
Doncaster	28	2	0	26	237	597	4

Yorkshire League 1966/67

	P	W	D	L	F	A	Ps
Leeds	28	25	0	3	586	275	50
Hull KR	28	23	2	3	598	262	48
Wakefield T.	28	23	0	5	528	259	46
Hull	28	18	1	9	430	329	37
Castleford	28	18	0	10	487	338	36
Bradford N.	28	17	2	9	412	286	36
Halifax	28	14	1	13	446	397	29
Dewsbury	28	11	1	16	275	357	23
Keighley	28	10	1	17	332	478	21
Bramley	28	10	0	18	316	402	20
Featherstone R.	28	9	1	18	318	414	19
York	28	9	0	19	345	531	18
Hunslet	28	6	1	21	321	481	13
Doncaster	28	6	0	22	293	593	12
Batley	28	6	0	22	229	514	12

Yorkshire League 1968/69

	P	W	D	L	F	A	Ps
Leeds	28	25	2	1	661	262	52
Castleford	28	19	1	8	370	222	39
Hull KR	28	19	0	9	499	333	38
Featherstone R	28	18	0	10	416	278	36
Wakefield T	28	17	1	10	389	278	35
Hull	28	15	2	11	408	347	32
Bradford N	28	15	0	13	444	358	30
York	28	15	0	13	339	388	30
Keighley	28	13	1	14	278	356	27
Halifax	28	12	2	14	370	413	26
Dewsbury	28	11	1	16	259	349	23
Hunslet	28	9	0	19	346	463	18
Huddersfield	28	8	1	19	233	422	17
Batley	28	5	1	22	230	501	11
Bramley	28	3	0	25	228	497	6

Yorkshire League 1969/70

	P	W	D	L	F	A	Ps
Leeds	28	25	0	3	584	267	50
Castleford	28	20	1	7	409	233	41
Featherstone R	28	20	0	8	509	317	40
Hull KR	28	18	2	8	476	324	38
Hull	28	17	2	9	348	275	36
Bradford N	28	15	0	13	428	347	30
Huddersfield	28	14	1	13	307	329	29
Halifax	28	14	0	14	312	336	28
Wakefield T	28	10	2	16	445	380	22
York	28	10	1	17	311	427	21
Bramley	28	10	1	17	296	425	21
Hunslet	28	10	1	17	317	495	21
Dewsbury	28	9	1	18	286	403	19
Keighley	28	9	0	19	289	449	18
Doncaster	28	3	0	25	187	497	6

INDEX OF NAMES IN MAIN TEXT

Adams, Butch 69, 152, 153, 178, 180, 182
Ashcroft, Kevin 100
Ashton, Eric 129, 133, 140, 142
Ashton, Gilbert 29
Ashurst, Bill 124
Astbury, Peter 30, 98
Atkinson, John 24, 31, 43, 44, 47, 48, 49, 53, 54, 55, 56, 57, 58, 60, 61, 64, 66, 68, 69, 73, 74, 81, 82, 83, 84, 85, 86, 87, 88, 91, 92, 93, 94, 95, 96, 99, 100, 106, 108, 109, 110, 113, 114, 115, 116, 117, 118, 119, 121, 122, 124, 125, 126, 127, 128, 129, 137, 138, 141, 142, 143, 145, 149, 150, 152, 153, 156, 157, 158, 159, 167, 168, 169, 170, 171, 172, 173, 175, 178, 179, 180, 181, 182, 183

Bamford, Maurice 174
Banner, Peter 162, 166
Barends, David 144, 175
Barham, David 106, 114, 122
Barnard, Ted 109
Batten, Ray 26, 31, 43, 44, 47, 48, 51, 52, 53, 54, 55, 60, 64, 67, 68, 69, 70, 71, 74, 82, 84, 86, 87, 88, 89, 91, 92, 93, 98, 99, 101, 108, 112, 115, 118, 124, 133, 136, 138, 141, 145, 146, 150, 152
Batty, Brian 137
Beetson, Artie 137
Bence, Alan 109
Bevan, John 147
Boston, Billy 12, 14
Bowden, Reggie 141
Bradshaw, Harry 113
Briggs, Trevor 30, 84, 87, 98
Broatch, Drew 27, 42, 44, 48
Brown, Frank 62, 67, 69
Brown, Gordon 11
Brown 30
Burke, John 30, 53, 108, 109
Burton, Bruce 143
Burton, Chris 163
Burton, Norman 13, 29

Canister 30
Casey, Len 143
Challinor, Jim 170
Chamberlain, Les 28, 41, 46, 48
Chambers, George 112
Clark, Mick 28, 41, 43, 53, 55, 57, 59, 60, 61, 65, 68, 71, 73, 83
Clarke, Colin 32
Clarkson, Geoff 123, 126, 140
Clay 30
Clay, Eric 109
Clawson, Terry 104, 106, 109, 110, 113, 114, 115, 116, 121, 129, 134, 157
Cookson, Phil 68, 69, 83, 84, 85, 86, 88, 91, 101, 109, 112, 116, 117, 121, 122, 129, 137, 138, 140, 141, 152, 154, 157, 161, 163, 164, 165, 166, 171, 172, 179, 182, 183, 184
Coulman, Mike 146
Coulthard, Stuart 30
Cowan, Ron 27, 31, 40, 41, 42, 43, 44, 46, 47, 48, 53, 64, 69, 70, 73, 74, 82, 83, 87, 91, 93, 99, 108
Crane, Mick 175, 179, 181, 183
Crosby, Tony 32, 49, 53, 54, 57, 61, 67, 69, 73, 74, 93
Crowther, Arthur 142

Dalby, Ken 29
Davidson, Chris 156
Davies, John 45, 58
Dewhurst, Robin 30, 33, 35, 51, 53, 98
Dick, Kevin 69, 152, 164, 165, 166, 167, 169, 171, 172, 178, 179, 180, 181, 183, 184
Dickens, Steve 169
Dickinson, Roy 149, 158, 164, 165, 167, 169, 170, 173, 178, 179, 181
Dixon, Colin 74, 96, 101, 107
Drake, Bill 28
Drewry, Alfred 123
Duke, Tony 113
Dunn, Peter 86, 91, 93, 96, 114
Duxbury, Jack 75
Dyl, Les 24, 69, 80, 89, 90, 92, 95, 102, 105, 106, 108, 110, 111, 112, 114, 115, 116, 117, 118, 120, 137, 139, 140, 141, 143, 147, 148, 149, 154, 157, 162, 164, 169, 172, 173, 175, 176, 179, 181, 182, 183

Eardley 30
Eccles, Graham 66, 69, 87, 106, 109, 114, 116, 119, 144, 145, 146, 157, 158, 159, 162, 164, 166, 171, 172, 174, 177, 180, 181, 183
Edwards, Derek 34, 104, 122, 123, 137, 142, 143
Evans, Colin 16
Evans, Steve 170
Eyre, Albert 54, 60, 62, 70, 71, 87, 127
Eyre, Ken 50, 54, 58, 82, 83

Fairbank, Jack 14, 18, 19
Fallowfield, Bill 116
Fearnley, Stan 168, 173
Firth, Albert 28
Fisher, Tony 96, 105, 106, 111, 113, 114, 115, 123, 139, 145, 147
Fletcher, Paul 163, 166, 170, 175, 179
Fletcher, Raymond 146